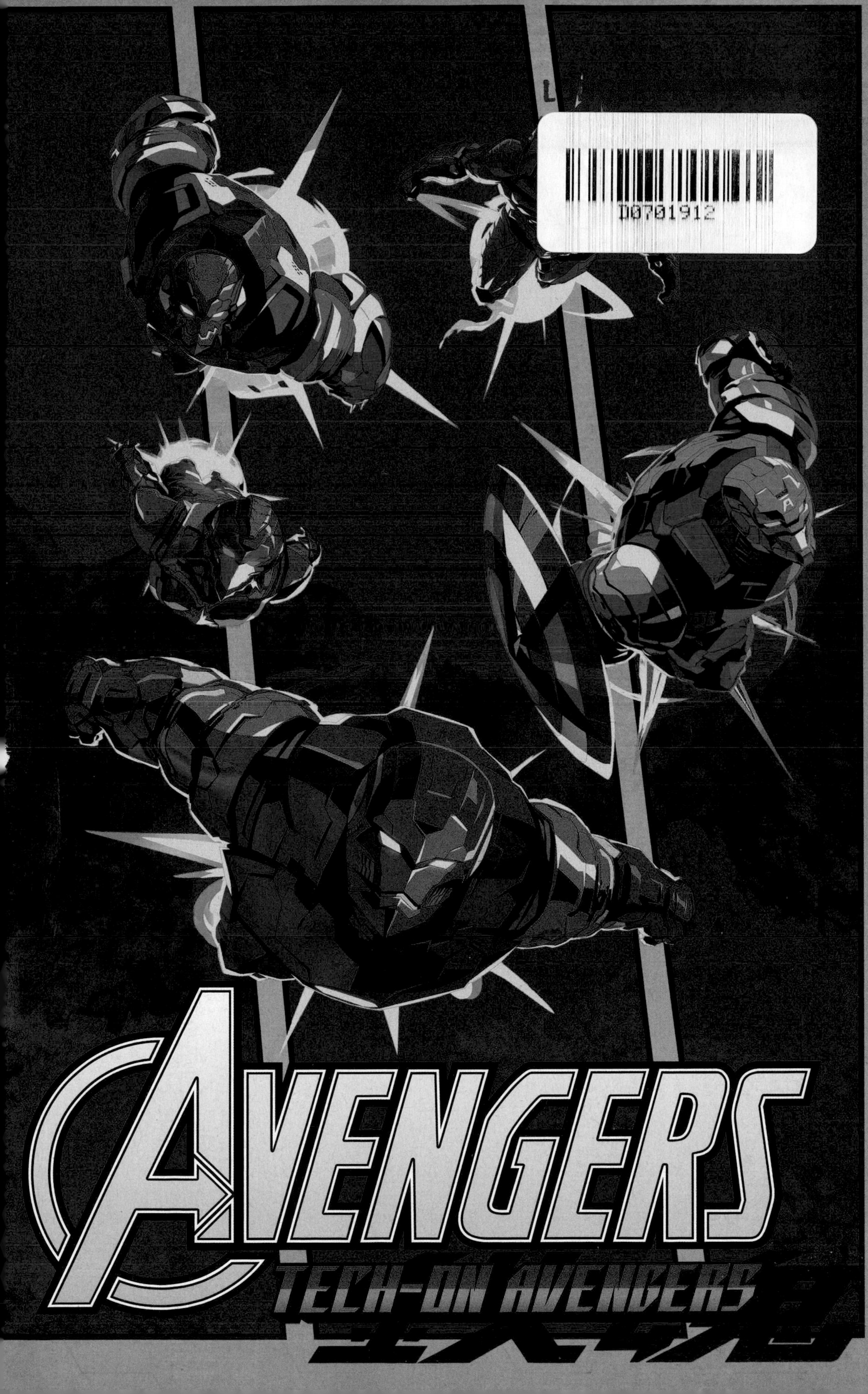
AVENGERS
TECH-ON AVENGERS

AVENGERS TECH-ON

AVENGERS: TECH-ON. Contains material originally published in magazine form as AVENGERS: TECH-ON (2021) #1-6. First printing 2022. ISBN 978-1-302-92444-7. Published by MARVEL WORLDWIDE, INC., a subsidiary of MARVEL ENTERTAINMENT, LLC. OFFICE OF PUBLICATION: 1290 Avenue of the Americas, New York, NY 10104. **Printed in Canada.** KEVIN FEIGE, Chief Creative Officer; DAN BUCKLEY, President, Marvel Entertainment; JOE QUESADA, EVP & Creative Director; DAVID BOGART, Associate Publisher & SVP of Talent Affairs; TOM BREVOORT, VP, Executive Editor; NICK LOWE, Executive Editor, VP of Content, Digital Publishing; DAVID GABRIEL, VP of Print & Digital Publishing; MARK ANNUNZIATO, VP of Planning & Forecasting; JEFF YOUNGQUIST, VP of Production & Special Projects; ALEX MORALES, Director of Publishing Operations; DAN EDINGTON, Director of Editorial Operations; RICKEY PURDIN, Director of Talent Relations; JENNIFER GRÜNWALD, Director of Production & Special Projects; SUSAN CRESPI, Production Manager; STAN LEE, Chairman Emeritus. For information regarding advertising in Marvel Comics or on Marvel.com, please contact Vit DeBellis, Custom Solutions & Integrated Advertising Manager, at vdebellis@marvel.com. For Marvel subscription inquiries, please call 888-511-5480. **Manufactured between 1/21/2022 and 2/22/2022 by SOLISCO PRINTERS, SCOTT, QC, CANADA.**

10987654321

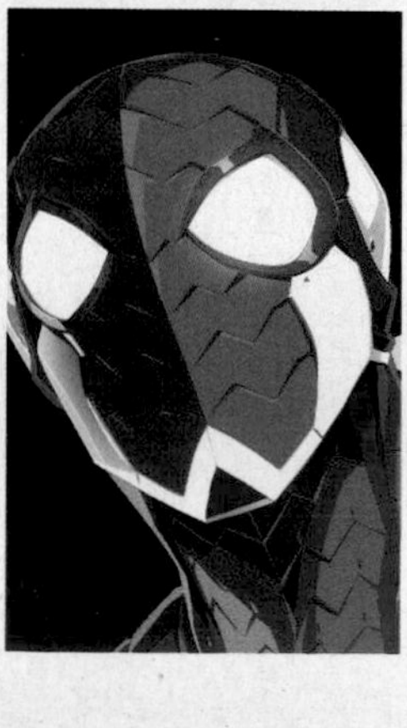

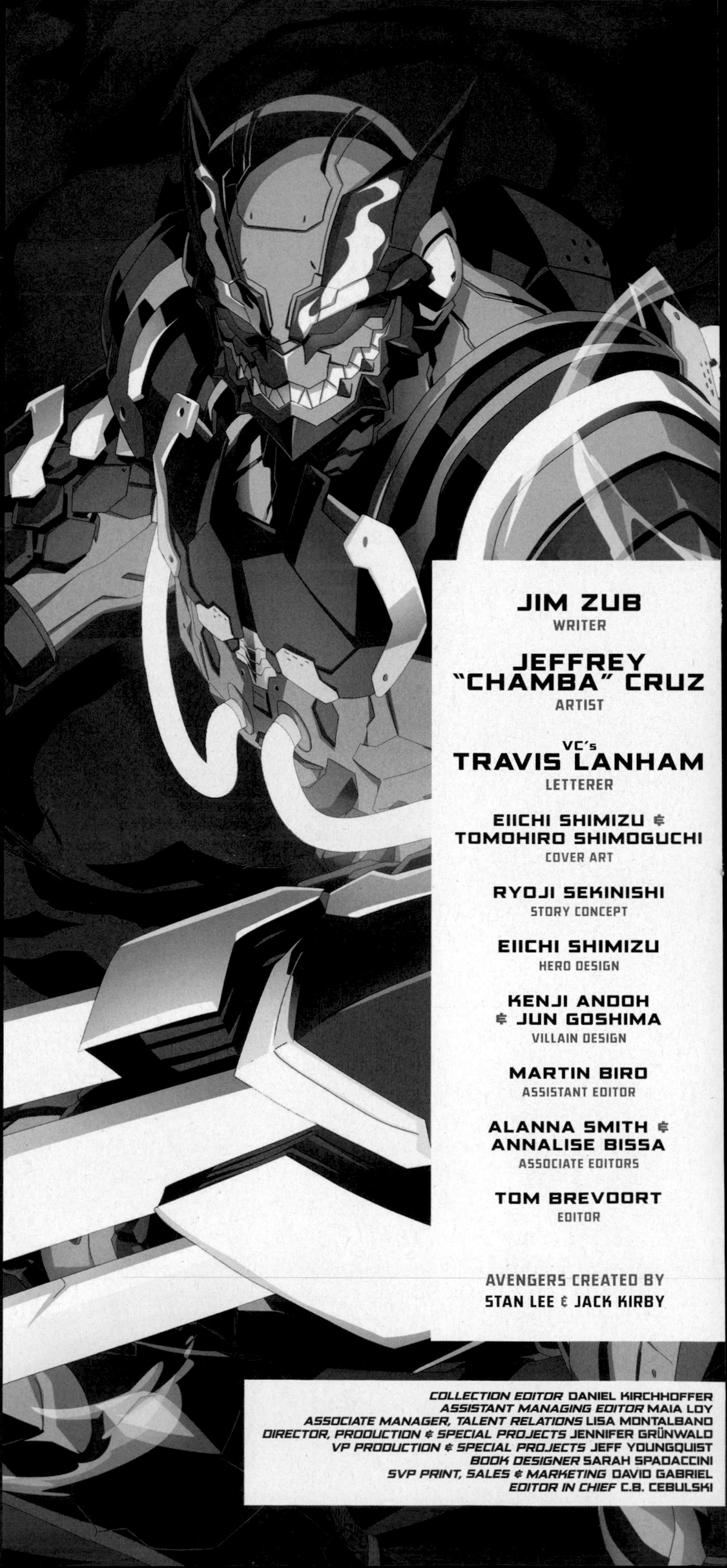

JIM ZUB
WRITER

JEFFREY "CHAMBA" CRUZ
ARTIST

VC's TRAVIS LANHAM
LETTERER

EIICHI SHIMIZU & TOMOHIRO SHIMOGUCHI
COVER ART

RYOJI SEKINISHI
STORY CONCEPT

EIICHI SHIMIZU
HERO DESIGN

KENJI ANDOH & JUN GOSHIMA
VILLAIN DESIGN

MARTIN BIRO
ASSISTANT EDITOR

ALANNA SMITH & ANNALISE BISSA
ASSOCIATE EDITORS

TOM BREVOORT
EDITOR

AVENGERS CREATED BY
STAN LEE & JACK KIRBY

COLLECTION EDITOR DANIEL KIRCHHOFFER
ASSISTANT MANAGING EDITOR MAIA LOY
ASSOCIATE MANAGER, TALENT RELATIONS LISA MONTALBANO
DIRECTOR, PRODUCTION & SPECIAL PROJECTS JENNIFER GRÜNWALD
VP PRODUCTION & SPECIAL PROJECTS JEFF YOUNGQUIST
BOOK DESIGNER SARAH SPADACCINI
SVP PRINT, SALES & MARKETING DAVID GABRIEL
EDITOR IN CHIEF C.B. CEBULSKI

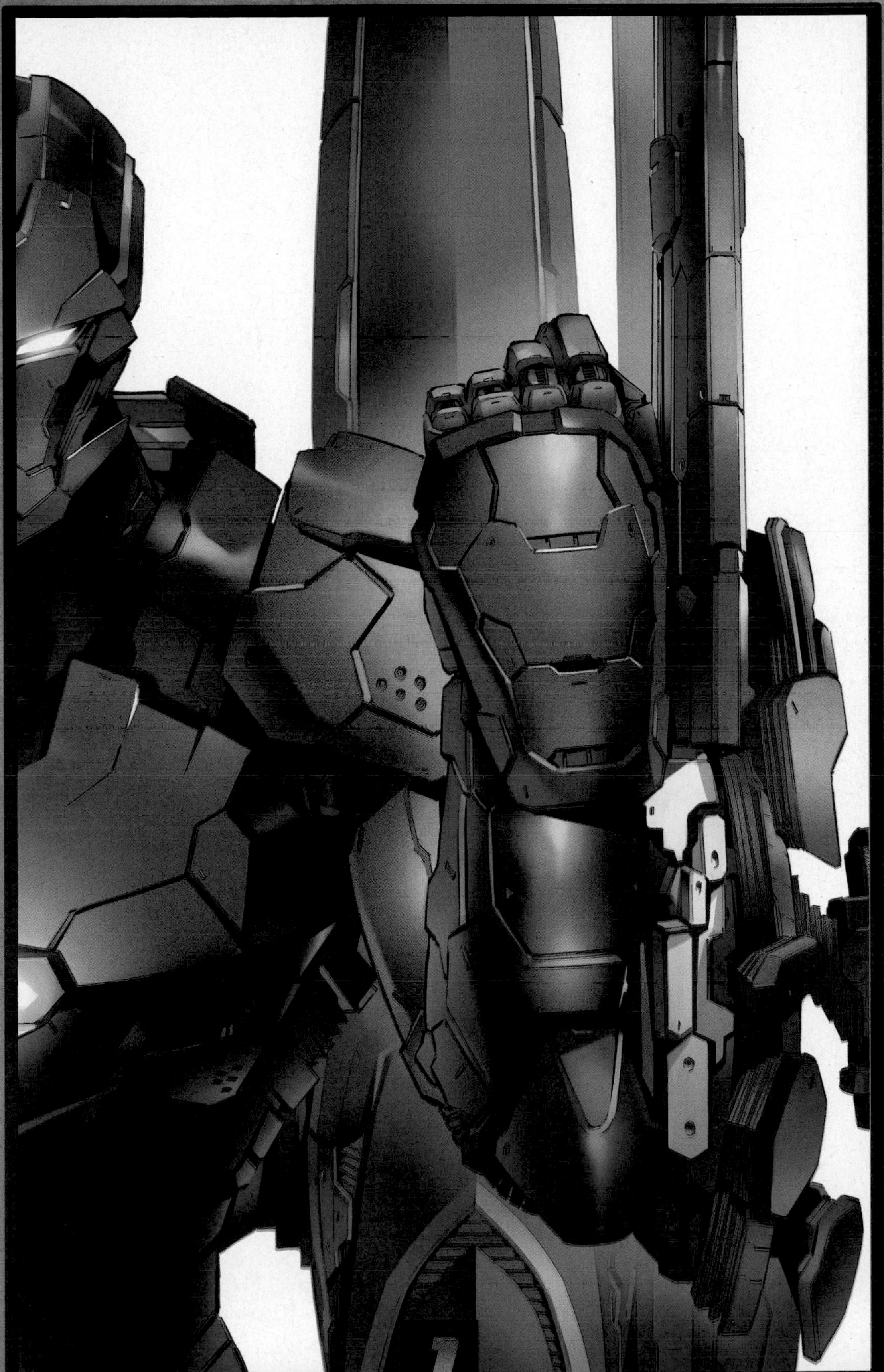

1

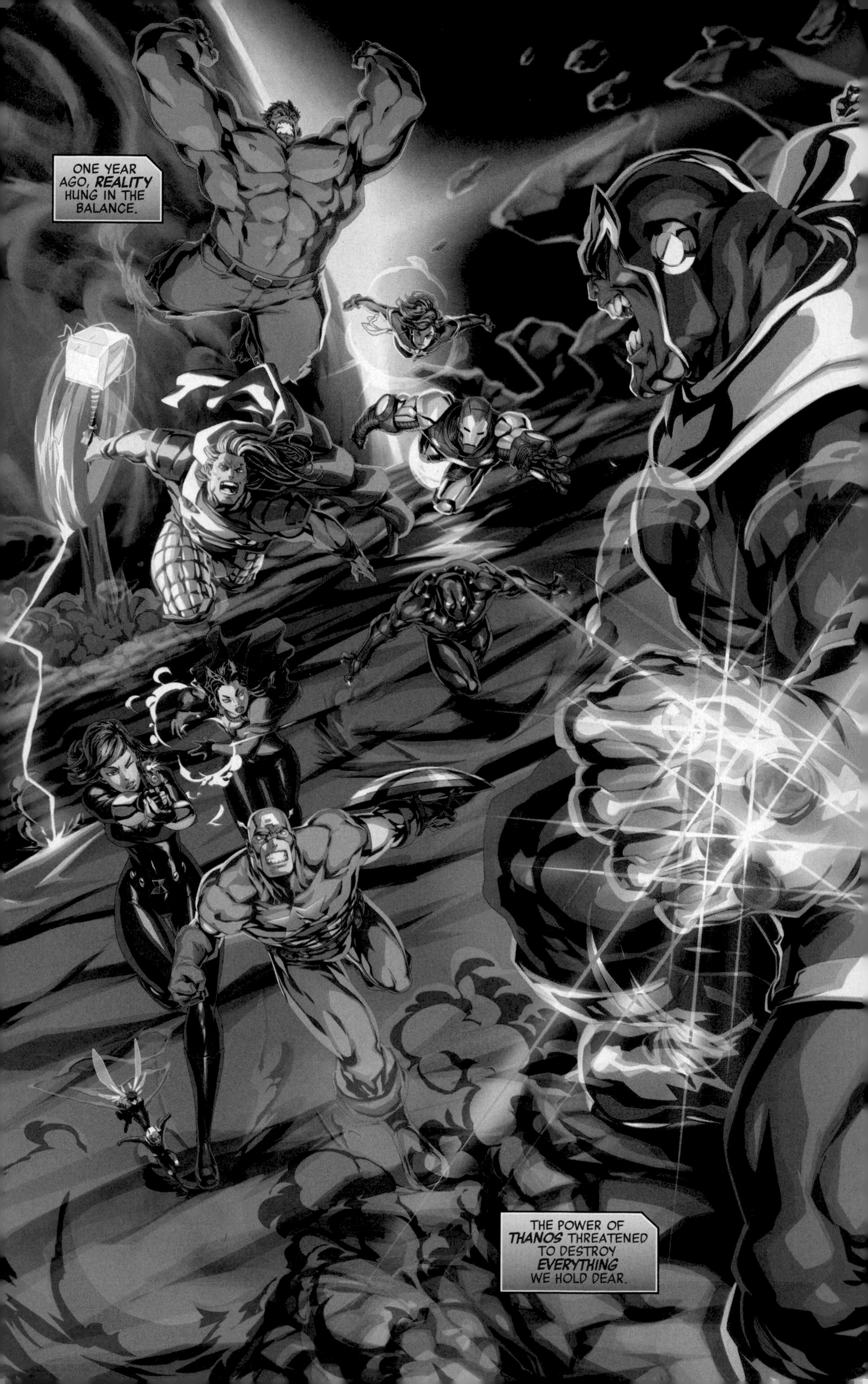
ONE YEAR AGO, REALITY HUNG IN THE BALANCE.
THE POWER OF THANOS THREATENED TO DESTROY EVERYTHING WE HOLD DEAR.

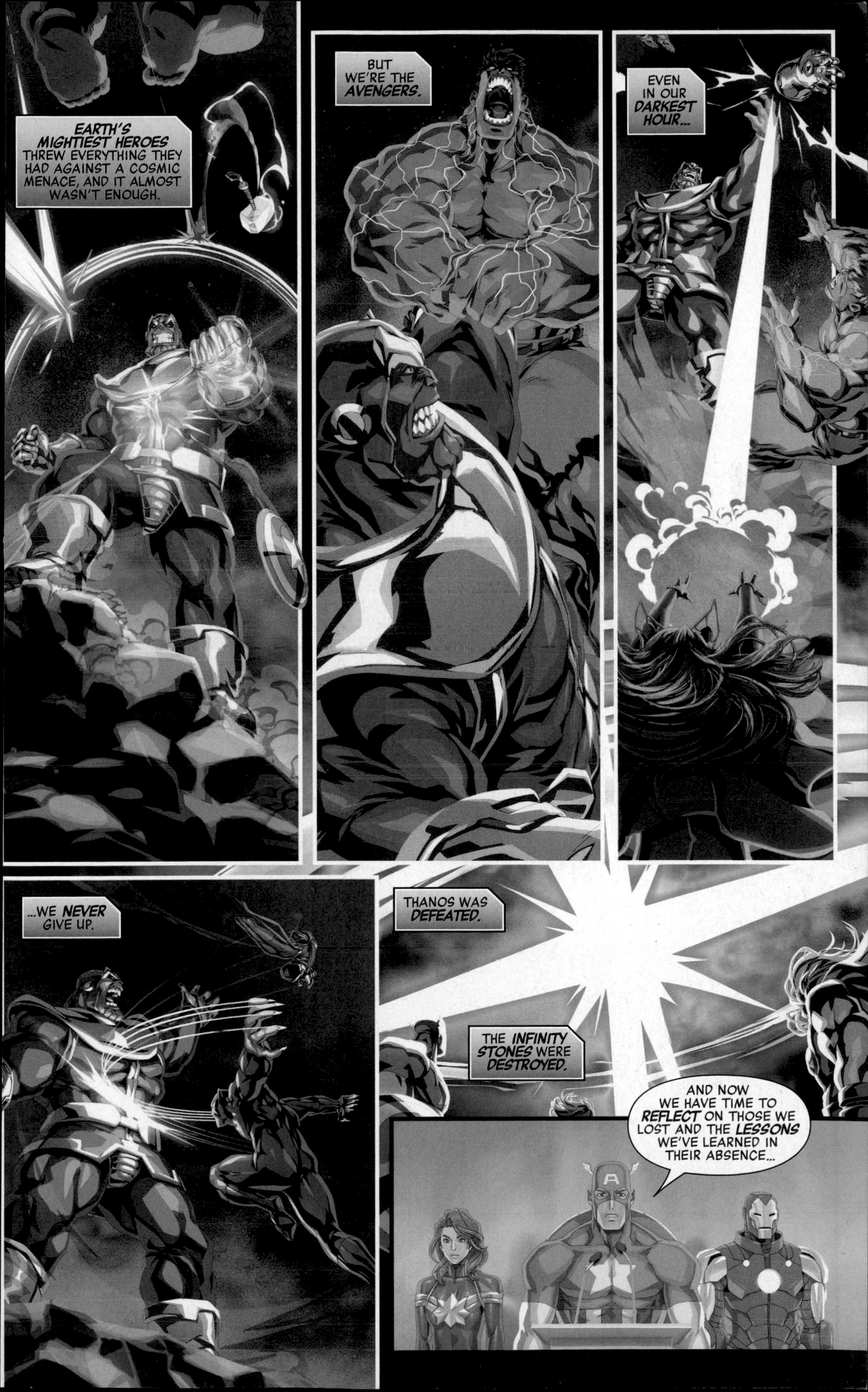
EARTH'S MIGHTIEST HEROES THREW EVERYTHING THEY HAD AGAINST A COSMIC MENACE, AND IT ALMOST WASN'T ENOUGH.
BUT WE'RE THE AVENGERS.
EVEN IN OUR DARKEST HOUR...
...WE NEVER GIVE UP.
THANOS WAS DEFEATED.
THE INFINITY STONES WERE DESTROYED.
AND NOW WE HAVE TIME TO REFLECT ON THOSE WE LOST AND THE LESSONS WE'VE LEARNED IN THEIR ABSENCE...

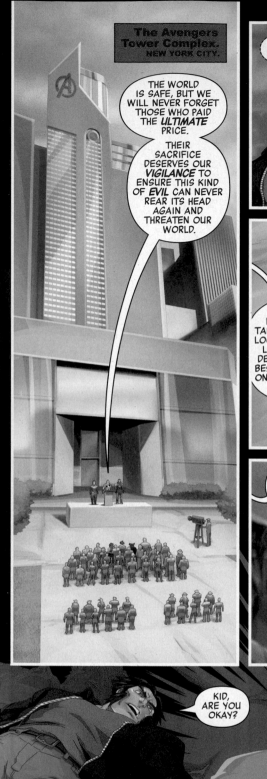

The Avengers Tower Complex. NEW YORK CITY.

THE WORLD IS SAFE, BUT WE WILL NEVER FORGET THOSE WHO PAID THE **ULTIMATE** PRICE.

THEIR SACRIFICE DESERVES OUR **VIGILANCE** TO ENSURE THIS KIND OF **EVIL** CAN NEVER REAR ITS HEAD AGAIN AND THREATEN OUR WORLD.

WE **ALL** NEED TO TAKE A GOOD LOOK AT OUR LIVES AND DECIDE HOW BEST TO **LIFT** ONE ANOTHER **UP**...

THAT'S WHY THE AVENGERS ENDURE-- BECAUSE **TOGETHER** WE CAN CONFRONT THREATS NO **INDIVIDUAL** COULD HANDLE ON THEIR OWN.

HECK OF A SPEECH.

YEAH, IT'S KIND OF WHAT CAP DOES.

HARD TO BELIEVE THAT HOT PIECE OF PATRIOTISM IS OVER A **HUNDRED YEARS** OLD.

MJ!

UNH!

PETER?

TONY!

UH, FRIDAY? I'M IN THE MIDDLE OF SOMETHI--

IT **CAN'T** WAIT! I'M READING A **MASSIVE ENERGY SURGE** FROM YOUR LOCATION!

KID, ARE YOU OKAY?

SPIDER-SENSE...GOING... **CRAZY!**

WE'VE GOT TO--

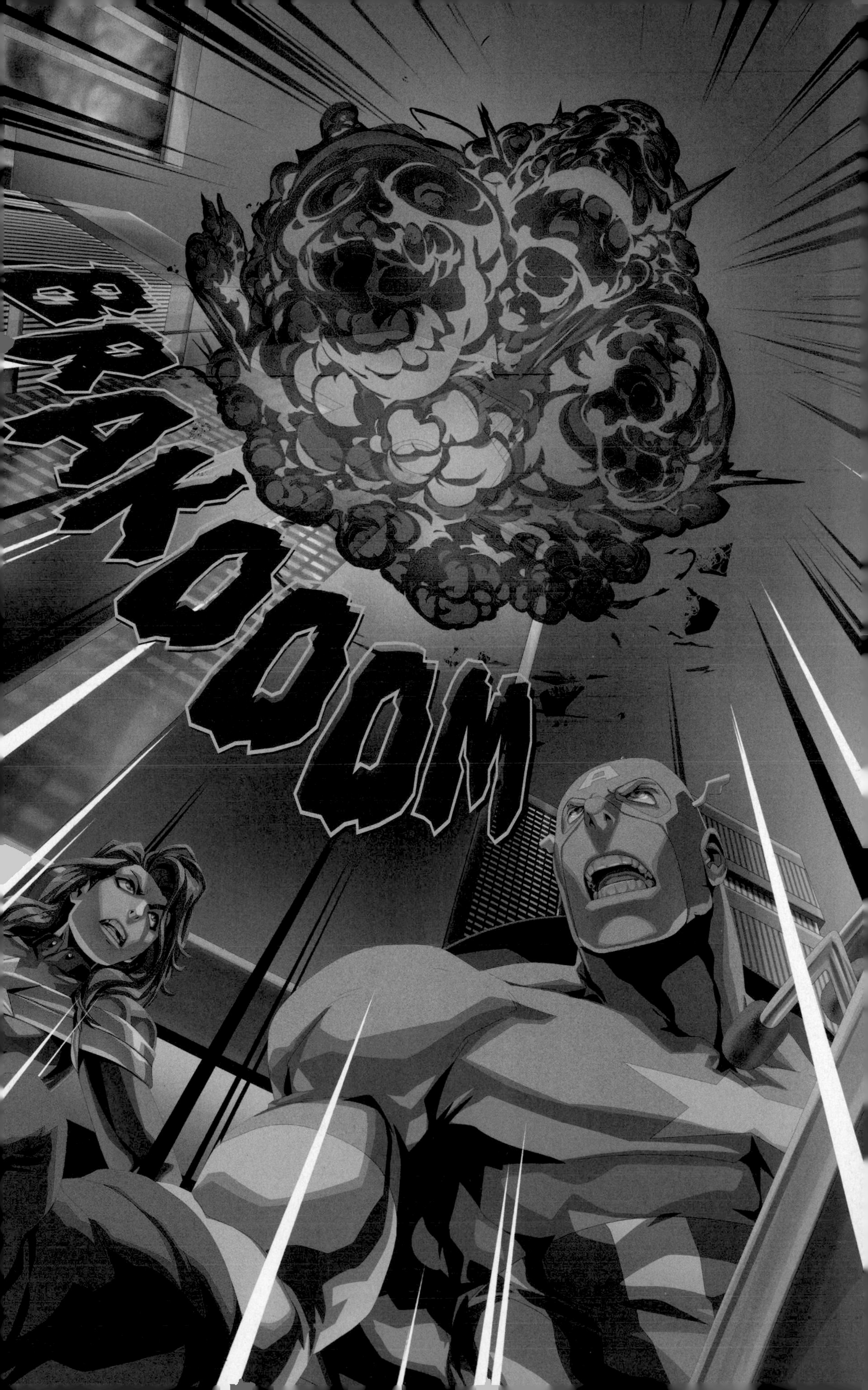
BRAKOOOM

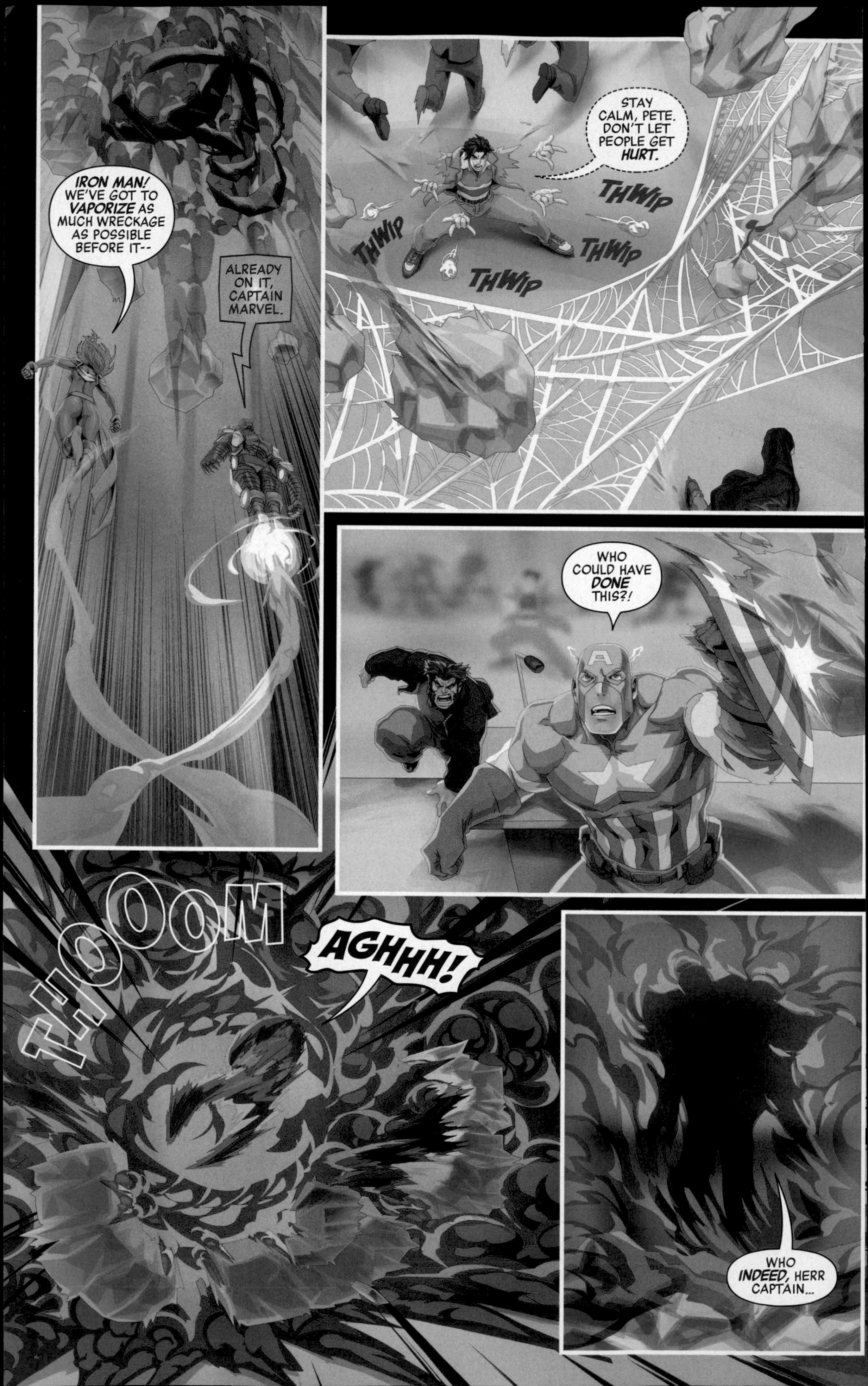
IRON MAN! WE'VE GOT TO VAPORIZE AS MUCH WRECKAGE AS POSSIBLE BEFORE IT--
ALREADY ON IT, CAPTAIN MARVEL.
STAY CALM, PETE. DON'T LET PEOPLE GET HURT.
THWIP
THWIP
THWIP
THWIP
WHO COULD HAVE DONE THIS?!
THOOOM
AGHHH!
WHO INDEED, HERR CAPTAIN...

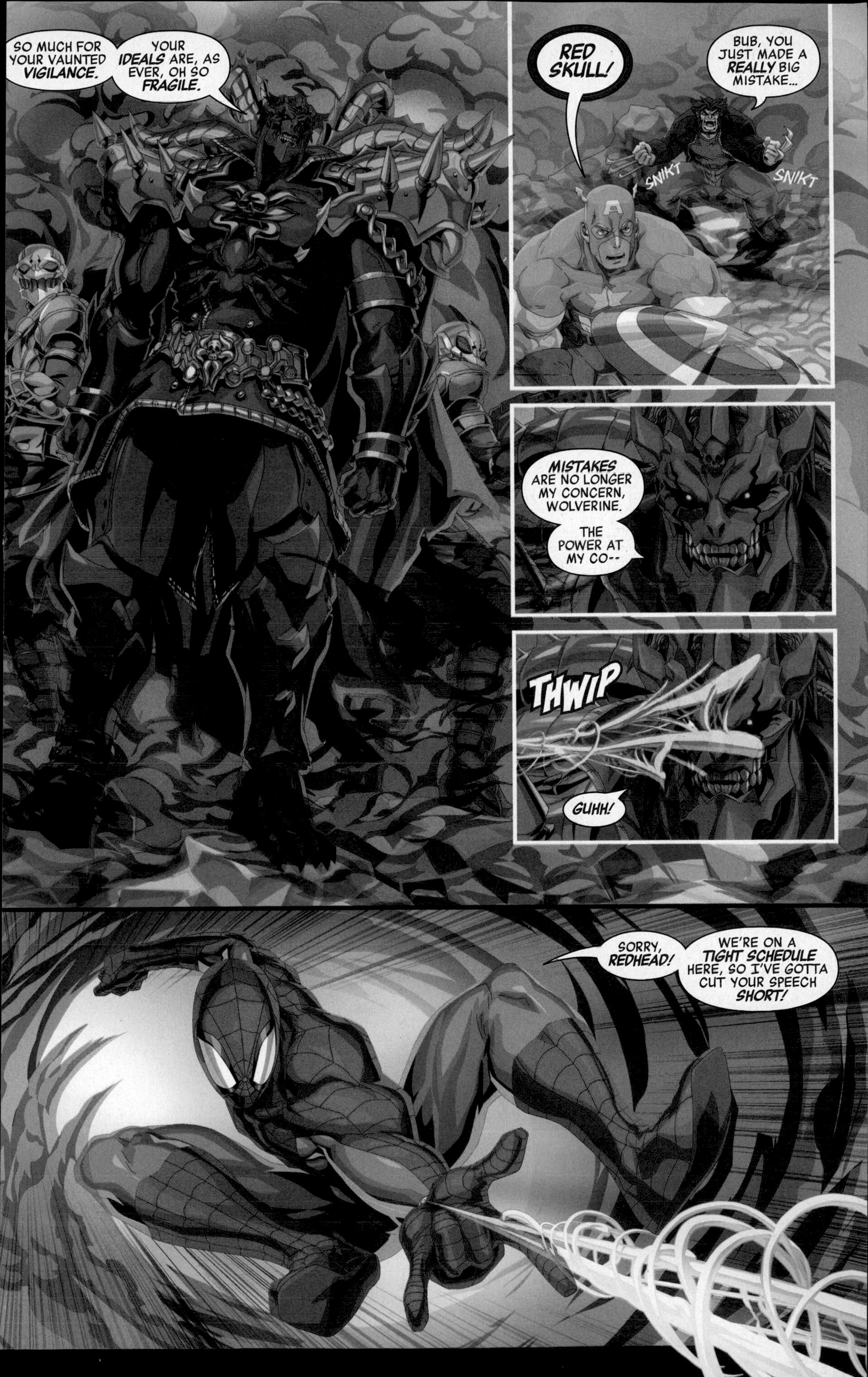
SO MUCH FOR YOUR VAUNTED VIGILANCE.
YOUR IDEALS ARE, AS EVER, OH SO FRAGILE.
RED SKULL!
BUB, YOU JUST MADE A REALLY BIG MISTAKE...
SNIKT
SNIKT
MISTAKES ARE NO LONGER MY CONCERN, WOLVERINE.
THE POWER AT MY CO--
THWIP
GUHH!
SORRY, REDHEAD!
WE'RE ON A TIGHT SCHEDULE HERE, SO I'VE GOTTA CUT YOUR SPEECH SHORT!

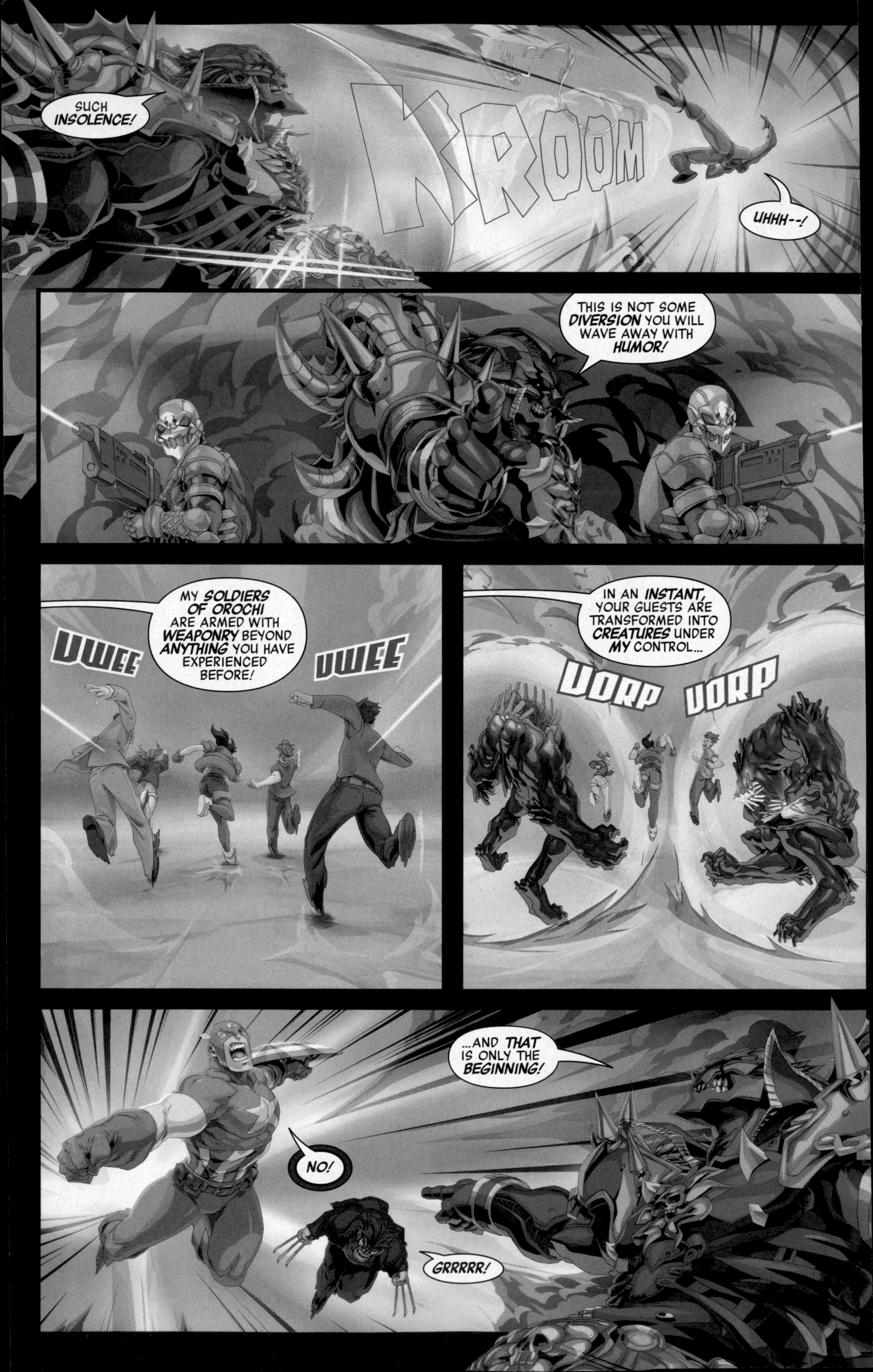
SUCH INSOLENCE!
KROOM
UHHH--!
THIS IS NOT SOME DIVERSION YOU WILL WAVE AWAY WITH HUMOR!
MY SOLDIERS OF OROCHI ARE ARMED WITH WEAPONRY BEYOND ANYTHING YOU HAVE EXPERIENCED BEFORE!
UWEE
UWEE
IN AN INSTANT, YOUR GUESTS ARE TRANSFORMED INTO CREATURES UNDER MY CONTROL...
VORP
VORP
...AND THAT IS ONLY THE BEGINNING!
NO!
GRRRRR!

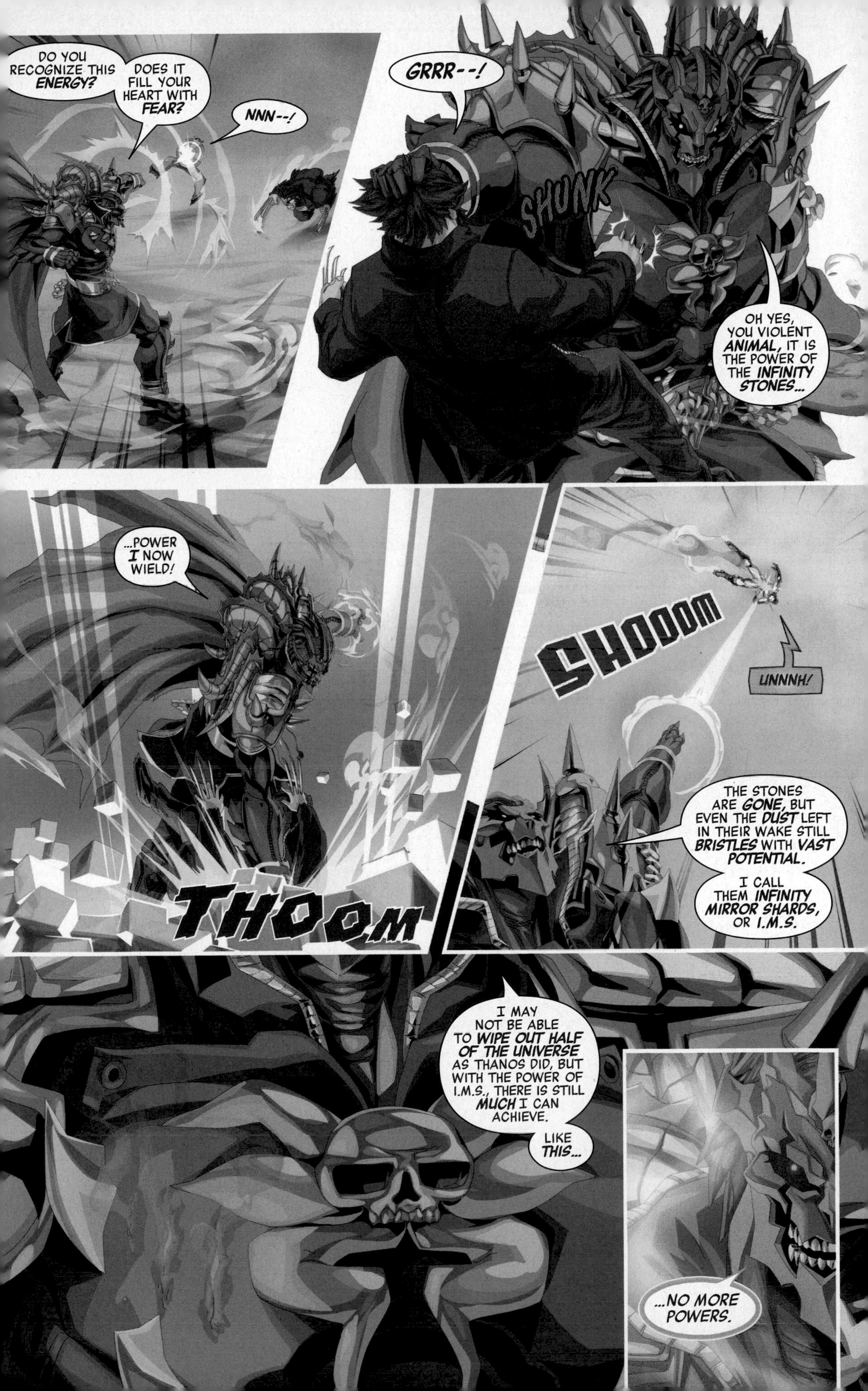

DO YOU RECOGNIZE THIS ENERGY?
DOES IT FILL YOUR HEART WITH FEAR?
NNN--!
GRRR--!
SHUNK
OH YES, YOU VIOLENT ANIMAL, IT IS THE POWER OF THE INFINITY STONES...
...POWER I NOW WIELD!
THOOM
SHOOOM
UNNNH!
THE STONES ARE GONE, BUT EVEN THE DUST LEFT IN THEIR WAKE STILL BRISTLES WITH VAST POTENTIAL.
I CALL THEM INFINITY MIRROR SHARDS, OR I.M.S.
I MAY NOT BE ABLE TO WIPE OUT HALF OF THE UNIVERSE AS THANOS DID, BUT WITH THE POWER OF I.M.S., THERE IS STILL MUCH I CAN ACHIEVE.
LIKE THIS...
...NO MORE POWERS.

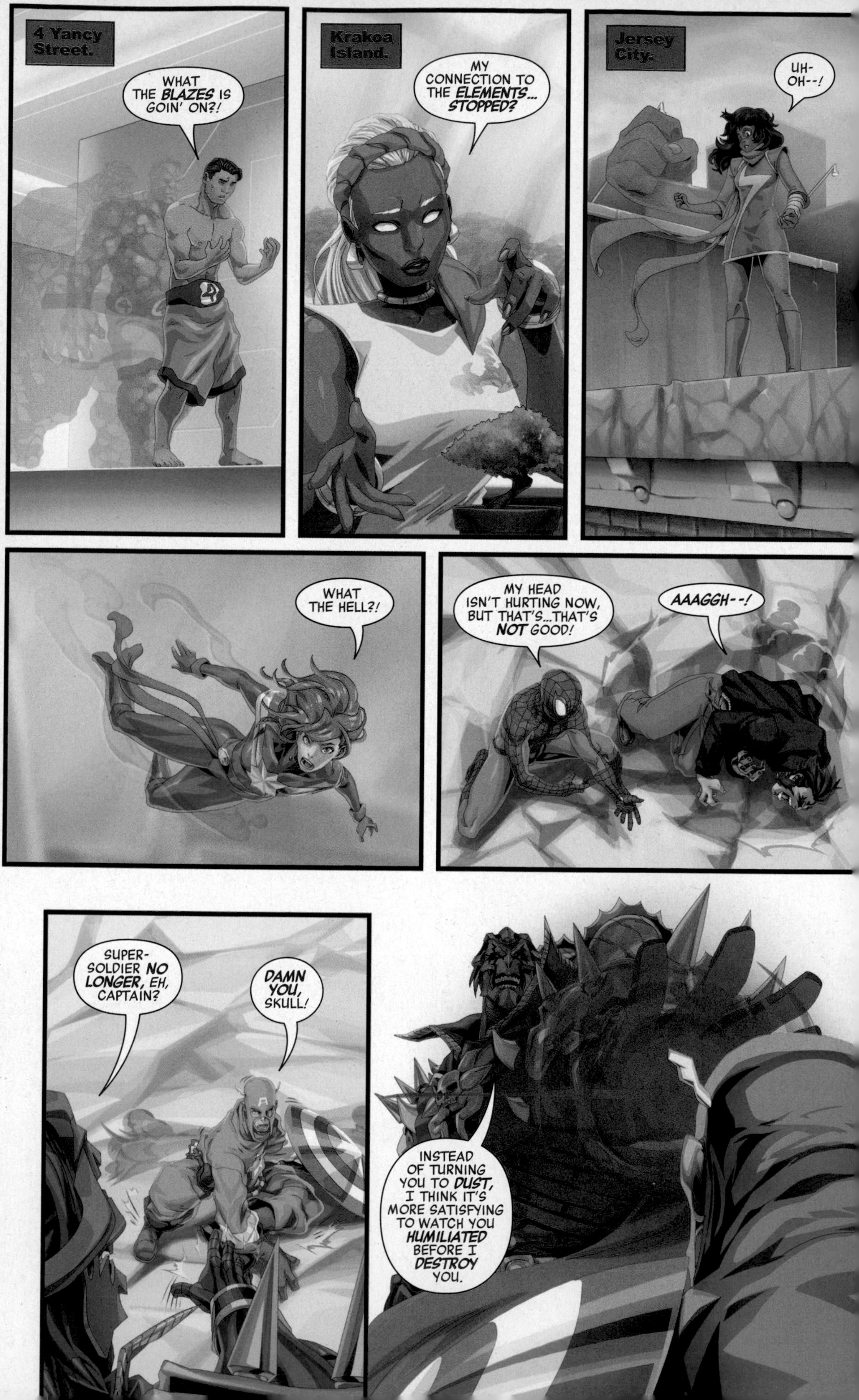
4 Yancy Street.
WHAT THE BLAZES IS GOIN' ON?!
Krakoa Island.
MY CONNECTION TO THE ELEMENTS... STOPPED?
Jersey City.
UH-OH--!
WHAT THE HELL?!
MY HEAD ISN'T HURTING NOW, BUT THAT'S...THAT'S NOT GOOD!
AAAGGH--!
SUPER-SOLDIER NO LONGER, EH, CAPTAIN?
DAMN YOU, SKULL!
INSTEAD OF TURNING YOU TO DUST, I THINK IT'S MORE SATISFYING TO WATCH YOU HUMILIATED BEFORE I DESTROY YOU.

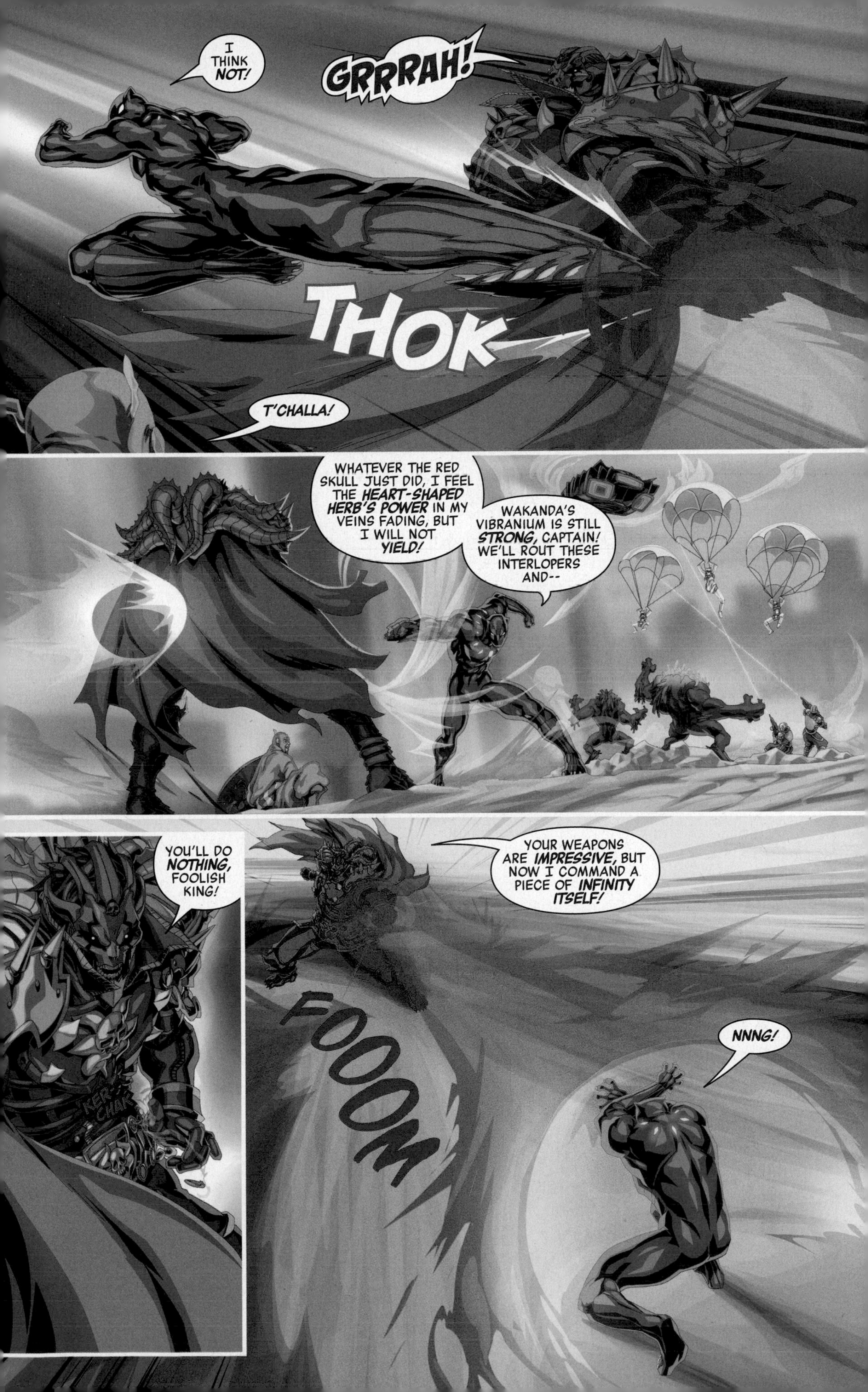
I THINK NOT!
GRRRAH!
THOK
T'CHALLA!
WHATEVER THE RED SKULL JUST DID, I FEEL THE HEART-SHAPED HERB'S POWER IN MY VEINS FADING, BUT I WILL NOT YIELD!
WAKANDA'S VIBRANIUM IS STILL STRONG, CAPTAIN! WE'LL ROUT THESE INTERLOPERS AND--
YOU'LL DO NOTHING, FOOLISH KING!
KER-CHAK
YOUR WEAPONS ARE IMPRESSIVE, BUT NOW I COMMAND A PIECE OF INFINITY ITSELF!
FOOOM
NNNG!

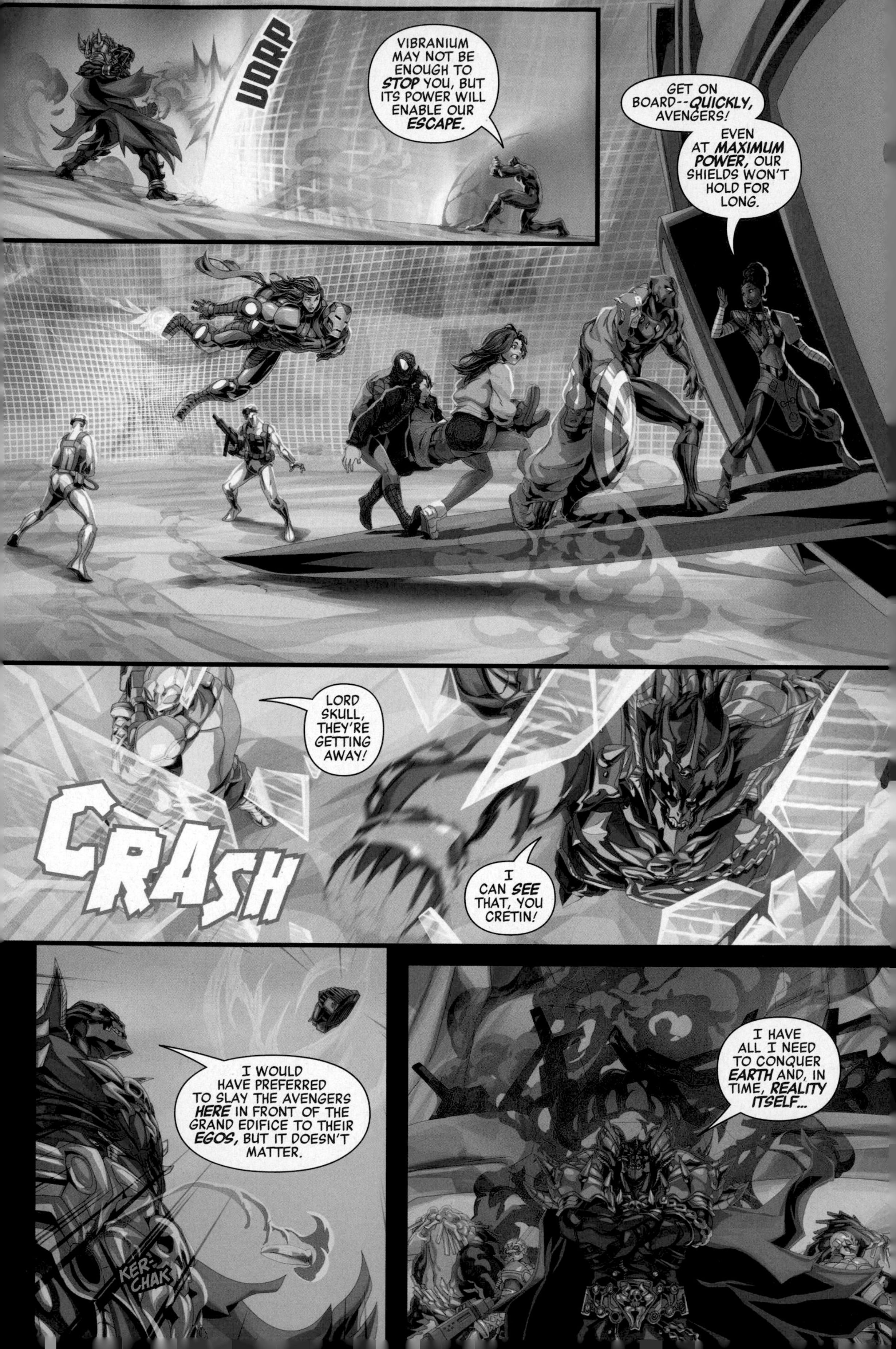
UORP
VIBRANIUM MAY NOT BE ENOUGH TO STOP YOU, BUT ITS POWER WILL ENABLE OUR ESCAPE.
GET ON BOARD--QUICKLY, AVENGERS!
EVEN AT MAXIMUM POWER, OUR SHIELDS WON'T HOLD FOR LONG.
LORD SKULL, THEY'RE GETTING AWAY!
CRASH
I CAN SEE THAT, YOU CRETIN!
I WOULD HAVE PREFERRED TO SLAY THE AVENGERS HERE IN FRONT OF THE GRAND EDIFICE TO THEIR EGOS, BUT IT DOESN'T MATTER.
KER-CHAK
I HAVE ALL I NEED TO CONQUER EARTH AND, IN TIME, REALITY ITSELF...

WE GOT **SHELLACKED** OUT THERE!

I BUILT DOZENS OF **DEFENSE SYSTEMS** PACKED WITH **REDUNDANCIES,** AND THE RED SKULL STILL WALKED **ALL OVER** US!

EVERY HERO ON EARTH **LOST THEIR SUPER-POWERS,** AND WE RAN WITH TAILS FIRMLY TUCKED BETWEEN OUR LEGS!

YOU CAN'T BLAME YOURSELF FOR THIS, TONY.

DAMN RIGHT I CAN!

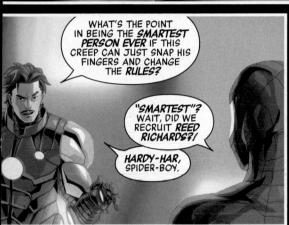

WHAT'S THE POINT IN BEING THE **SMARTEST PERSON EVER** IF THIS CREEP CAN JUST SNAP HIS FINGERS AND CHANGE THE **RULES?**

"SMARTEST"? WAIT, DID WE RECRUIT **REED RICHARDS?!**

HARDY-HAR, SPIDER-BOY.

TEARING INTO EACH OTHER WON'T FIX THIS.

I KNOW. I JUST NEED TO FIGURE OUT THE **RULES** TO THE NEW GAME THE SKULL IS PLAYING.

IF I RUN SOME TESTS ON THE **ENERGY** THAT HIT MY ARMOR, I CAN FIGURE OUT WHAT HE USED TO KNOCK US DOWN.

NO NEED. HE GLOATED ABOUT IT AS HE PUMMELED ME. HE GATHERED **STRAY DUST** FROM THE SHATTERED **INFINITY STONES.**

IT'S NOT THE SAME AS **THANOS,** BUT--

BUT STILL MORE THAN ENOUGH TO SHIFT **REALITY** IN HIS FAVOR AND **KICK OUR BUTTS.**

YEAH.

WHEN THE SKULL UNLEASHED THAT ENERGY, HIS EXOSKELETON EJECTED **THIS.**

I GRABBED IT OFF THE GROUND AS WE BEAT OUR HASTY **RETREAT.**

THAT'S **GREAT,** KID. I CAN **ANALYZE** THAT AND SEE IF IT'S--

NOT SO FAST, **MR. BILLIONS. I'M** A SCIENTIST TOO, AND I'M **NOT** A KID.

WHATEVER YOU'RE DOING, **I** GET TO BE PART OF IT.

PETER, I'M **WORRIED.** YOUR SUPER-POWERS... THEY'RE **GONE.**

I KNOW, MJ, BUT I CAN'T LET THAT STOP ME FROM DOING WHAT'S **RIGHT.**

MAYBE I CAN FIND A WAY TO EVEN THE ODDS.

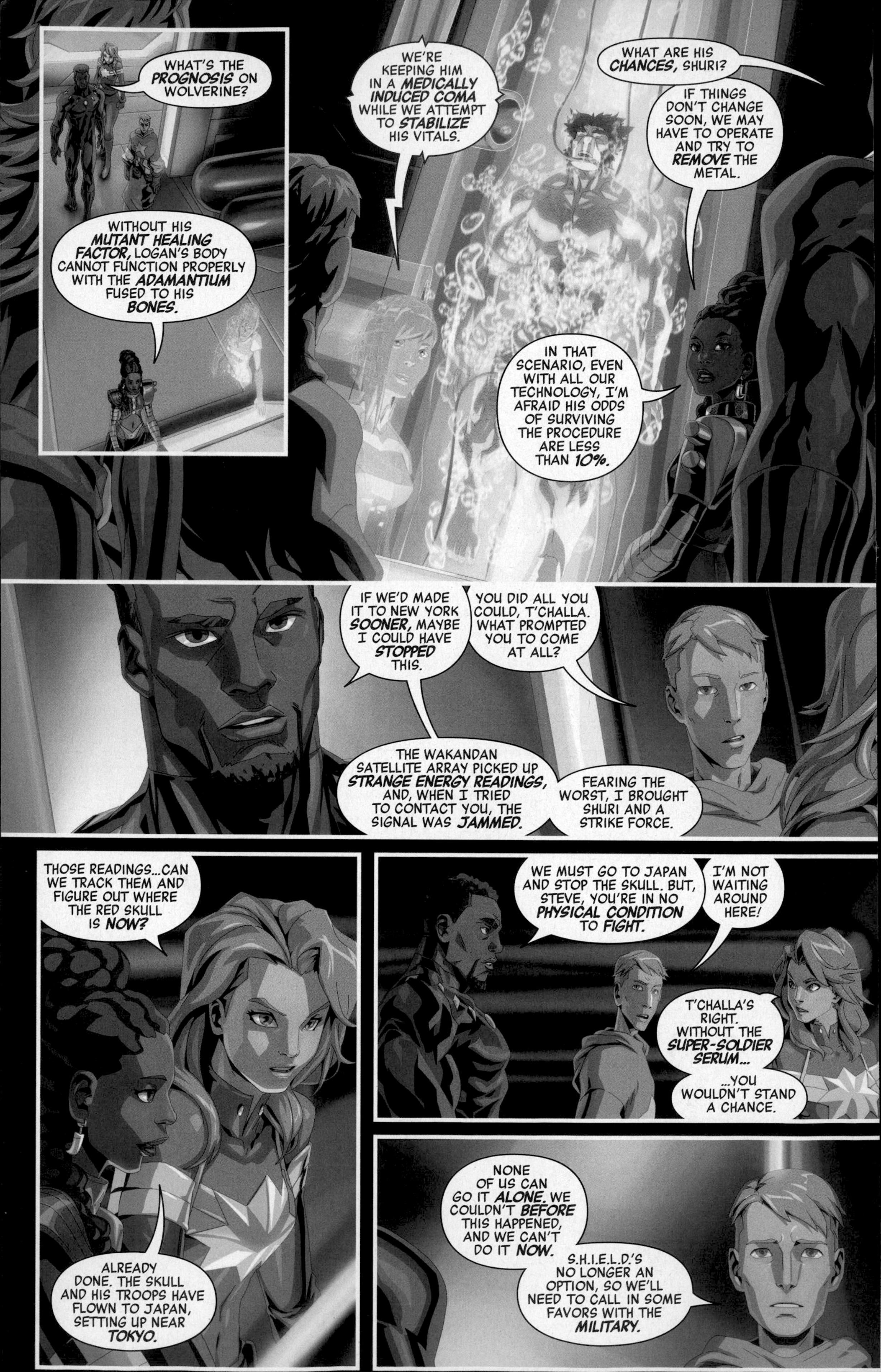
WHAT'S THE PROGNOSIS ON WOLVERINE?
WITHOUT HIS MUTANT HEALING FACTOR, LOGAN'S BODY CANNOT FUNCTION PROPERLY WITH THE ADAMANTIUM FUSED TO HIS BONES.
WE'RE KEEPING HIM IN A MEDICALLY INDUCED COMA WHILE WE ATTEMPT TO STABILIZE HIS VITALS.
WHAT ARE HIS CHANCES, SHURI?
IF THINGS DON'T CHANGE SOON, WE MAY HAVE TO OPERATE AND TRY TO REMOVE THE METAL.
IN THAT SCENARIO, EVEN WITH ALL OUR TECHNOLOGY, I'M AFRAID HIS ODDS OF SURVIVING THE PROCEDURE ARE LESS THAN 10%.
IF WE'D MADE IT TO NEW YORK SOONER, MAYBE I COULD HAVE STOPPED THIS.
YOU DID ALL YOU COULD, T'CHALLA. WHAT PROMPTED YOU TO COME AT ALL?
THE WAKANDAN SATELLITE ARRAY PICKED UP STRANGE ENERGY READINGS, AND, WHEN I TRIED TO CONTACT YOU, THE SIGNAL WAS JAMMED.
FEARING THE WORST, I BROUGHT SHURI AND A STRIKE FORCE.
THOSE READINGS...CAN WE TRACK THEM AND FIGURE OUT WHERE THE RED SKULL IS NOW?
ALREADY DONE. THE SKULL AND HIS TROOPS HAVE FLOWN TO JAPAN, SETTING UP NEAR TOKYO.
WE MUST GO TO JAPAN AND STOP THE SKULL. BUT, STEVE, YOU'RE IN NO PHYSICAL CONDITION TO FIGHT.
I'M NOT WAITING AROUND HERE!
T'CHALLA'S RIGHT. WITHOUT THE SUPER-SOLDIER SERUM...
...YOU WOULDN'T STAND A CHANCE.
NONE OF US CAN GO IT ALONE. WE COULDN'T BEFORE THIS HAPPENED, AND WE CAN'T DO IT NOW.
S.H.I.E.L.D.'S NO LONGER AN OPTION, SO WE'LL NEED TO CALL IN SOME FAVORS WITH THE MILITARY.

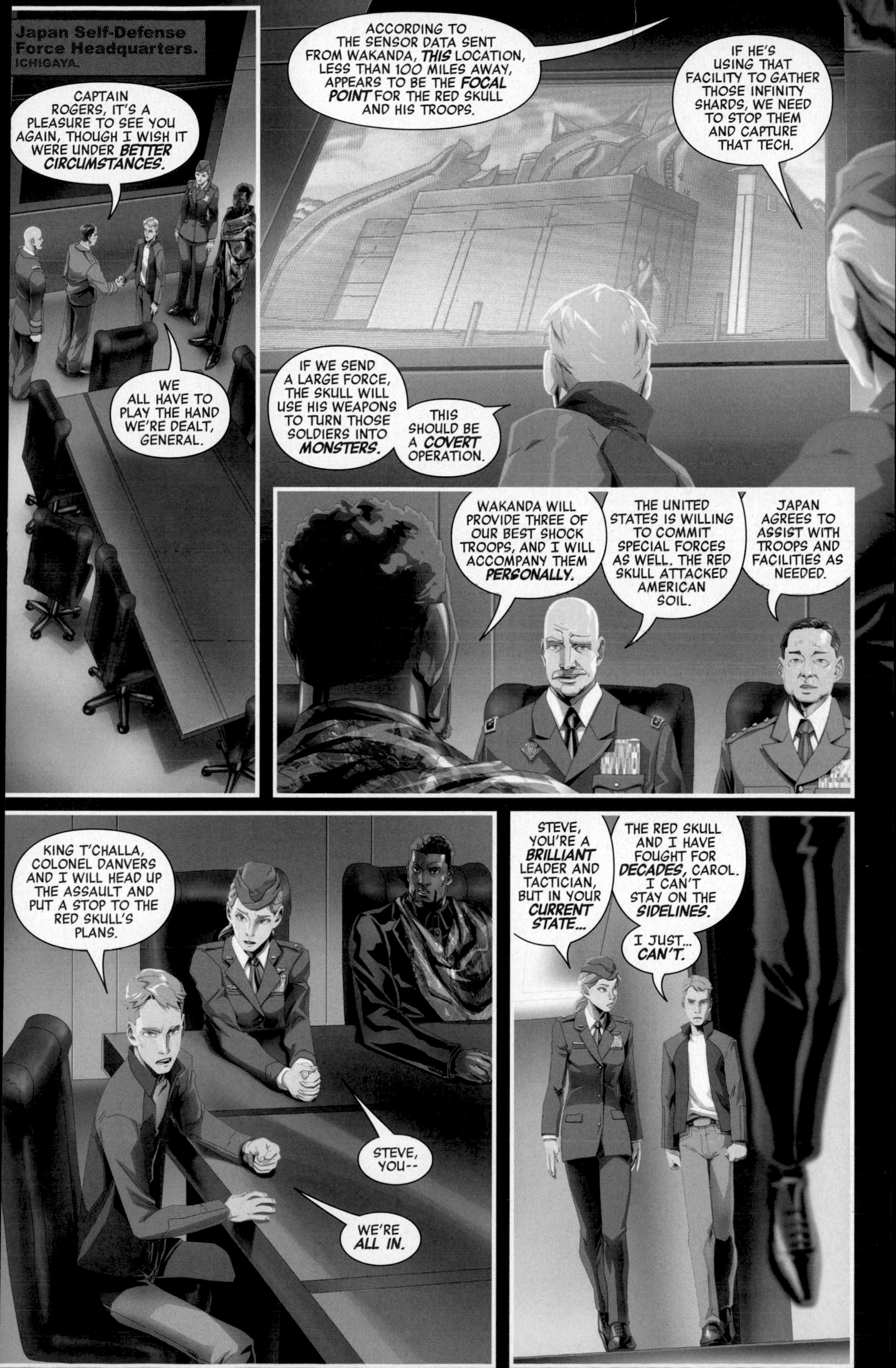
Japan Self-Defense Force Headquarters.
ICHIGAYA.
CAPTAIN ROGERS, IT'S A PLEASURE TO SEE YOU AGAIN, THOUGH I WISH IT WERE UNDER BETTER CIRCUMSTANCES.
WE ALL HAVE TO PLAY THE HAND WE'RE DEALT, GENERAL.
ACCORDING TO THE SENSOR DATA SENT FROM WAKANDA, THIS LOCATION, LESS THAN 100 MILES AWAY, APPEARS TO BE THE FOCAL POINT FOR THE RED SKULL AND HIS TROOPS.
IF HE'S USING THAT FACILITY TO GATHER THOSE INFINITY SHARDS, WE NEED TO STOP THEM AND CAPTURE THAT TECH.
IF WE SEND A LARGE FORCE, THE SKULL WILL USE HIS WEAPONS TO TURN THOSE SOLDIERS INTO MONSTERS.
THIS SHOULD BE A COVERT OPERATION.
WAKANDA WILL PROVIDE THREE OF OUR BEST SHOCK TROOPS, AND I WILL ACCOMPANY THEM PERSONALLY.
THE UNITED STATES IS WILLING TO COMMIT SPECIAL FORCES AS WELL. THE RED SKULL ATTACKED AMERICAN SOIL.
JAPAN AGREES TO ASSIST WITH TROOPS AND FACILITIES AS NEEDED.
KING T'CHALLA, COLONEL DANVERS AND I WILL HEAD UP THE ASSAULT AND PUT A STOP TO THE RED SKULL'S PLANS.
STEVE, YOU--
WE'RE ALL IN.
STEVE, YOU'RE A BRILLIANT LEADER AND TACTICIAN, BUT IN YOUR CURRENT STATE...
THE RED SKULL AND I HAVE FOUGHT FOR DECADES, CAROL. I CAN'T STAY ON THE SIDELINES.
I JUST... CAN'T.

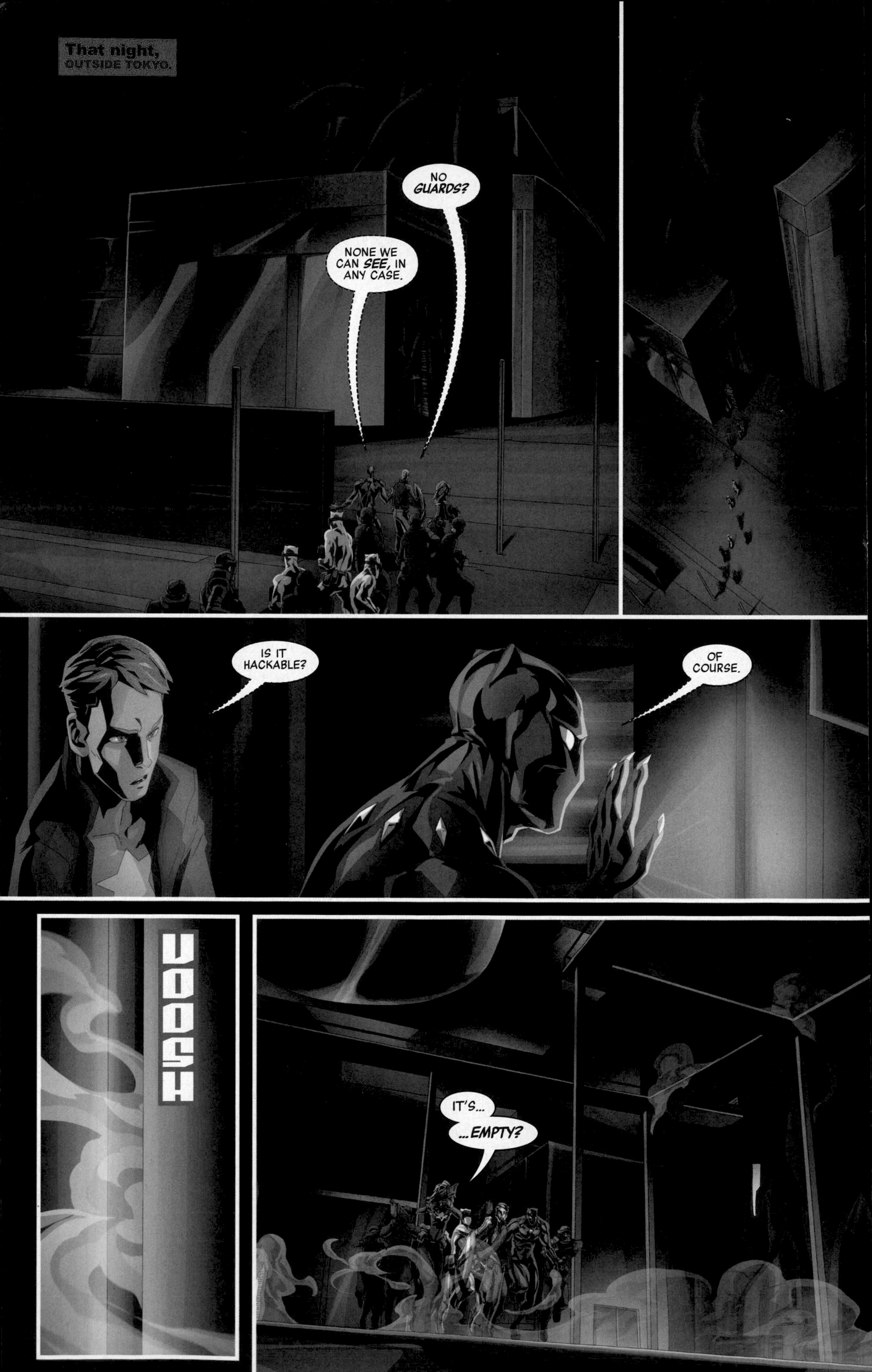
That night,
OUTSIDE TOKYO.
NO GUARDS?
NONE WE CAN SEE, IN ANY CASE.
IS IT HACKABLE?
OF COURSE.
VOOSH
IT'S...
...EMPTY?

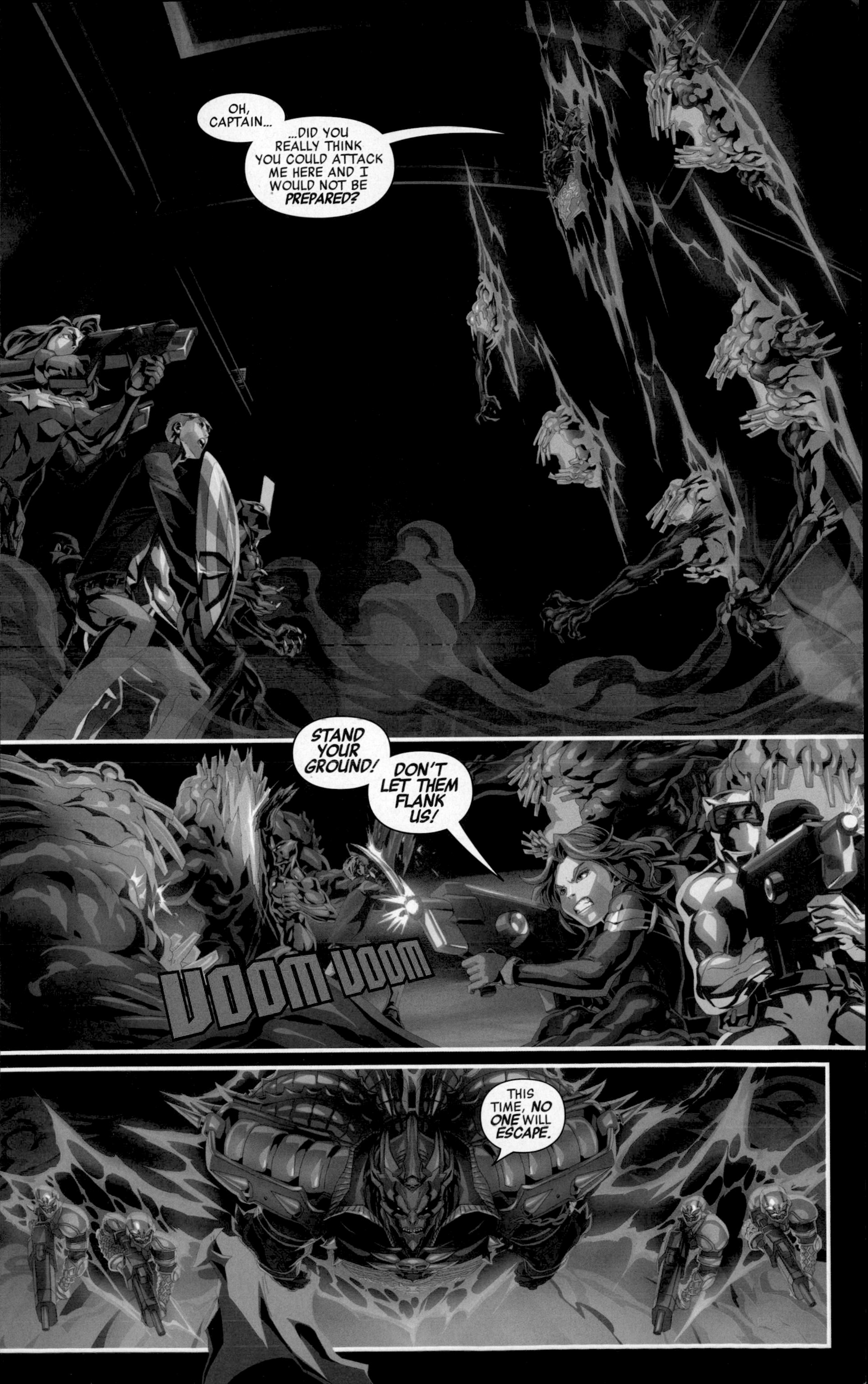
OH, CAPTAIN...
...DID YOU REALLY THINK YOU COULD ATTACK ME HERE AND I WOULD NOT BE PREPARED?
STAND YOUR GROUND!
DON'T LET THEM FLANK US!
VOOM VOOM
THIS TIME, NO ONE WILL ESCAPE.

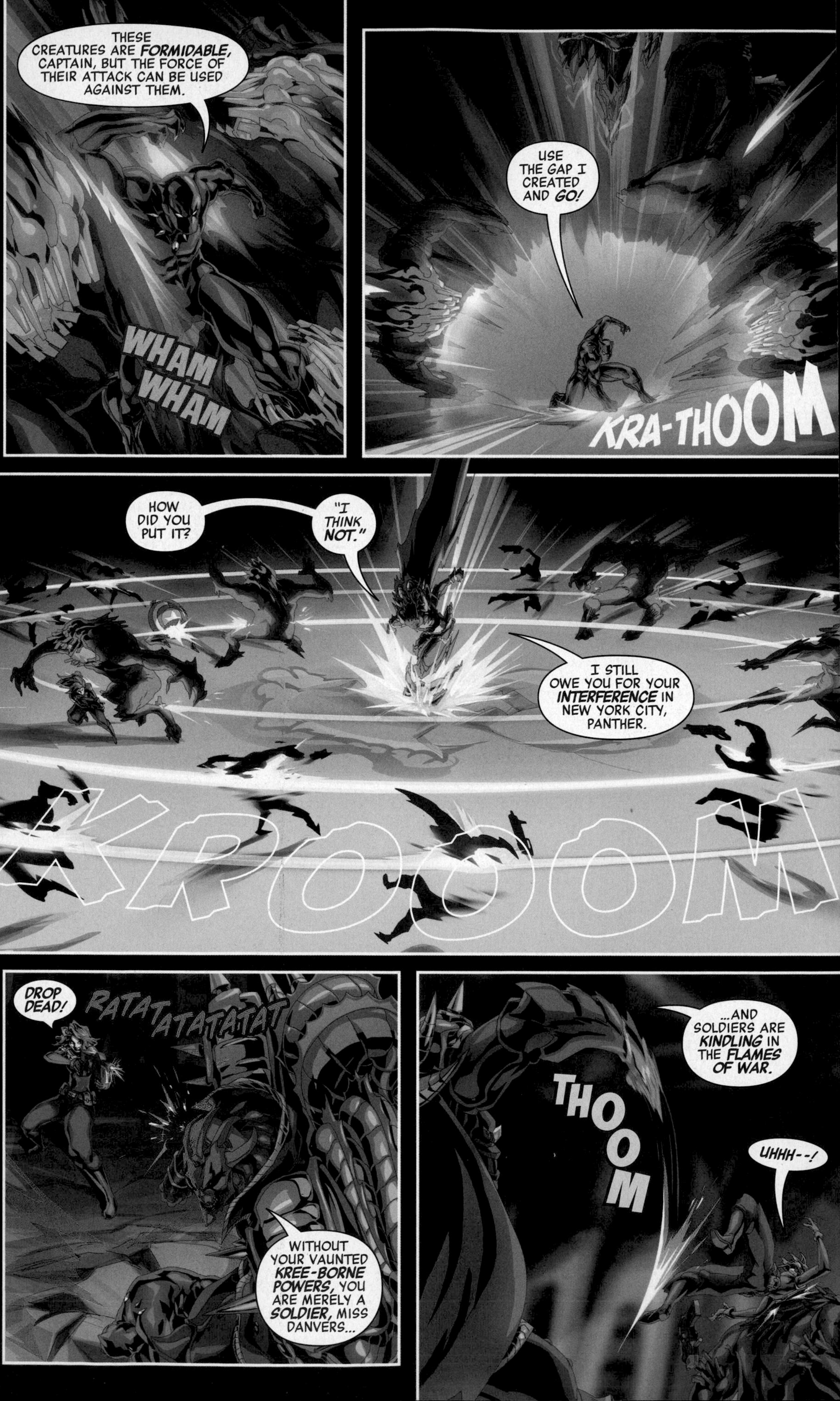
THESE CREATURES ARE FORMIDABLE, CAPTAIN, BUT THE FORCE OF THEIR ATTACK CAN BE USED AGAINST THEM.
WHAM
WHAM
USE THE GAP I CREATED AND GO!
KRA-THOOM
HOW DID YOU PUT IT?
"I THINK NOT."
I STILL OWE YOU FOR YOUR INTERFERENCE IN NEW YORK CITY, PANTHER.
KROOOM
DROP DEAD!
RATATATATATAT
WITHOUT YOUR VAUNTED KREE-BORNE POWERS, YOU ARE MERELY A SOLDIER, MISS DANVERS...
...AND SOLDIERS ARE KINDLING IN THE FLAMES OF WAR.
THOOM
UHHH--!

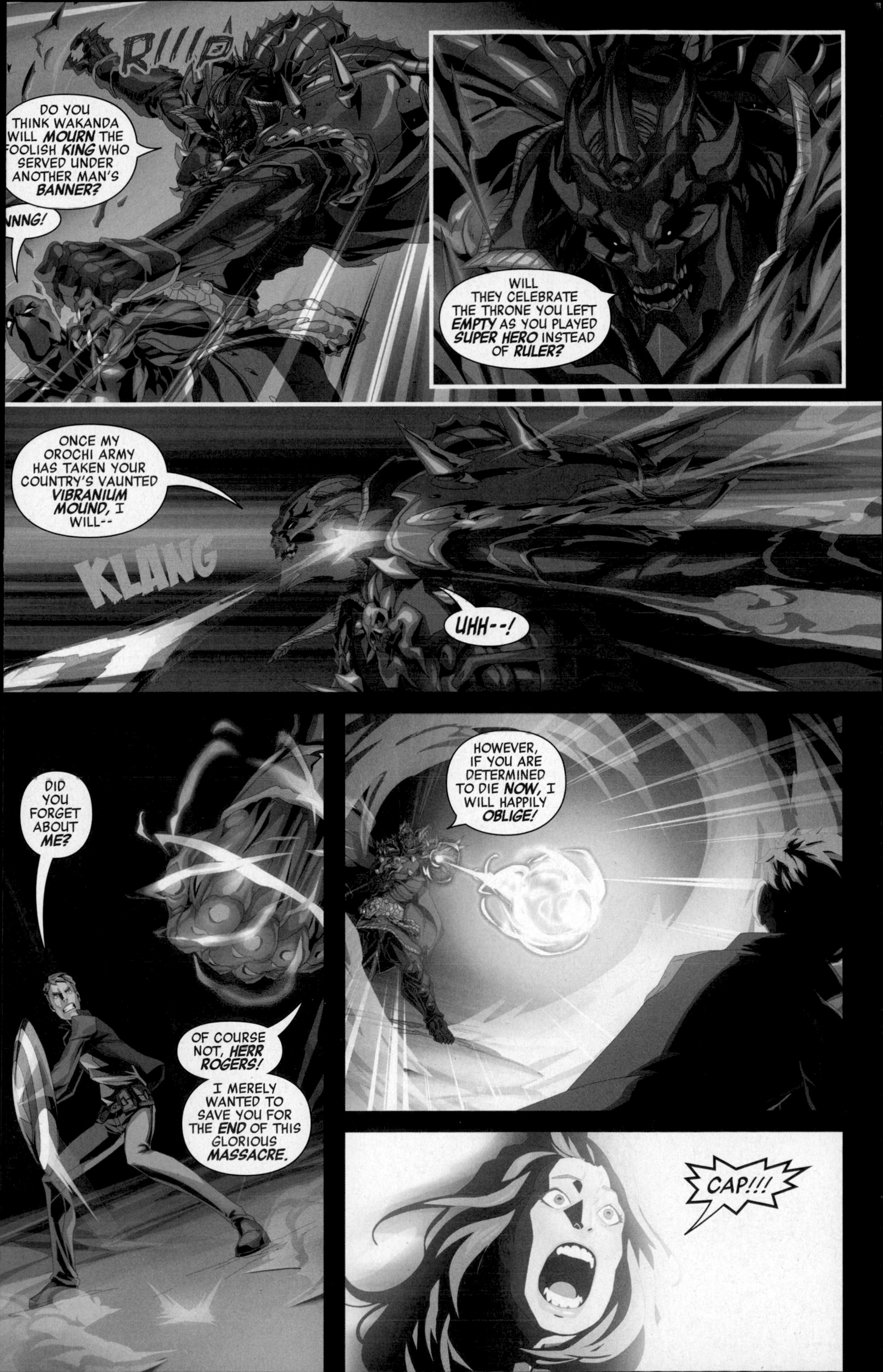
RIIIP
DO YOU THINK WAKANDA WILL MOURN THE FOOLISH KING WHO SERVED UNDER ANOTHER MAN'S BANNER?
NNNG!
WILL THEY CELEBRATE THE THRONE YOU LEFT EMPTY AS YOU PLAYED SUPER HERO INSTEAD OF RULER?
ONCE MY OROCHI ARMY HAS TAKEN YOUR COUNTRY'S VAUNTED VIBRANIUM MOUND, I WILL--
KLANG
UHH--!
DID YOU FORGET ABOUT ME?
OF COURSE NOT, HERR ROGERS!
I MERELY WANTED TO SAVE YOU FOR THE END OF THIS GLORIOUS MASSACRE.
HOWEVER, IF YOU ARE DETERMINED TO DIE NOW, I WILL HAPPILY OBLIGE!
CAP!!!

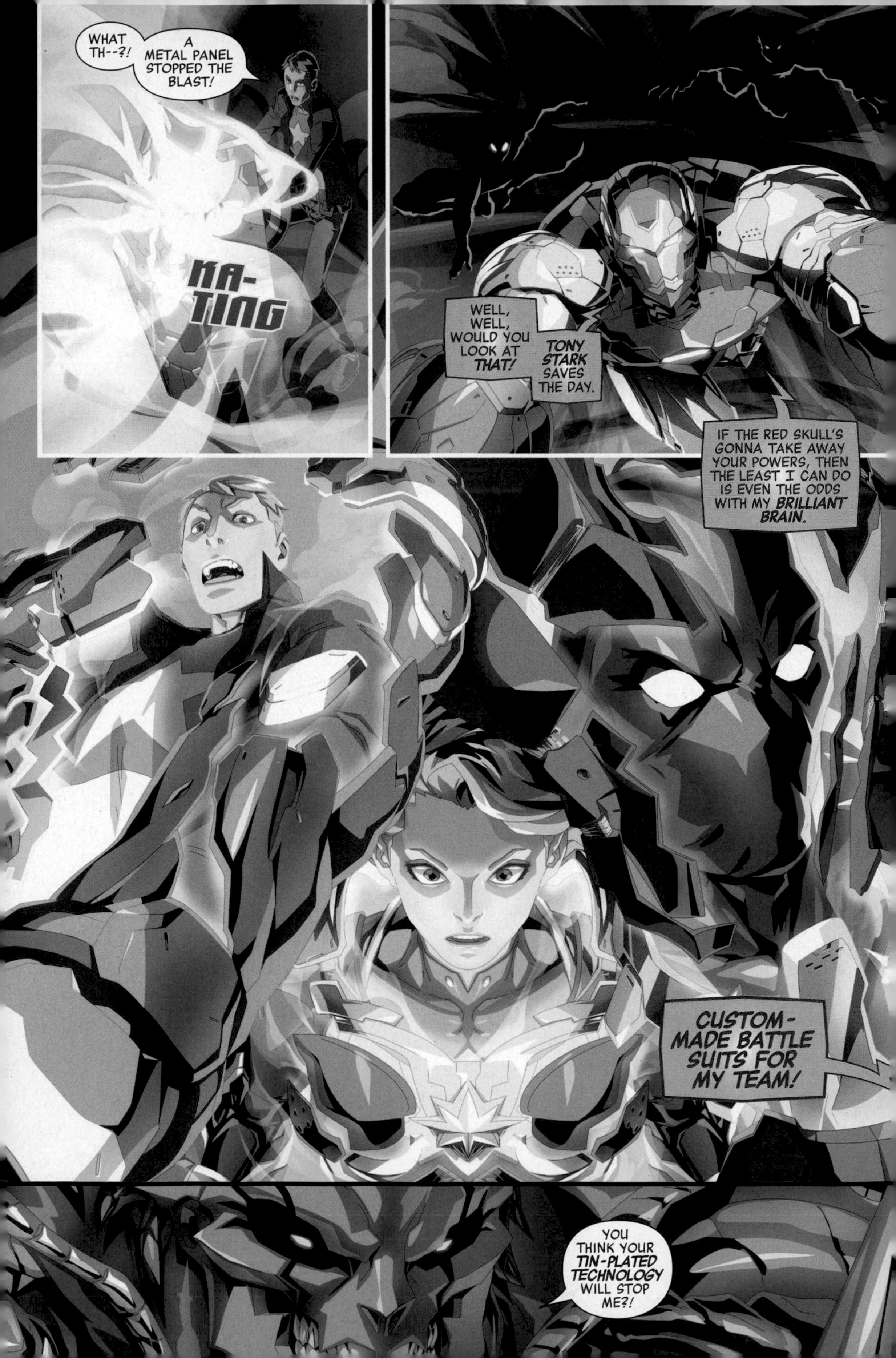
WHAT TH--?!
A METAL PANEL STOPPED THE BLAST!
KA-TING
WELL, WELL, WOULD YOU LOOK AT THAT!
TONY STARK SAVES THE DAY.
IF THE RED SKULL'S GONNA TAKE AWAY YOUR POWERS, THEN THE LEAST I CAN DO IS EVEN THE ODDS WITH MY BRILLIANT BRAIN.
CUSTOM-MADE BATTLE SUITS FOR MY TEAM!
YOU THINK YOUR TIN-PLATED TECHNOLOGY WILL STOP ME?!

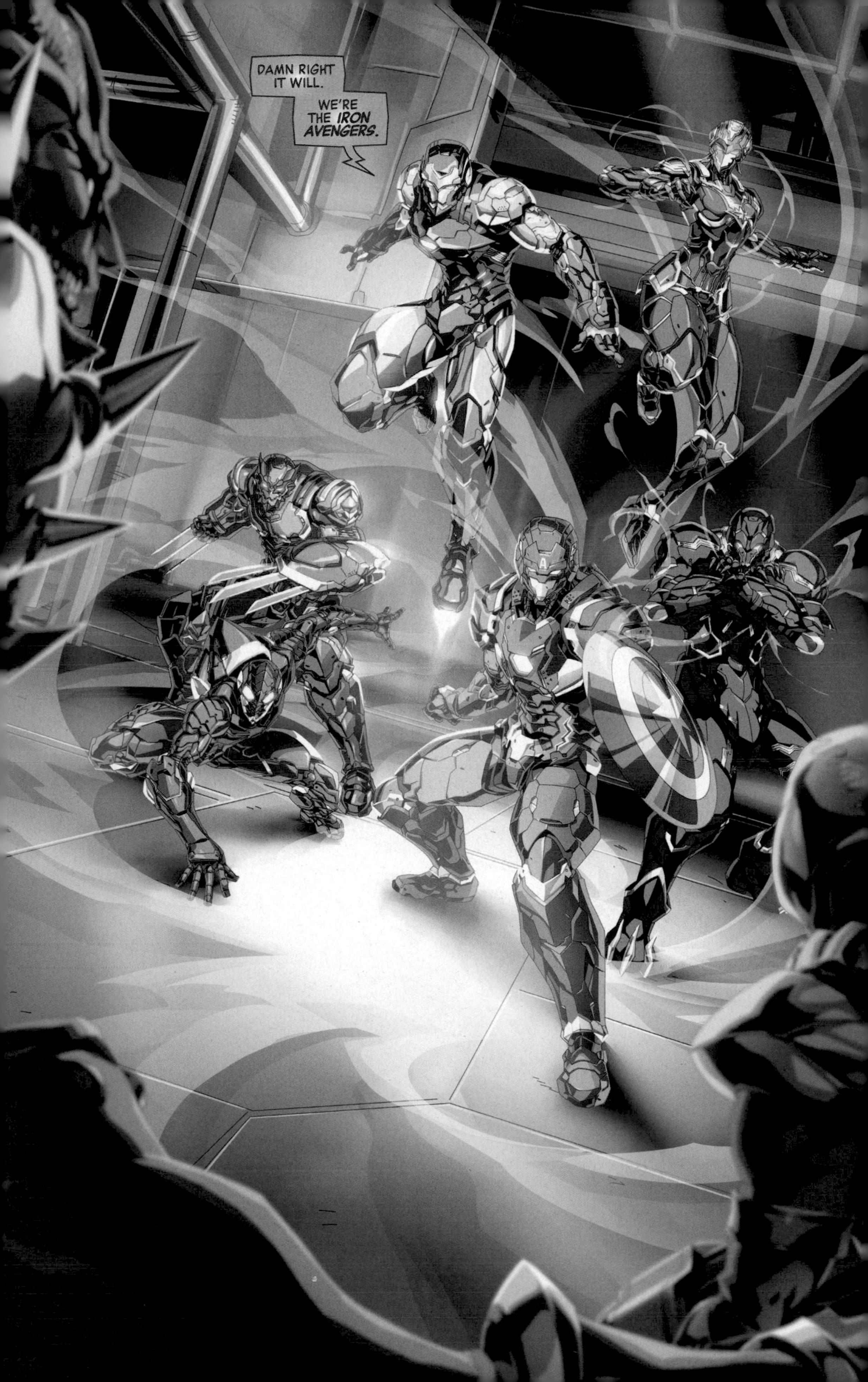
DAMN RIGHT IT WILL.
WE'RE THE IRON AVENGERS.

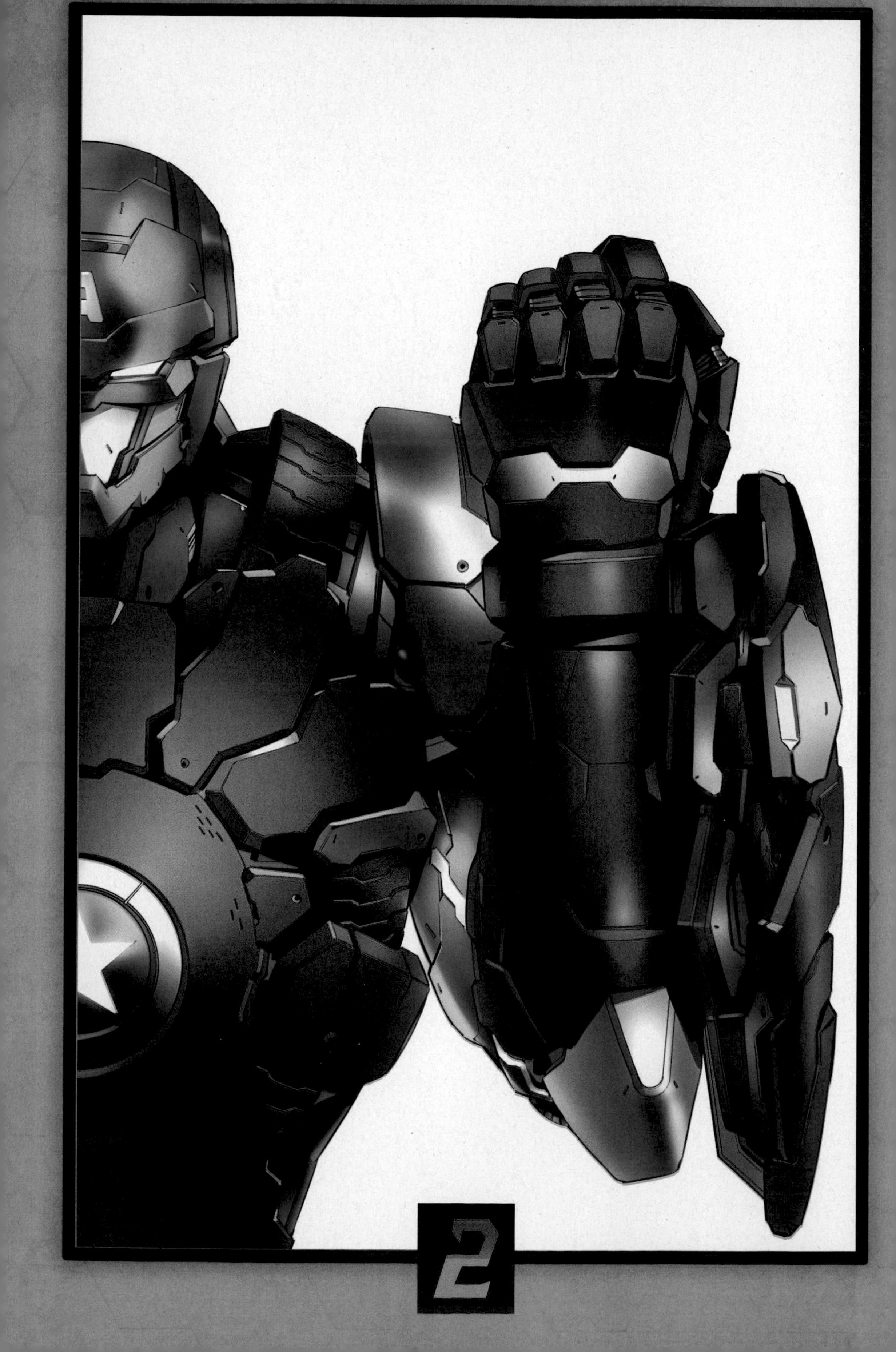

2

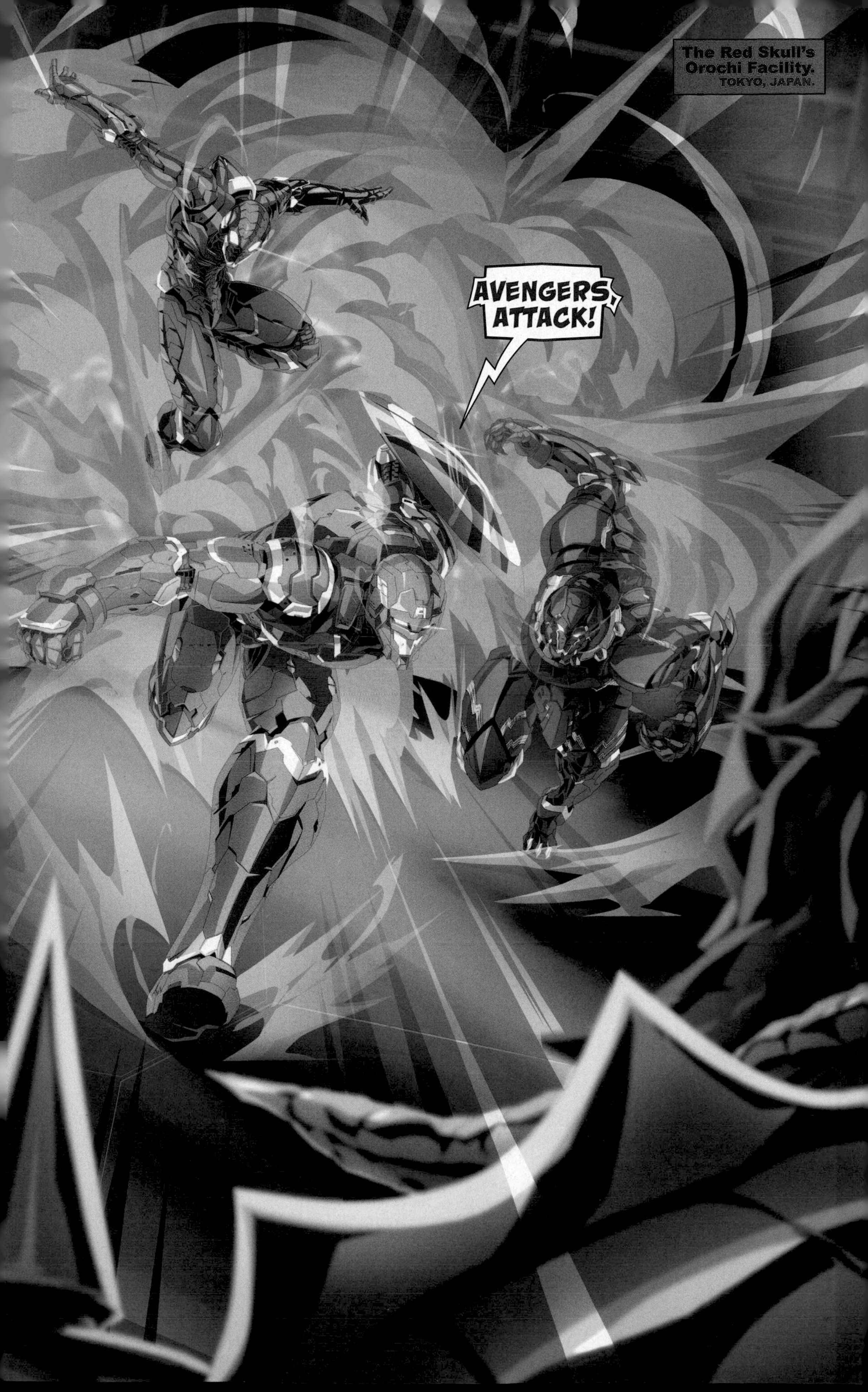
The Red Skull's Orochi Facility. TOKYO, JAPAN.
AVENGERS, ATTACK!

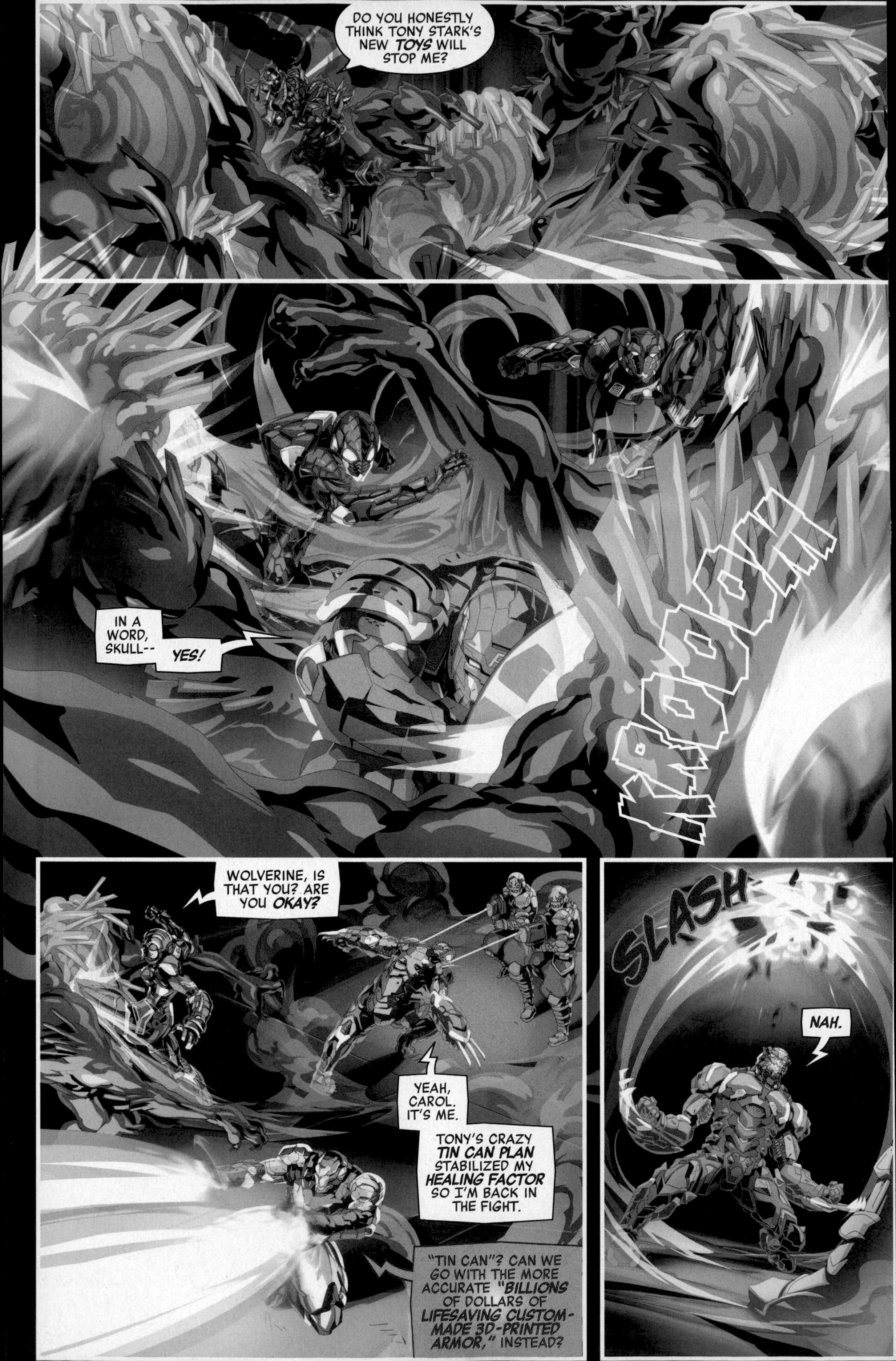
DO YOU HONESTLY THINK TONY STARK'S NEW *TOYS* WILL STOP ME?
IN A WORD, SKULL--
YES!
WOLVERINE, IS THAT YOU? ARE YOU *OKAY?*
YEAH, CAROL. IT'S ME.
TONY'S CRAZY *TIN CAN PLAN* STABILIZED MY *HEALING FACTOR* SO I'M BACK IN THE FIGHT.
"TIN CAN"? CAN WE GO WITH THE MORE ACCURATE *"BILLIONS* OF DOLLARS OF *LIFESAVING CUSTOM-MADE 3D-PRINTED ARMOR,"* INSTEAD?
SLASH
NAH.

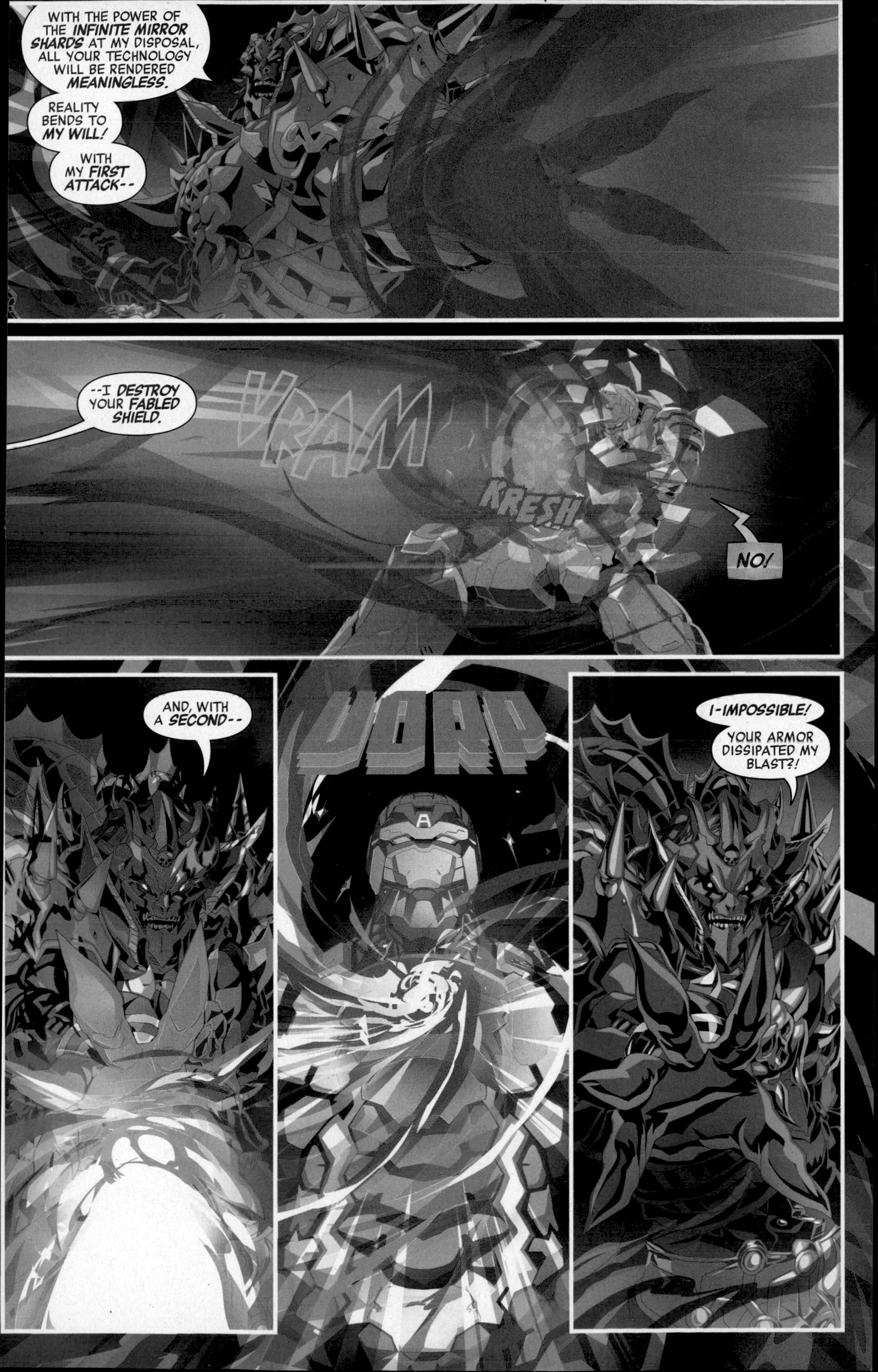
WITH THE POWER OF THE INFINITE MIRROR SHARDS AT MY DISPOSAL, ALL YOUR TECHNOLOGY WILL BE RENDERED MEANINGLESS.
REALITY BENDS TO MY WILL!
WITH MY FIRST ATTACK--
--I DESTROY YOUR FABLED SHIELD.
VRAM
KRESH
NO!
AND, WITH A SECOND--
VORP
I-IMPOSSIBLE!
YOUR ARMOR DISSIPATED MY BLAST?!

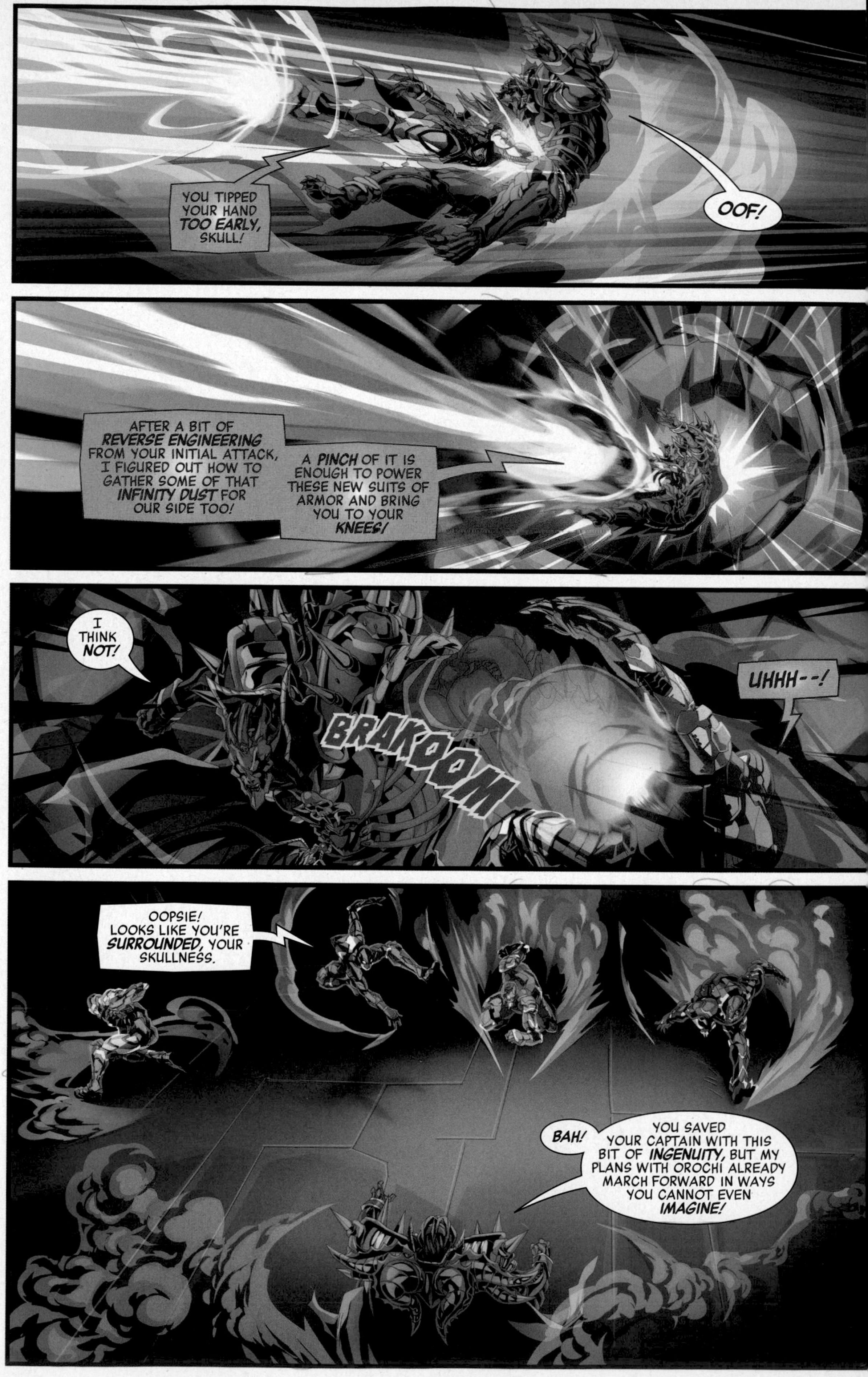
YOU TIPPED YOUR HAND TOO EARLY, SKULL!
OOF!
AFTER A BIT OF REVERSE ENGINEERING FROM YOUR INITIAL ATTACK, I FIGURED OUT HOW TO GATHER SOME OF THAT INFINITY DUST FOR OUR SIDE TOO!
A PINCH OF IT IS ENOUGH TO POWER THESE NEW SUITS OF ARMOR AND BRING YOU TO YOUR KNEES!
I THINK NOT!
BRAKOOM
UHHH--!
OOPSIE! LOOKS LIKE YOU'RE SURROUNDED, YOUR SKULLNESS.
BAH!
YOU SAVED YOUR CAPTAIN WITH THIS BIT OF INGENUITY, BUT MY PLANS WITH OROCHI ALREADY MARCH FORWARD IN WAYS YOU CANNOT EVEN IMAGINE!

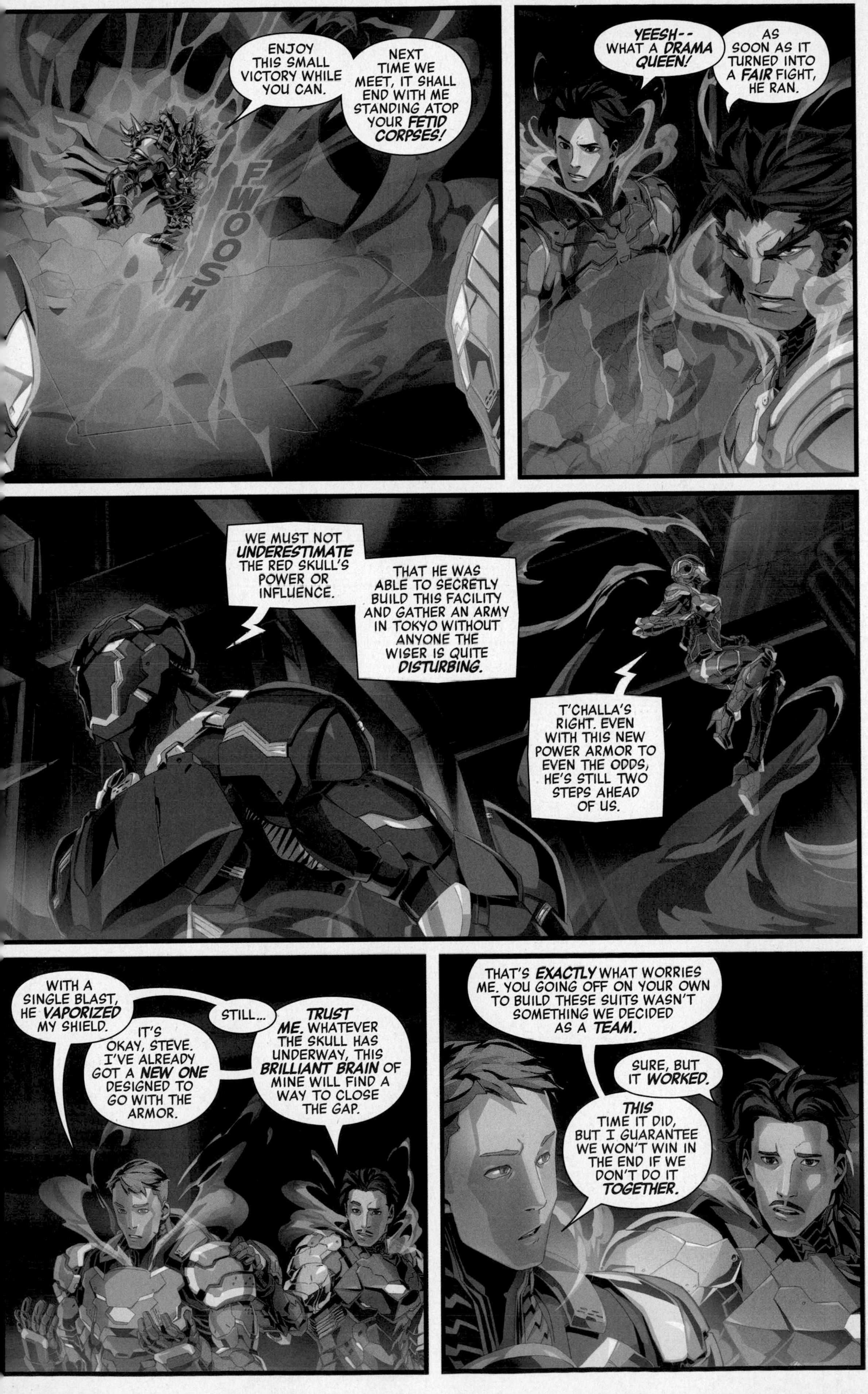
ENJOY THIS SMALL VICTORY WHILE YOU CAN.
NEXT TIME WE MEET, IT SHALL END WITH ME STANDING ATOP YOUR FETID CORPSES!
FWOOSH
YEESH-- WHAT A DRAMA QUEEN!
AS SOON AS IT TURNED INTO A FAIR FIGHT, HE RAN.
WE MUST NOT UNDERESTIMATE THE RED SKULL'S POWER OR INFLUENCE.
THAT HE WAS ABLE TO SECRETLY BUILD THIS FACILITY AND GATHER AN ARMY IN TOKYO WITHOUT ANYONE THE WISER IS QUITE DISTURBING.
T'CHALLA'S RIGHT. EVEN WITH THIS NEW POWER ARMOR TO EVEN THE ODDS, HE'S STILL TWO STEPS AHEAD OF US.
WITH A SINGLE BLAST, HE VAPORIZED MY SHIELD.
IT'S OKAY, STEVE. I'VE ALREADY GOT A NEW ONE DESIGNED TO GO WITH THE ARMOR.
STILL...
TRUST ME. WHATEVER THE SKULL HAS UNDERWAY, THIS BRILLIANT BRAIN OF MINE WILL FIND A WAY TO CLOSE THE GAP.
THAT'S EXACTLY WHAT WORRIES ME. YOU GOING OFF ON YOUR OWN TO BUILD THESE SUITS WASN'T SOMETHING WE DECIDED AS A TEAM.
SURE, BUT IT WORKED.
THIS TIME IT DID, BUT I GUARANTEE WE WON'T WIN IN THE END IF WE DON'T DO IT TOGETHER.

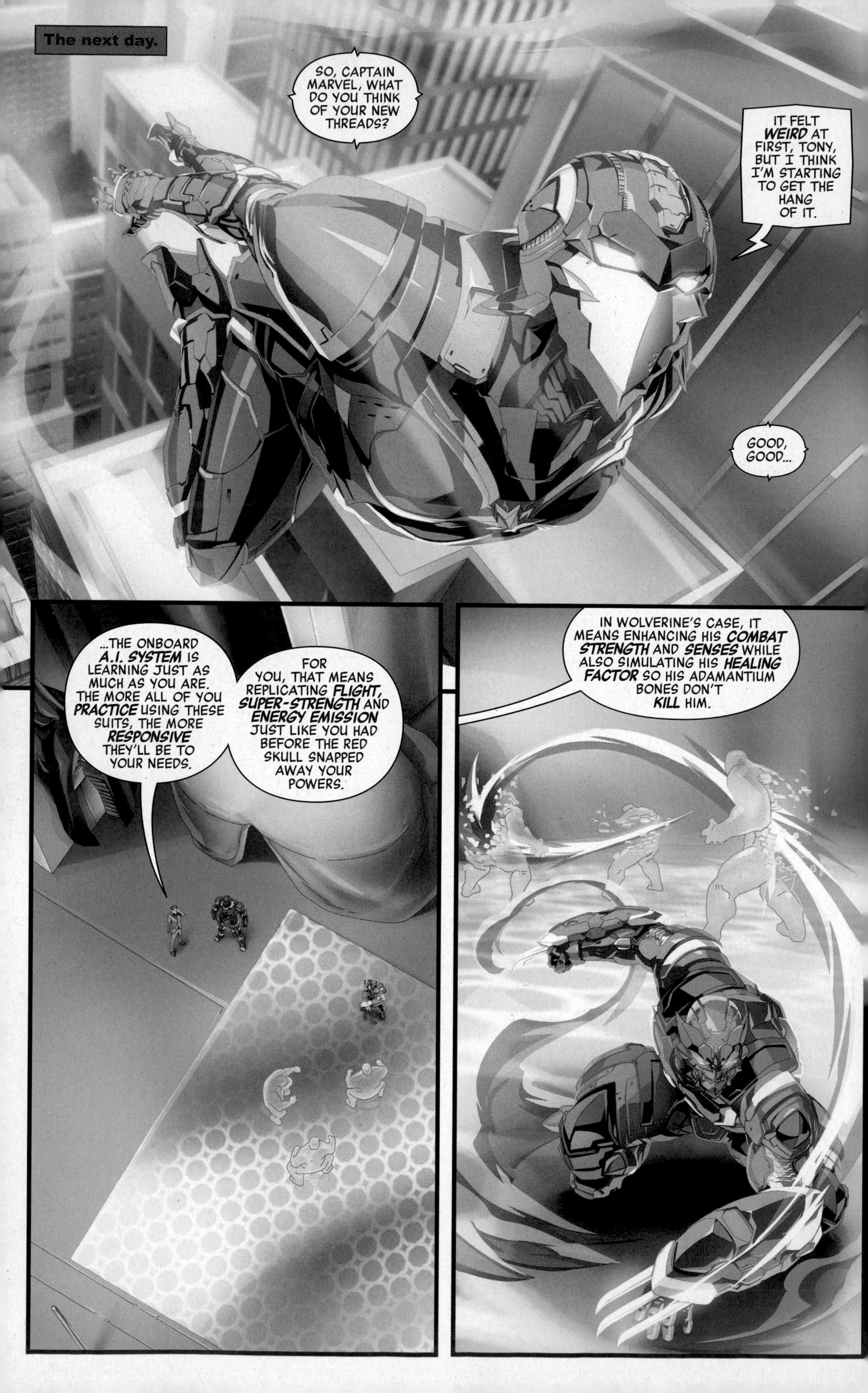

The next day.
SO, CAPTAIN MARVEL, WHAT DO YOU THINK OF YOUR NEW THREADS?
IT FELT WEIRD AT FIRST, TONY, BUT I THINK I'M STARTING TO GET THE HANG OF IT.
GOOD, GOOD...
...THE ONBOARD A.I. SYSTEM IS LEARNING JUST AS MUCH AS YOU ARE. THE MORE ALL OF YOU PRACTICE USING THESE SUITS, THE MORE RESPONSIVE THEY'LL BE TO YOUR NEEDS.
FOR YOU, THAT MEANS REPLICATING FLIGHT, SUPER-STRENGTH AND ENERGY EMISSION JUST LIKE YOU HAD BEFORE THE RED SKULL SNAPPED AWAY YOUR POWERS.
IN WOLVERINE'S CASE, IT MEANS ENHANCING HIS COMBAT STRENGTH AND SENSES WHILE ALSO SIMULATING HIS HEALING FACTOR SO HIS ADAMANTIUM BONES DON'T KILL HIM.

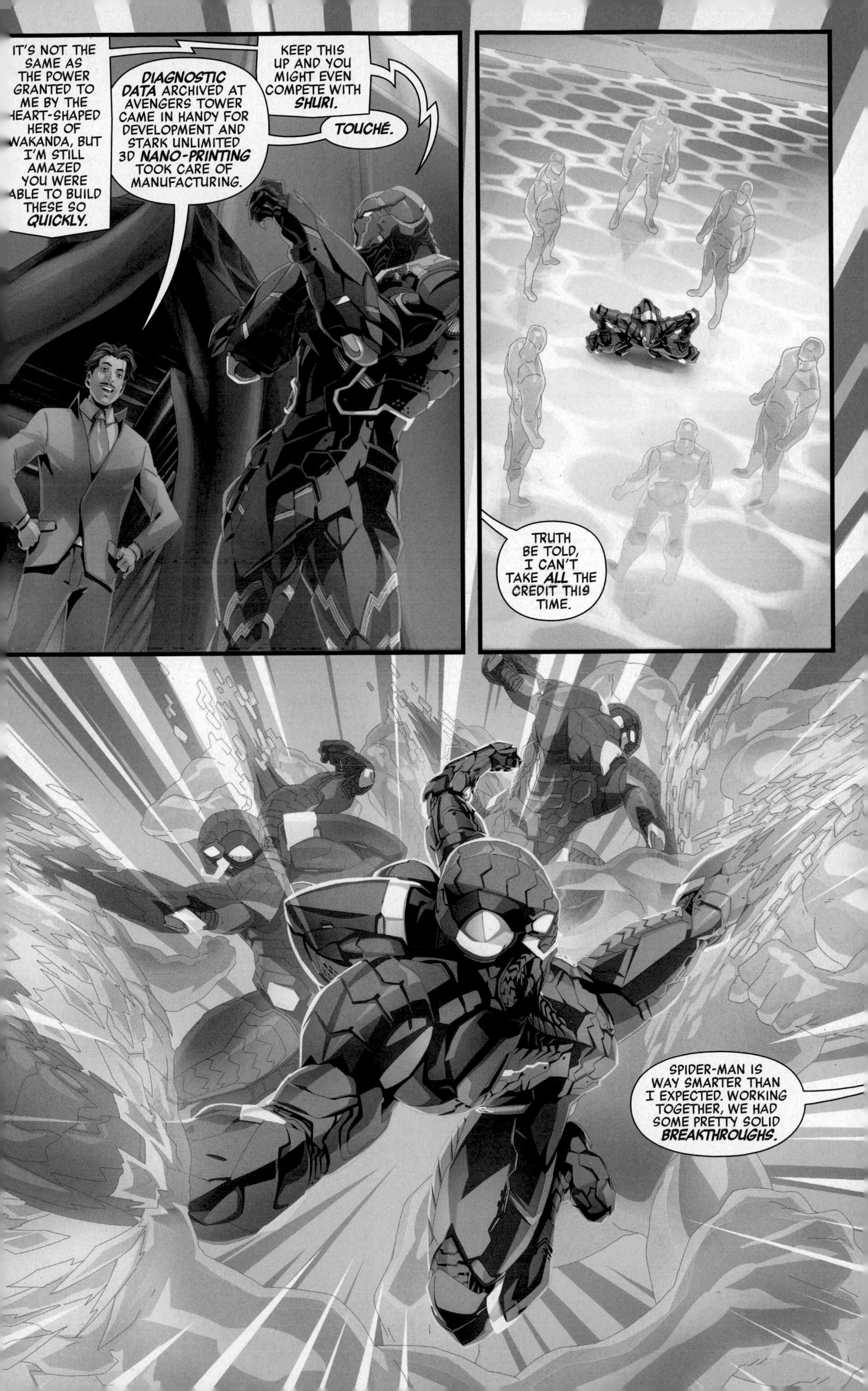
IT'S NOT THE SAME AS THE POWER GRANTED TO ME BY THE HEART-SHAPED HERB OF WAKANDA, BUT I'M STILL AMAZED YOU WERE ABLE TO BUILD THESE SO QUICKLY.
DIAGNOSTIC DATA ARCHIVED AT AVENGERS TOWER CAME IN HANDY FOR DEVELOPMENT AND STARK UNLIMITED 3D NANO-PRINTING TOOK CARE OF MANUFACTURING.
KEEP THIS UP AND YOU MIGHT EVEN COMPETE WITH SHURI.
TOUCHÉ.
TRUTH BE TOLD, I CAN'T TAKE ALL THE CREDIT THIS TIME.
SPIDER-MAN IS WAY SMARTER THAN I EXPECTED. WORKING TOGETHER, WE HAD SOME PRETTY SOLID BREAKTHROUGHS.

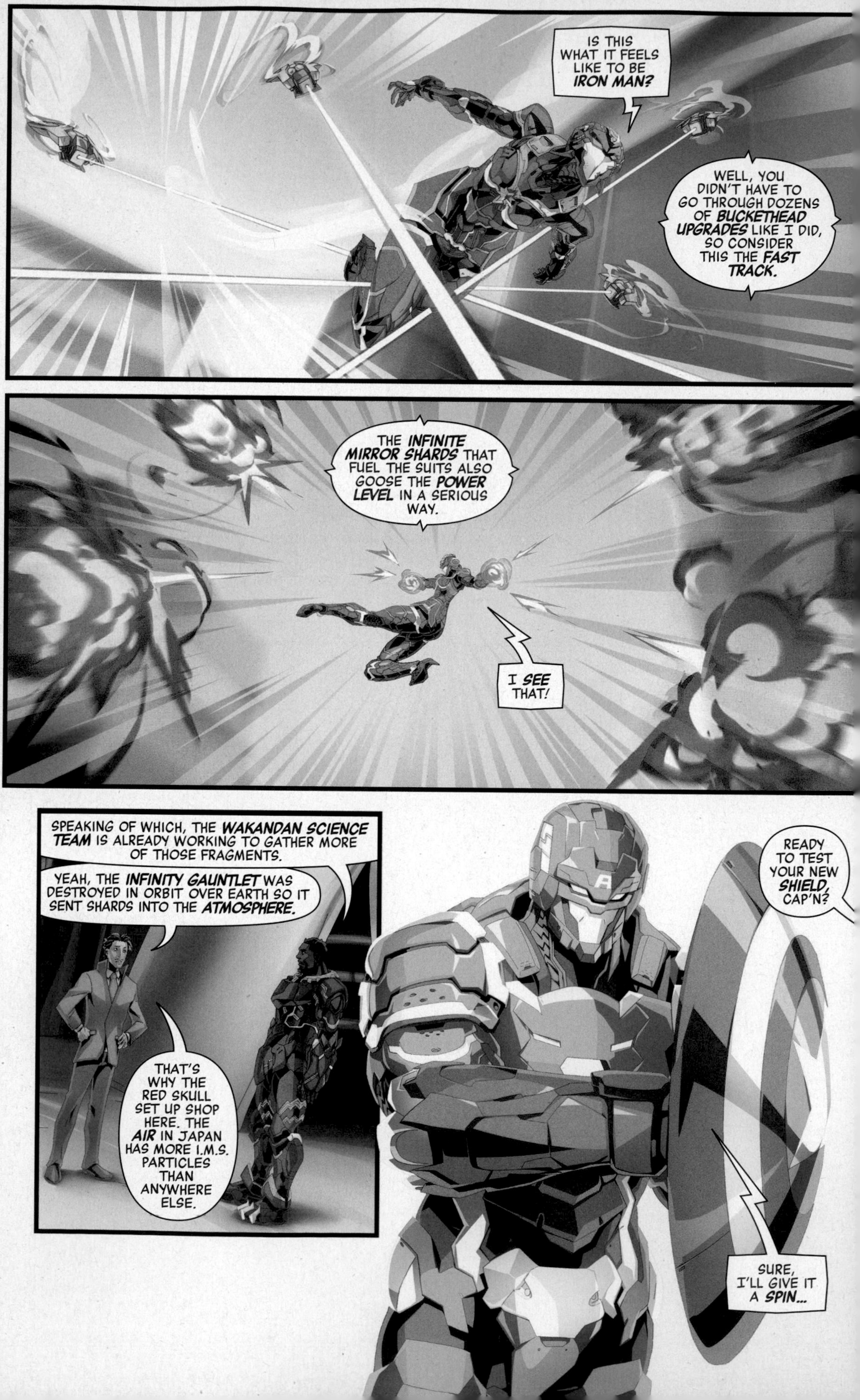
IS THIS WHAT IT FEELS LIKE TO BE IRON MAN?
WELL, YOU DIDN'T HAVE TO GO THROUGH DOZENS OF BUCKETHEAD UPGRADES LIKE I DID, SO CONSIDER THIS THE FAST TRACK.
THE INFINITE MIRROR SHARDS THAT FUEL THE SUITS ALSO GOOSE THE POWER LEVEL IN A SERIOUS WAY.
I SEE THAT!
SPEAKING OF WHICH, THE WAKANDAN SCIENCE TEAM IS ALREADY WORKING TO GATHER MORE OF THOSE FRAGMENTS.
YEAH, THE INFINITY GAUNTLET WAS DESTROYED IN ORBIT OVER EARTH SO IT SENT SHARDS INTO THE ATMOSPHERE.
THAT'S WHY THE RED SKULL SET UP SHOP HERE. THE AIR IN JAPAN HAS MORE I.M.S. PARTICLES THAN ANYWHERE ELSE.
READY TO TEST YOUR NEW SHIELD, CAP'N?
SURE, I'LL GIVE IT A SPIN...

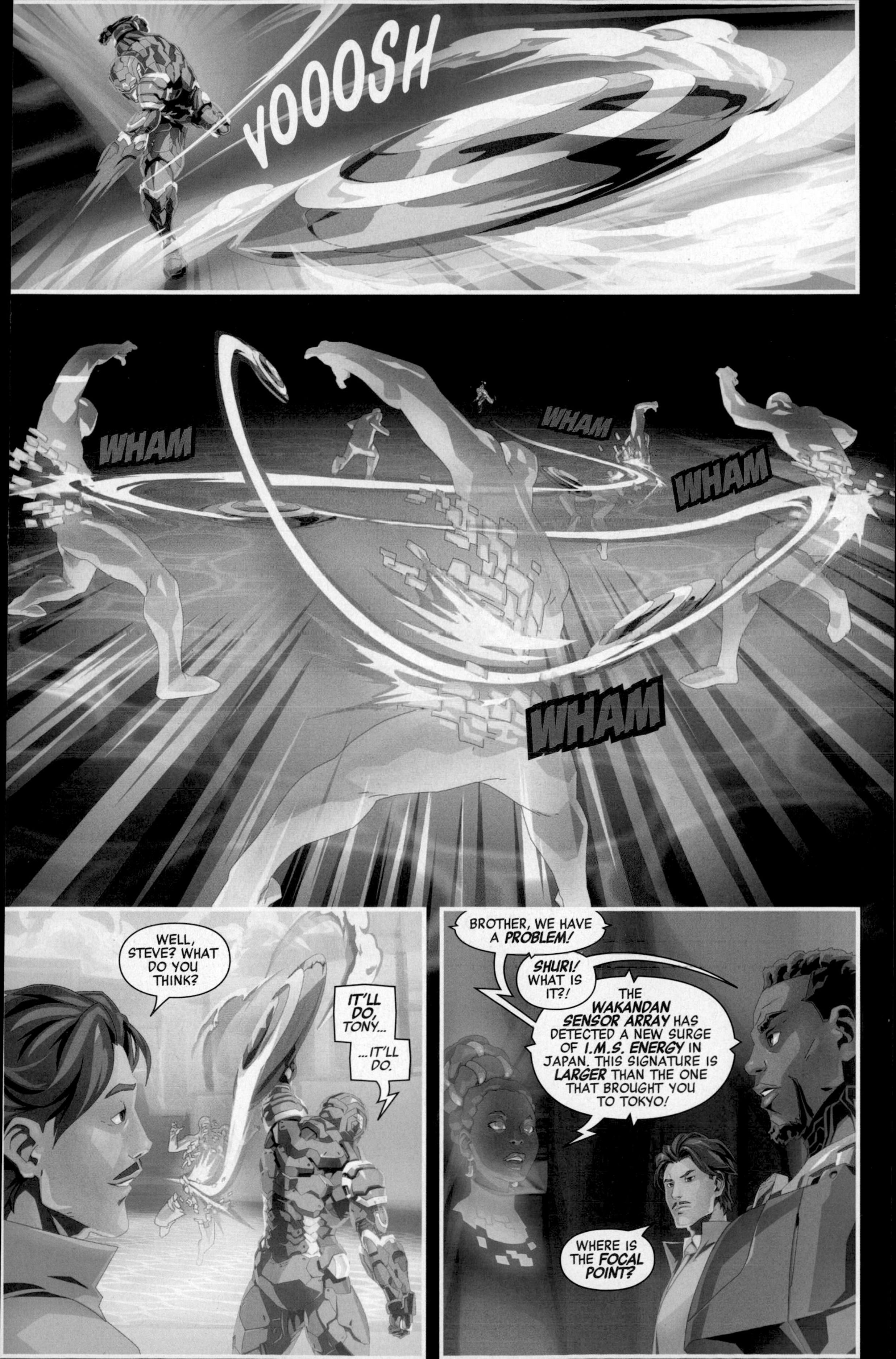
VOOOSH
WHAM
WHAM
WHAM
WHAM
WELL, STEVE? WHAT DO YOU THINK?
IT'LL DO, TONY...
...IT'LL DO.
BROTHER, WE HAVE A PROBLEM!
SHURI! WHAT IS IT?!
THE WAKANDAN SENSOR ARRAY HAS DETECTED A NEW SURGE OF I.M.S. ENERGY IN JAPAN. THIS SIGNATURE IS LARGER THAN THE ONE THAT BROUGHT YOU TO TOKYO!
WHERE IS THE FOCAL POINT?

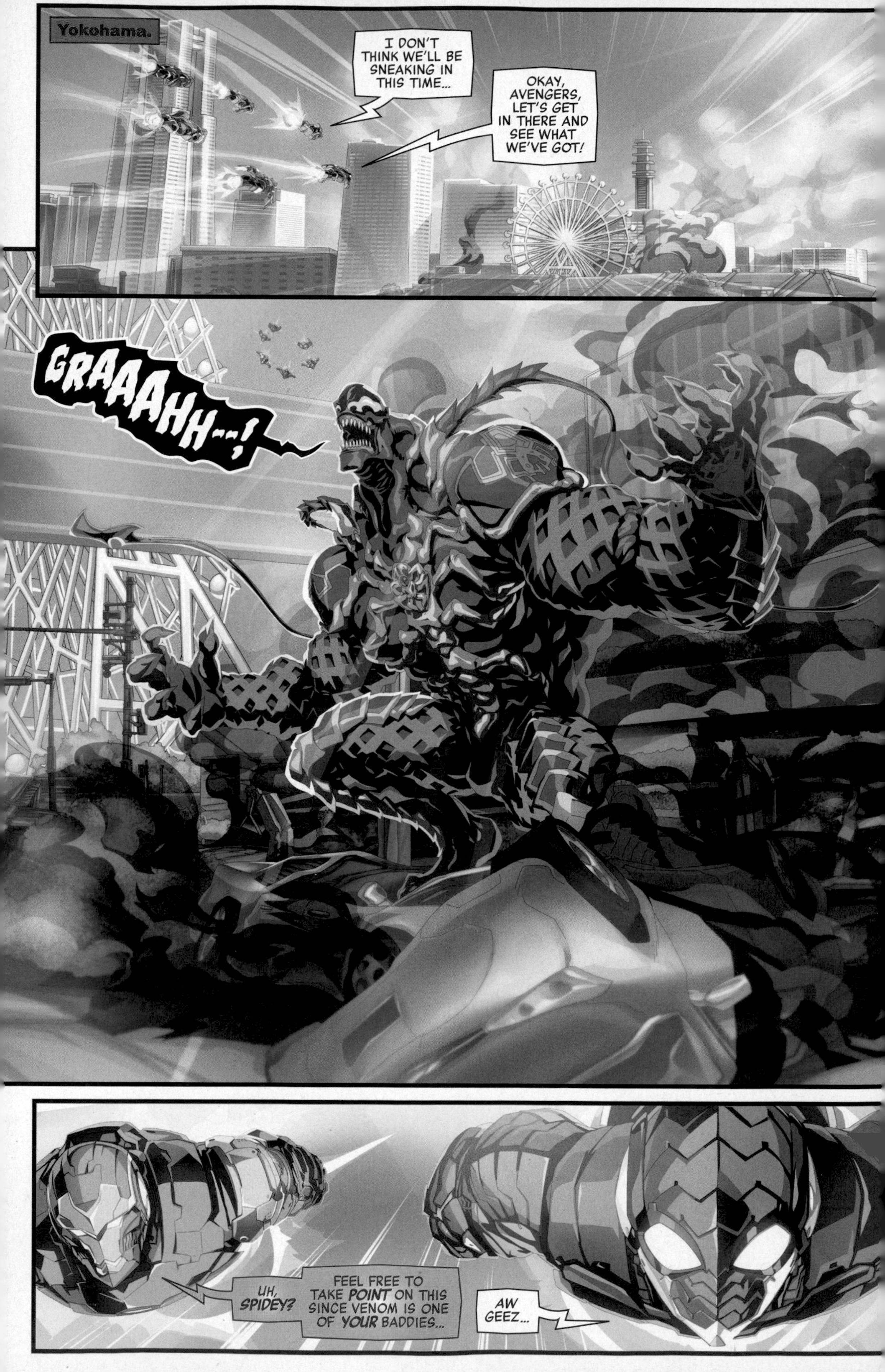
Yokohama.
I DON'T THINK WE'LL BE SNEAKING IN THIS TIME...
OKAY, AVENGERS, LET'S GET IN THERE AND SEE WHAT WE'VE GOT!
GRAAAHH--!
UH, SPIDEY?
FEEL FREE TO TAKE POINT ON THIS SINCE VENOM IS ONE OF YOUR BADDIES...
AW GEEZ...

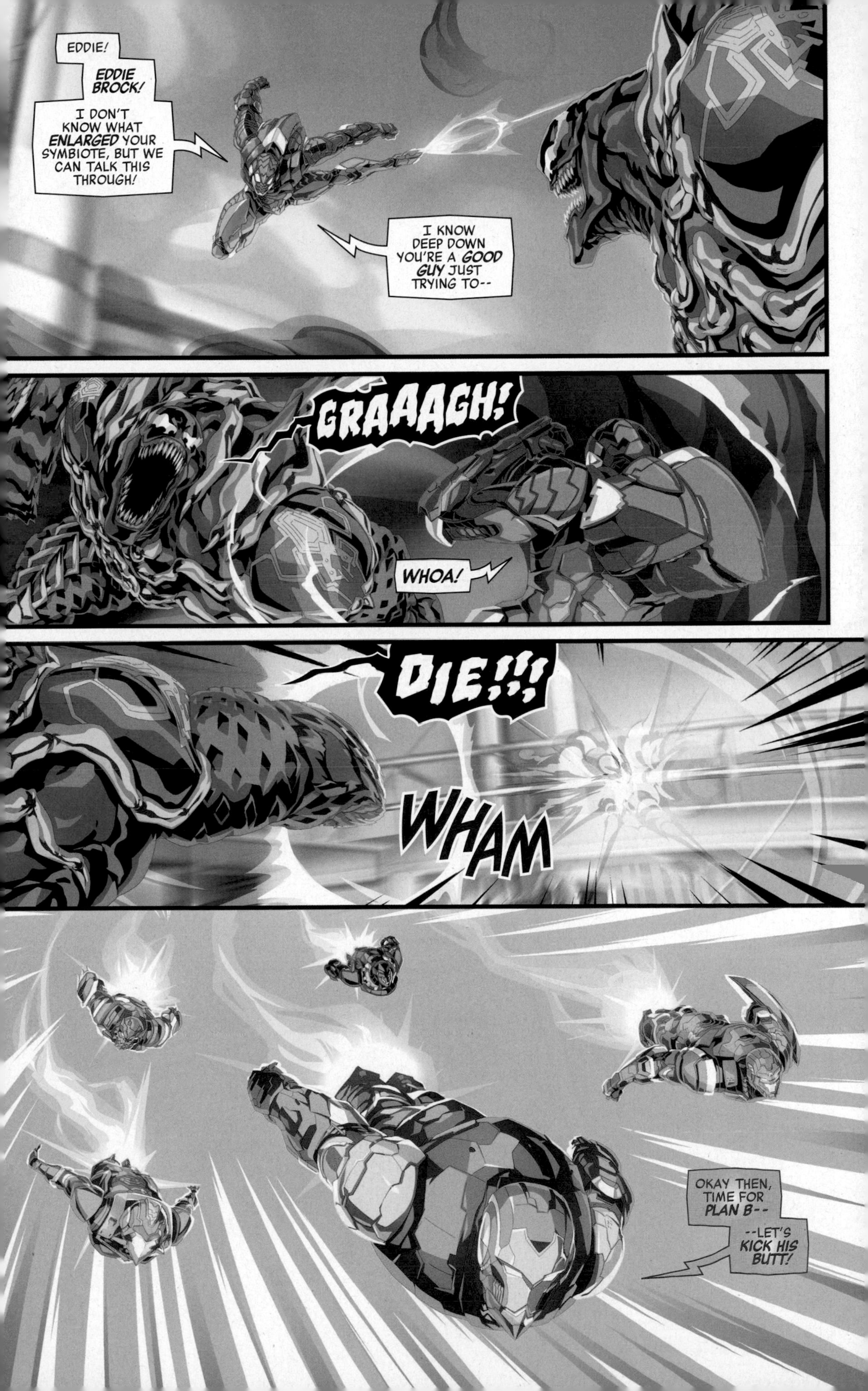
EDDIE!
EDDIE BROCK!
I DON'T KNOW WHAT ENLARGED YOUR SYMBIOTE, BUT WE CAN TALK THIS THROUGH!
I KNOW DEEP DOWN YOU'RE A GOOD GUY JUST TRYING TO--
GRAAAGH!
WHOA!
DIE!!!
WHAM
OKAY THEN, TIME FOR PLAN B--
--LET'S KICK HIS BUTT!

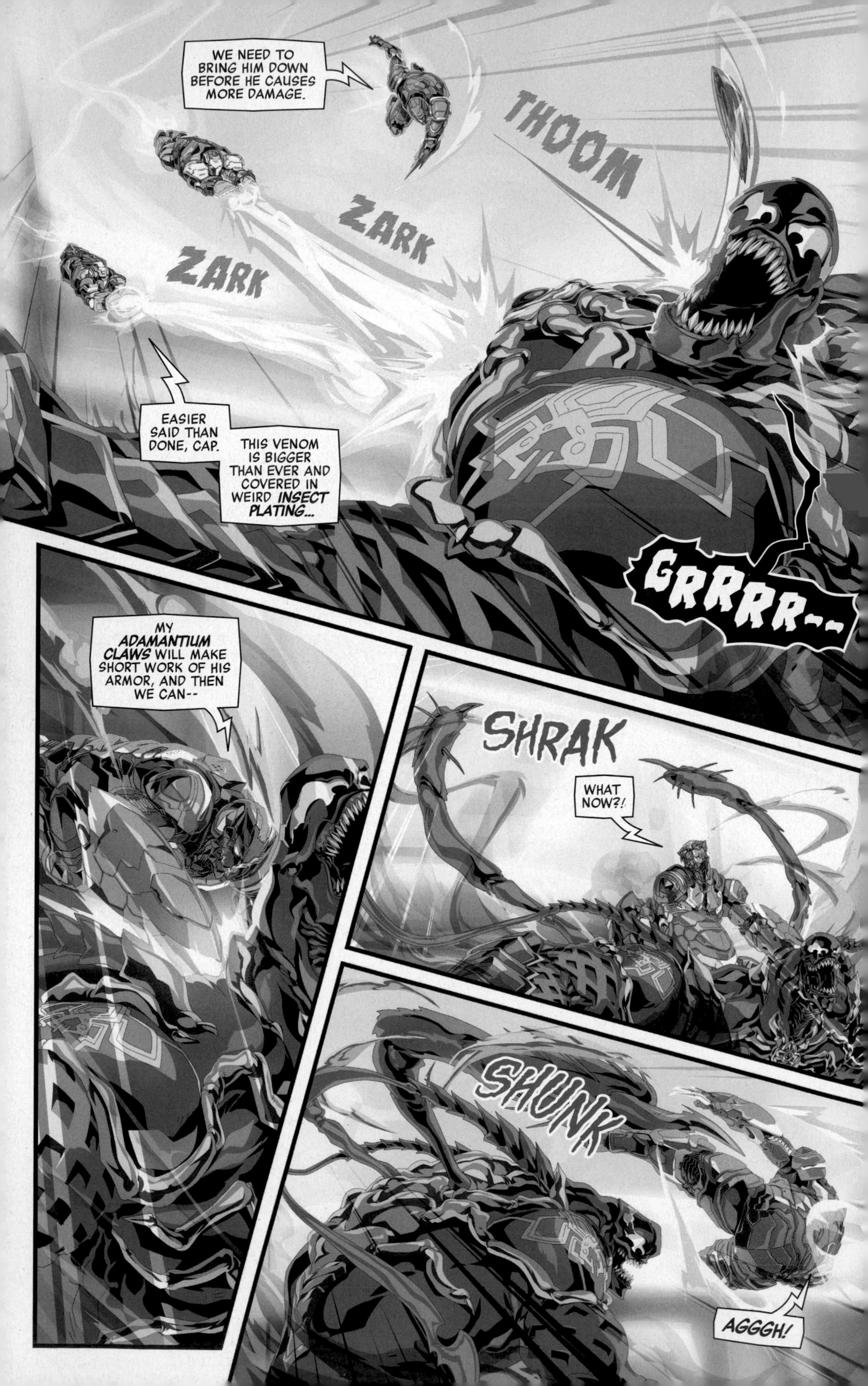

WE NEED TO BRING HIM DOWN BEFORE HE CAUSES MORE DAMAGE.
THOOM
ZARK
ZARK
EASIER SAID THAN DONE, CAP.
THIS VENOM IS BIGGER THAN EVER AND COVERED IN WEIRD *INSECT PLATING*...
GRRRRR--
MY *ADAMANTIUM CLAWS* WILL MAKE SHORT WORK OF HIS ARMOR, AND THEN WE CAN--
SHRAK
WHAT NOW?!
SHUNK
AGGGH!

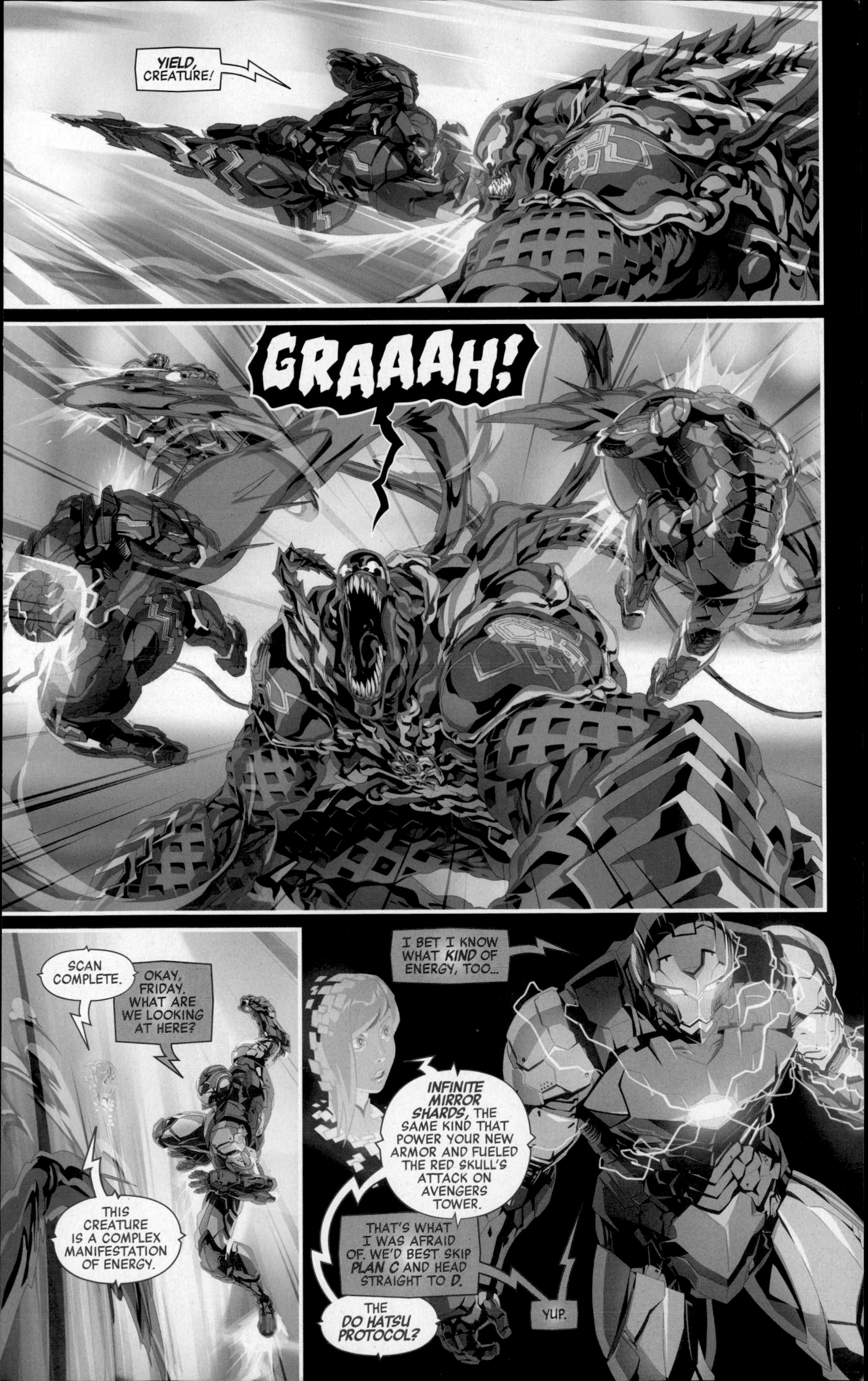

YIELD, CREATURE!
GRAAAH!
SCAN COMPLETE.
OKAY, FRIDAY. WHAT ARE WE LOOKING AT HERE?
THIS CREATURE IS A COMPLEX MANIFESTATION OF ENERGY.
I BET I KNOW WHAT KIND OF ENERGY, TOO...
INFINITE MIRROR SHARDS, THE SAME KIND THAT POWER YOUR NEW ARMOR AND FUELED THE RED SKULL'S ATTACK ON AVENGERS TOWER.
THAT'S WHAT I WAS AFRAID OF. WE'D BEST SKIP PLAN C AND HEAD STRAIGHT TO D.
THE DO HATSU PROTOCOL?
YUP.

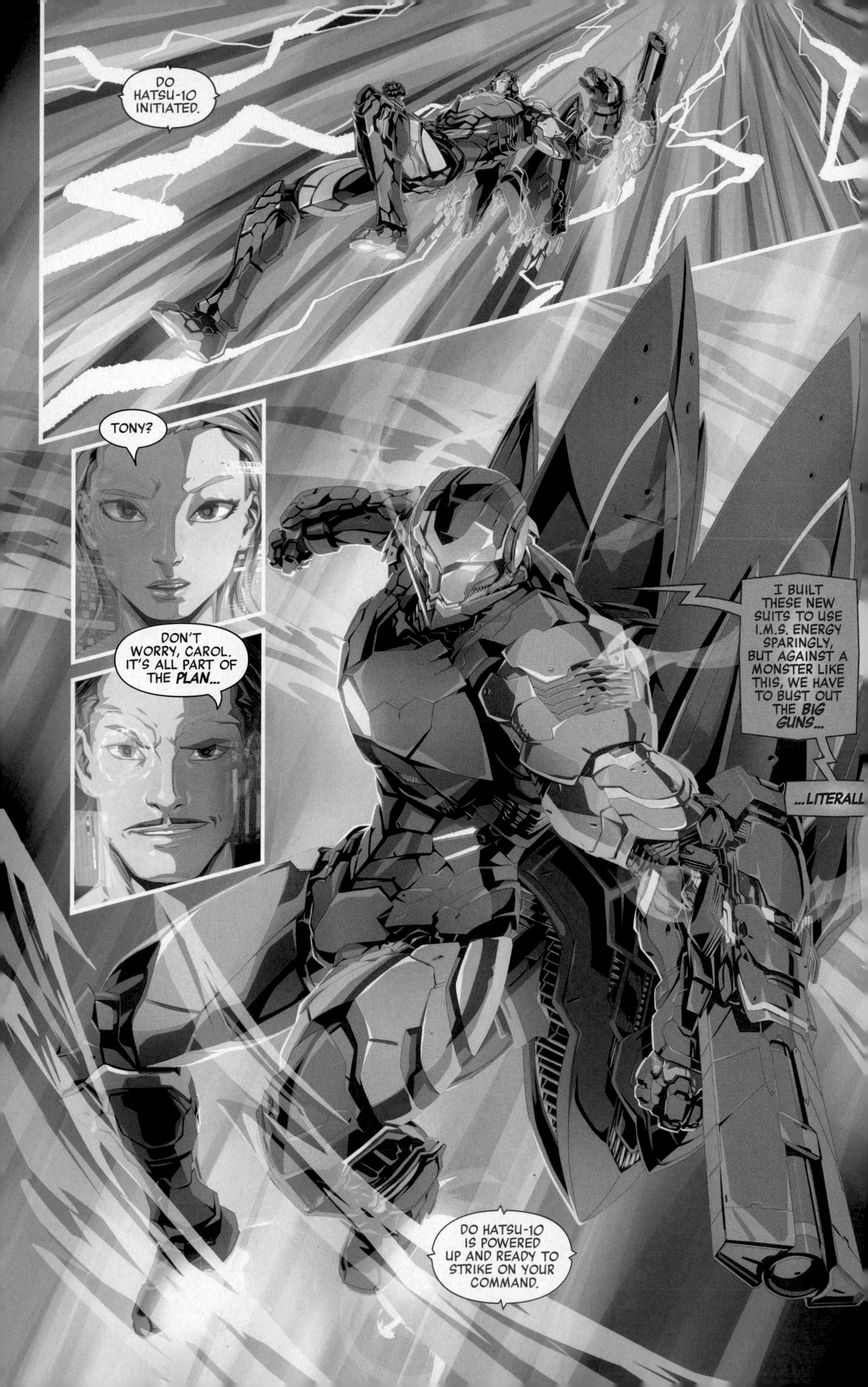
DO HATSU-10 INITIATED.
TONY?
DON'T WORRY, CAROL. IT'S ALL PART OF THE PLAN...
I BUILT THESE NEW SUITS TO USE I.M.S. ENERGY SPARINGLY, BUT AGAINST A MONSTER LIKE THIS, WE HAVE TO BUST OUT THE BIG GUNS...
...LITERALL
DO HATSU-10 IS POWERED UP AND READY TO STRIKE ON YOUR COMMAND.

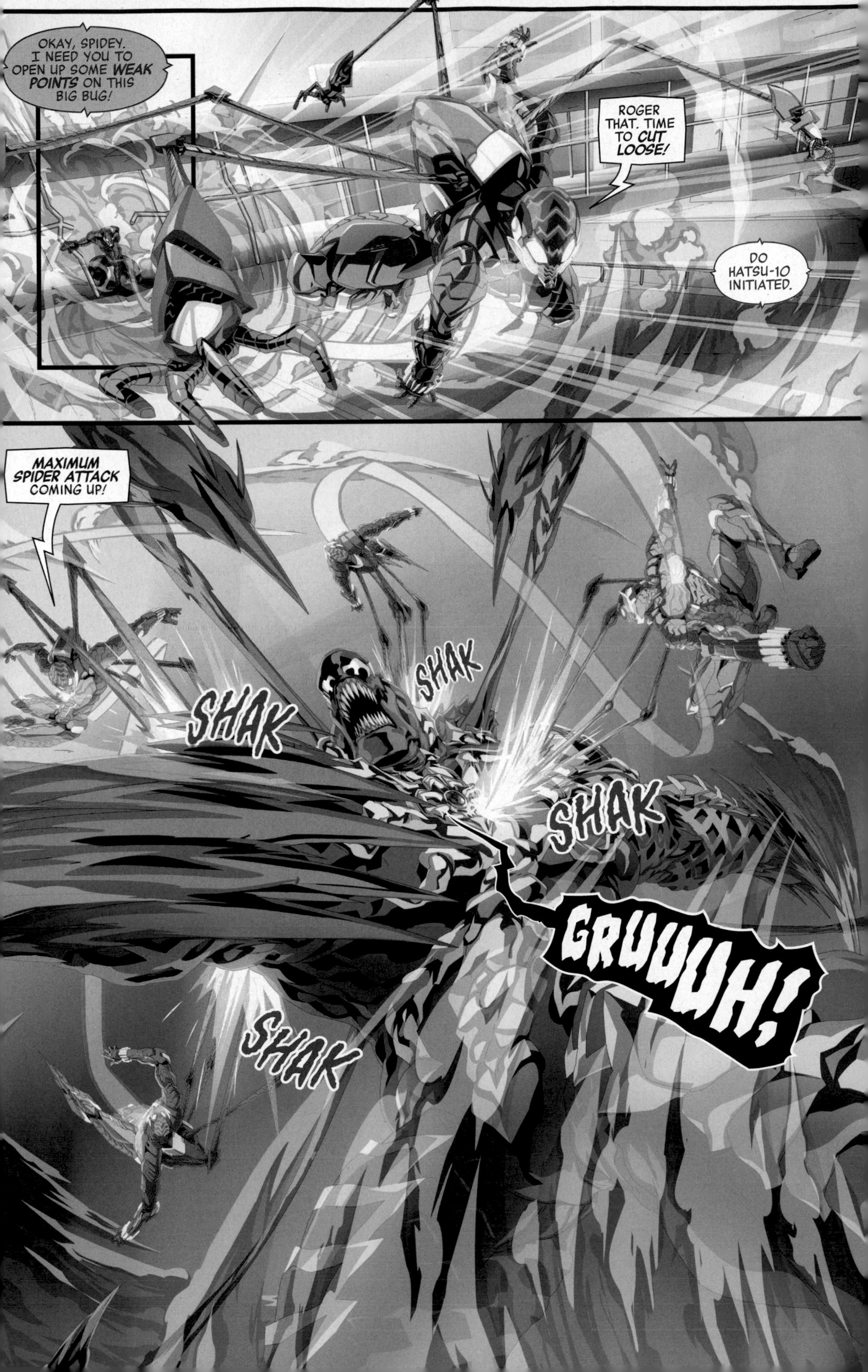
OKAY, SPIDEY. I NEED YOU TO OPEN UP SOME WEAK POINTS ON THIS BIG BUG!
ROGER THAT. TIME TO CUT LOOSE!
DO HATSU-10 INITIATED.
MAXIMUM SPIDER ATTACK COMING UP!
SHAK
SHAK
SHAK
SHAK
GRUUUH!

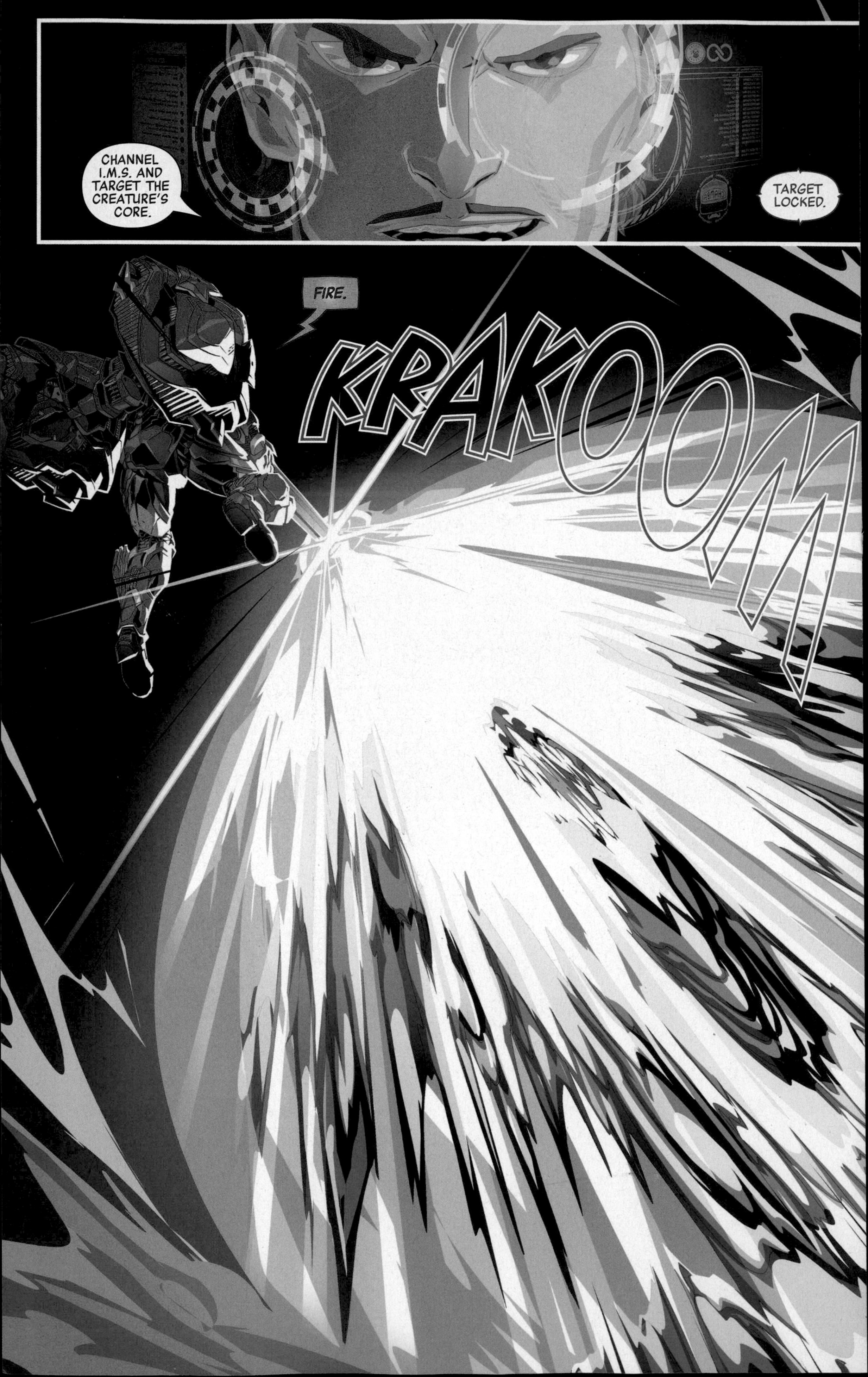
CHANNEL I.M.S. AND TARGET THE CREATURE'S CORE.
TARGET LOCKED.
FIRE.
KRAKOOOM

UH, DID YOU JUST... *DISINTEGRATE* HIM?

DON'T WORRY, SPIDEY. I DIDN'T *KILL* ANYONE.

EDDIE BROCK WASN'T *IN* THAT THING. IT WAS INFINITE MIRROR SHARD ENERGY TURNED INTO A MONSTER. A WALKING NIGHTMARE CONJURED UP BY OUR PAL THE *RED SKULL*.

OKAY, BUT WHAT DID YOU AND SPIDEY HIT IT WITH TO *SHRED* IT?

WE HAD TO FIGHT FIRE *WITH* FIRE AND THAT MEANT USING A BUNCH OF OUR OWN INFINITE MIRROR SHARD ENERGY TO STOP "*VENOM*."

KER-CHAK

THESE "*COINS*" IMBUED WITH PURE I.M.S. ARE IN *SHORT SUPPLY*. THEY'RE POWERFUL, BUT ALSO QUITE *VOLATILE*.

THE *DO HATSU-10 MODE* BUILT INTO EACH SUIT CAN ONLY LAST A MAXIMUM OF *TEN MINUTES*-- AND WITH A BIG ENOUGH ATTACK, IT CAN BURN OUT AND CAUSE *INJURY* OR EVEN *DEATH*.

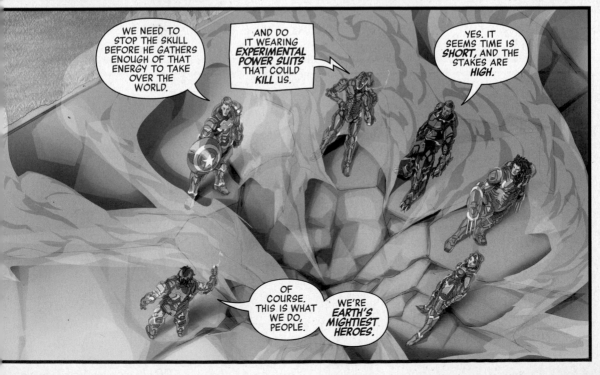

WE NEED TO STOP THE SKULL BEFORE HE GATHERS ENOUGH OF THAT ENERGY TO TAKE OVER THE WORLD.

AND DO IT WEARING *EXPERIMENTAL POWER SUITS* THAT COULD *KILL* US.

YES. IT SEEMS TIME IS *SHORT*, AND THE STAKES ARE *HIGH*.

OF COURSE. THIS IS WHAT WE DO, PEOPLE.

WE'RE *EARTH'S MIGHTIEST HEROES*.

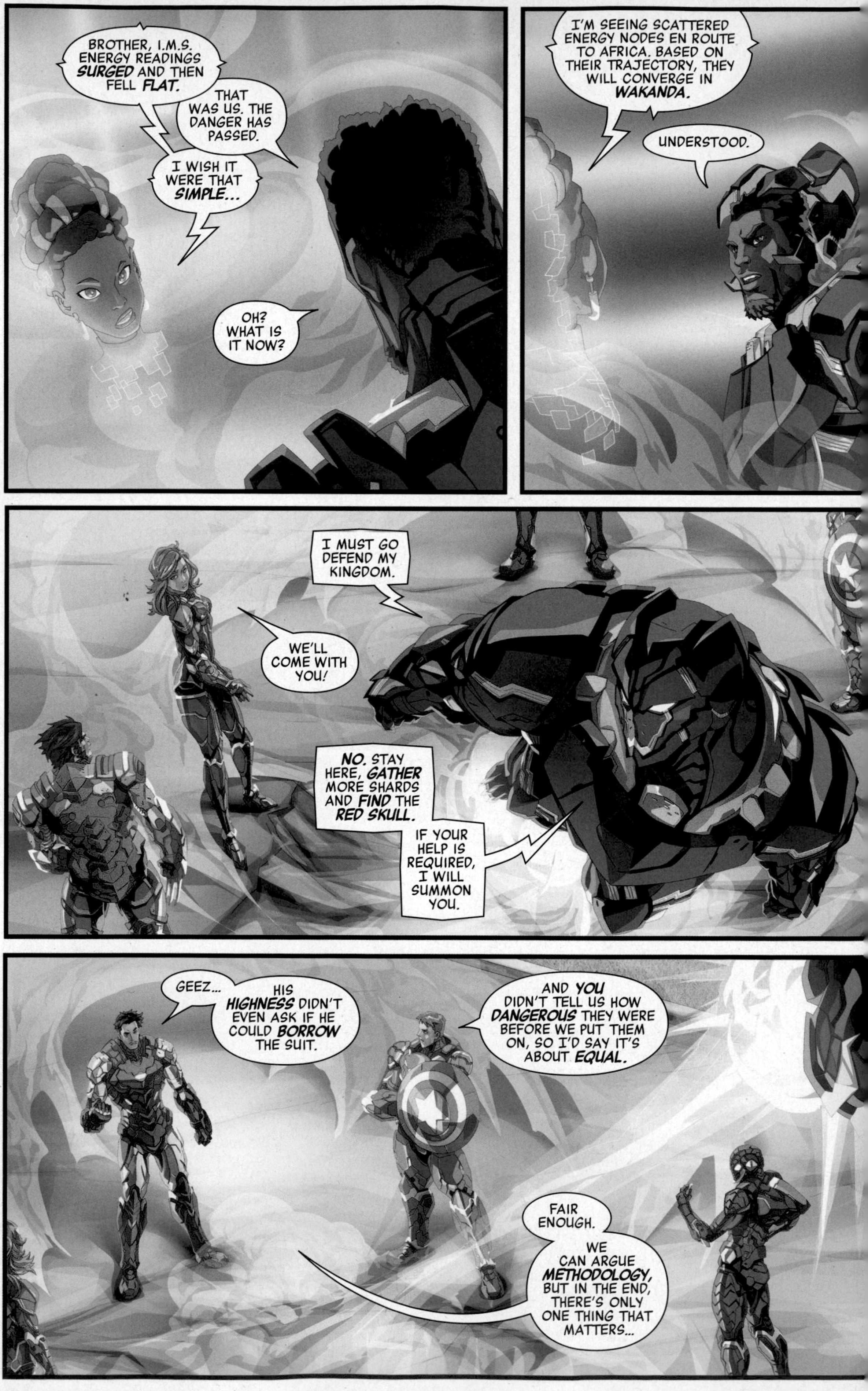

BROTHER, I.M.S. ENERGY READINGS SURGED AND THEN FELL FLAT.
THAT WAS US. THE DANGER HAS PASSED.
I WISH IT WERE THAT SIMPLE...
OH? WHAT IS IT NOW?
I'M SEEING SCATTERED ENERGY NODES EN ROUTE TO AFRICA. BASED ON THEIR TRAJECTORY, THEY WILL CONVERGE IN WAKANDA.
UNDERSTOOD.
I MUST GO DEFEND MY KINGDOM.
WE'LL COME WITH YOU!
NO. STAY HERE, GATHER MORE SHARDS AND FIND THE RED SKULL.
IF YOUR HELP IS REQUIRED, I WILL SUMMON YOU.
GEEZ...
HIS HIGHNESS DIDN'T EVEN ASK IF HE COULD BORROW THE SUIT.
AND YOU DIDN'T TELL US HOW DANGEROUS THEY WERE BEFORE WE PUT THEM ON, SO I'D SAY IT'S ABOUT EQUAL.
FAIR ENOUGH.
WE CAN ARGUE METHODOLOGY, BUT IN THE END, THERE'S ONLY ONE THING THAT MATTERS...

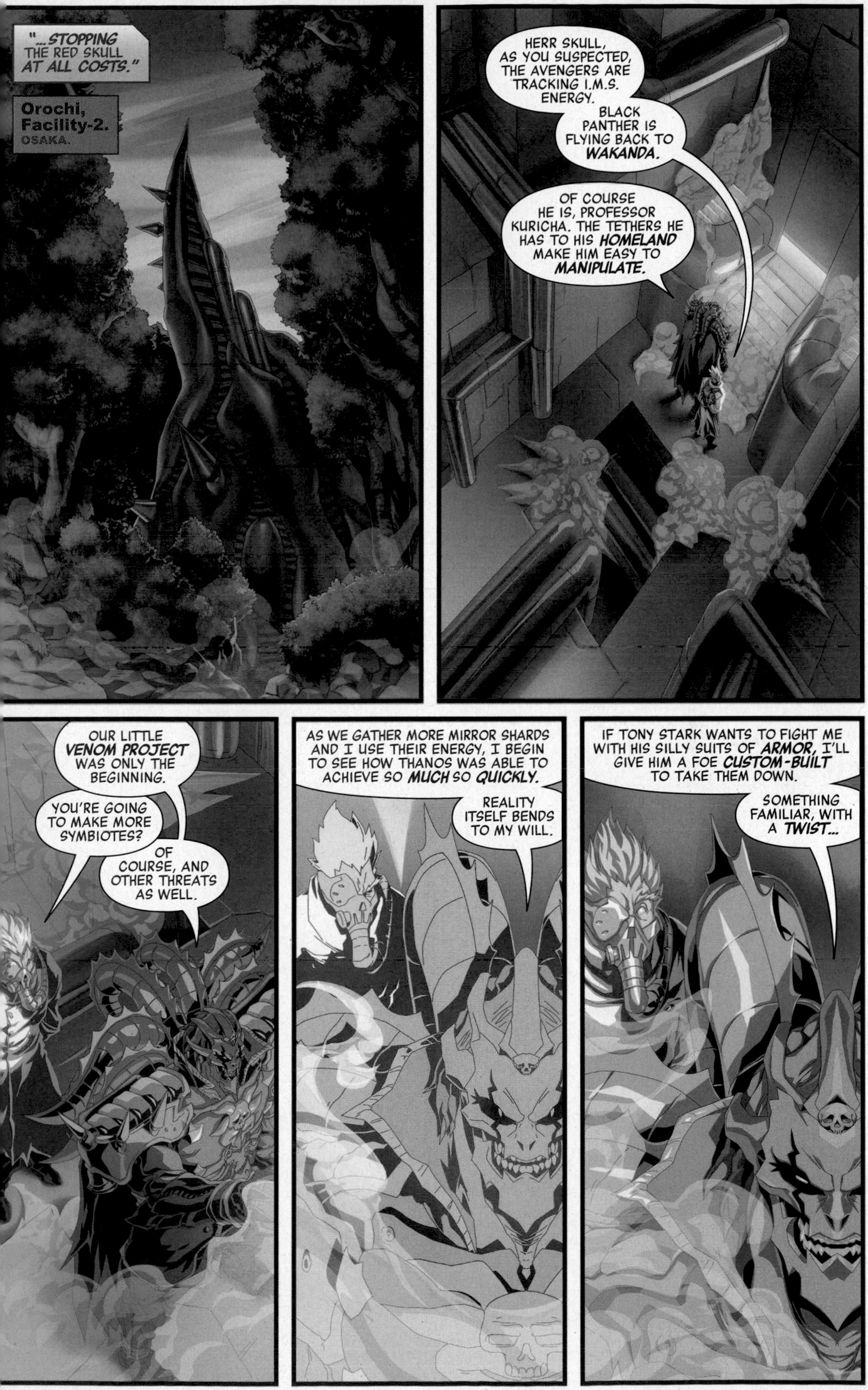
"...STOPPING THE RED SKULL AT ALL COSTS."
Orochi, Facility-2. OSAKA.
HERR SKULL, AS YOU SUSPECTED, THE AVENGERS ARE TRACKING I.M.S. ENERGY.
BLACK PANTHER IS FLYING BACK TO WAKANDA.
OF COURSE HE IS, PROFESSOR KURICHA. THE TETHERS HE HAS TO HIS HOMELAND MAKE HIM EASY TO MANIPULATE.
OUR LITTLE VENOM PROJECT WAS ONLY THE BEGINNING.
YOU'RE GOING TO MAKE MORE SYMBIOTES?
OF COURSE, AND OTHER THREATS AS WELL.
AS WE GATHER MORE MIRROR SHARDS AND I USE THEIR ENERGY, I BEGIN TO SEE HOW THANOS WAS ABLE TO ACHIEVE SO MUCH SO QUICKLY.
REALITY ITSELF BENDS TO MY WILL.
IF TONY STARK WANTS TO FIGHT ME WITH HIS SILLY SUITS OF ARMOR, I'LL GIVE HIM A FOE CUSTOM-BUILT TO TAKE THEM DOWN.
SOMETHING FAMILIAR, WITH A TWIST...

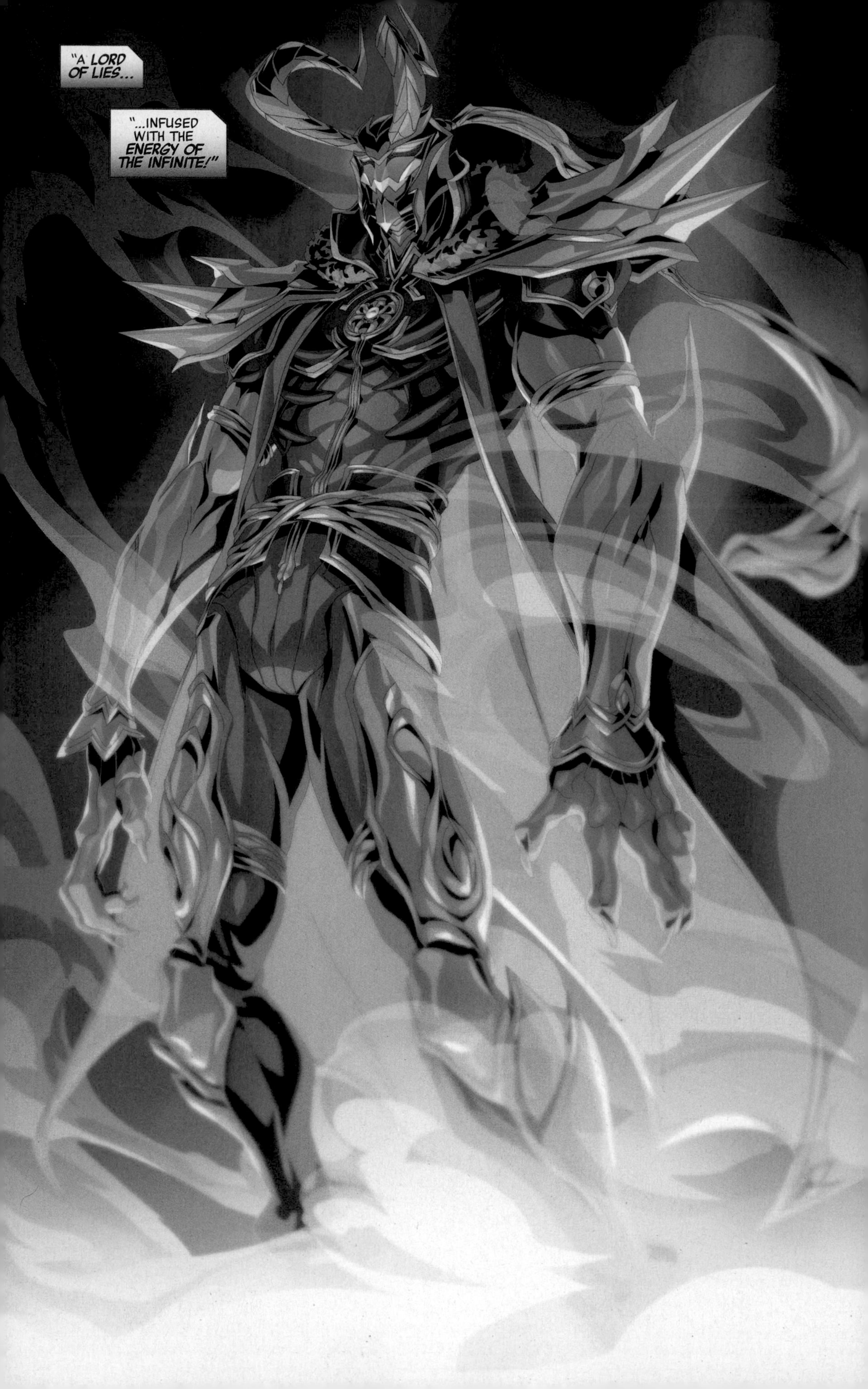
"A LORD OF LIES...
"...INFUSED WITH THE ENERGY OF THE INFINITE!"

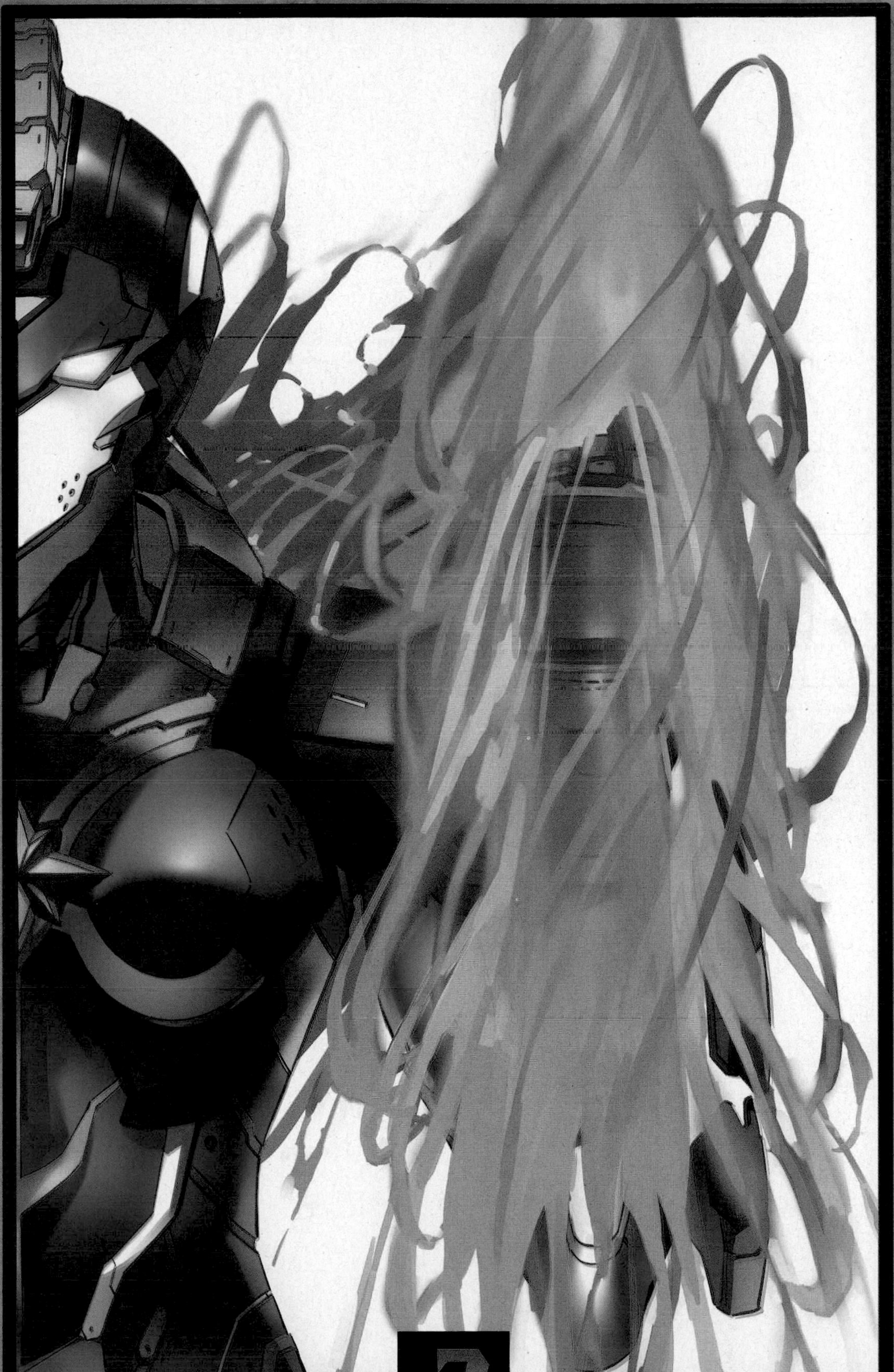

3

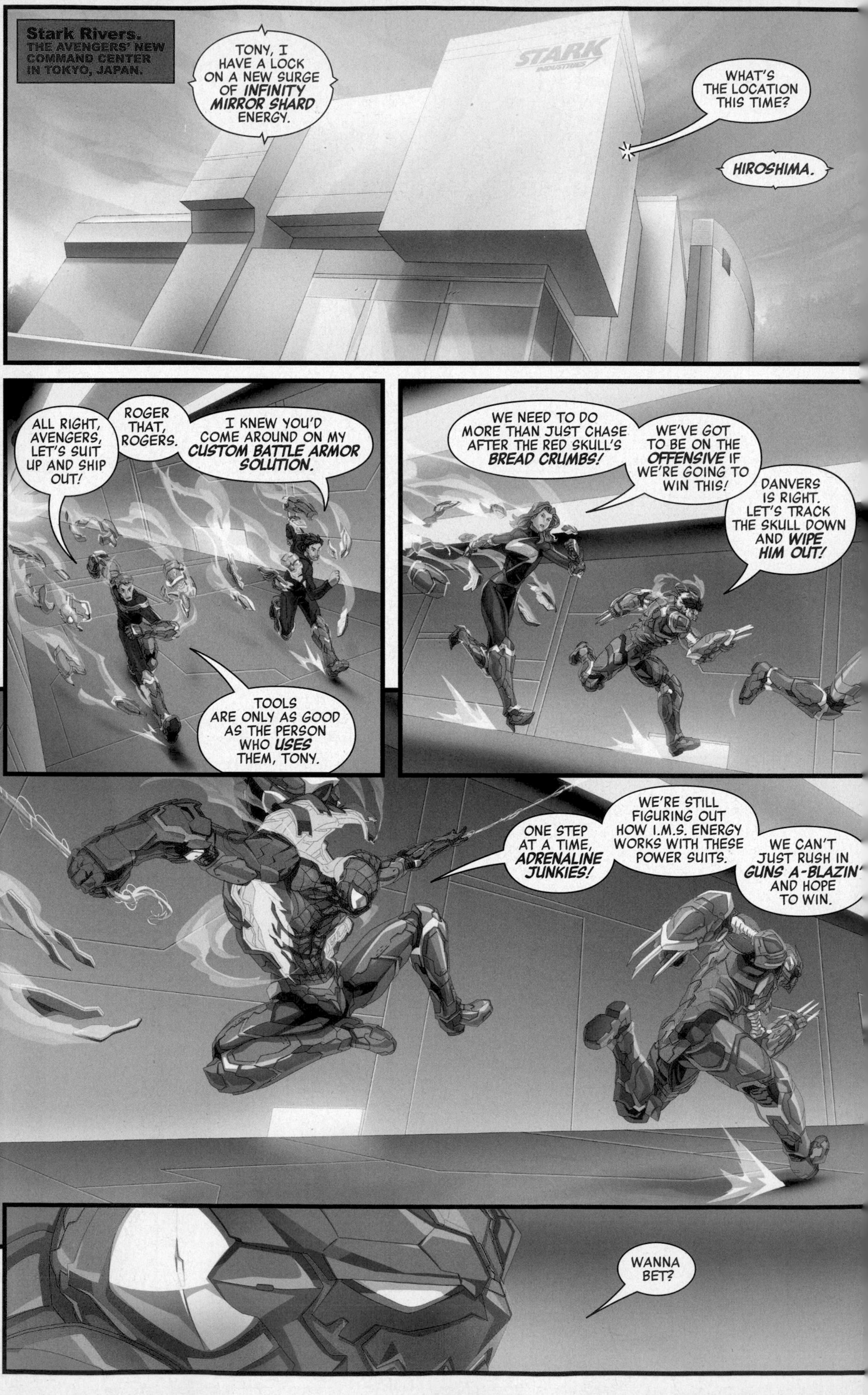
Stark Rivers.
THE AVENGERS' NEW COMMAND CENTER IN TOKYO, JAPAN.
TONY, I HAVE A LOCK ON A NEW SURGE OF INFINITY MIRROR SHARD ENERGY.
STARK INDUSTRIES
WHAT'S THE LOCATION THIS TIME?
HIROSHIMA.
ALL RIGHT, AVENGERS, LET'S SUIT UP AND SHIP OUT!
ROGER THAT, ROGERS.
I KNEW YOU'D COME AROUND ON MY CUSTOM BATTLE ARMOR SOLUTION.
TOOLS ARE ONLY AS GOOD AS THE PERSON WHO USES THEM, TONY.
WE NEED TO DO MORE THAN JUST CHASE AFTER THE RED SKULL'S BREAD CRUMBS!
WE'VE GOT TO BE ON THE OFFENSIVE IF WE'RE GOING TO WIN THIS!
DANVERS IS RIGHT. LET'S TRACK THE SKULL DOWN AND WIPE HIM OUT!
ONE STEP AT A TIME, ADRENALINE JUNKIES!
WE'RE STILL FIGURING OUT HOW I.M.S. ENERGY WORKS WITH THESE POWER SUITS.
WE CAN'T JUST RUSH IN GUNS A-BLAZIN' AND HOPE TO WIN.
WANNA BET?

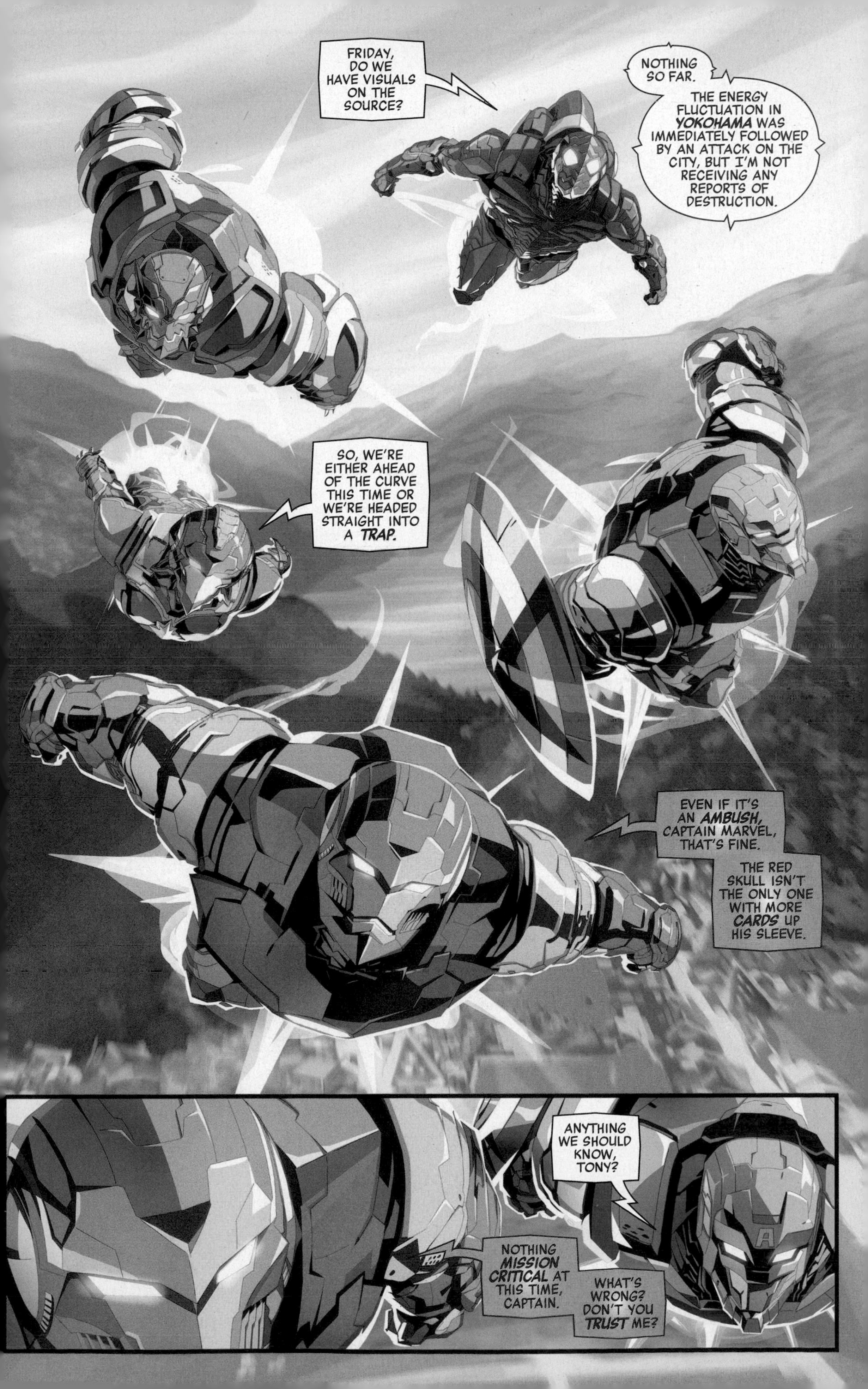
FRIDAY, DO WE HAVE VISUALS ON THE SOURCE?
NOTHING SO FAR.
THE ENERGY FLUCTUATION IN YOKOHAMA WAS IMMEDIATELY FOLLOWED BY AN ATTACK ON THE CITY, BUT I'M NOT RECEIVING ANY REPORTS OF DESTRUCTION.
SO, WE'RE EITHER AHEAD OF THE CURVE THIS TIME OR WE'RE HEADED STRAIGHT INTO A TRAP.
EVEN IF IT'S AN AMBUSH, CAPTAIN MARVEL, THAT'S FINE.
THE RED SKULL ISN'T THE ONLY ONE WITH MORE CARDS UP HIS SLEEVE.
ANYTHING WE SHOULD KNOW, TONY?
NOTHING MISSION CRITICAL AT THIS TIME, CAPTAIN.
WHAT'S WRONG? DON'T YOU TRUST ME?

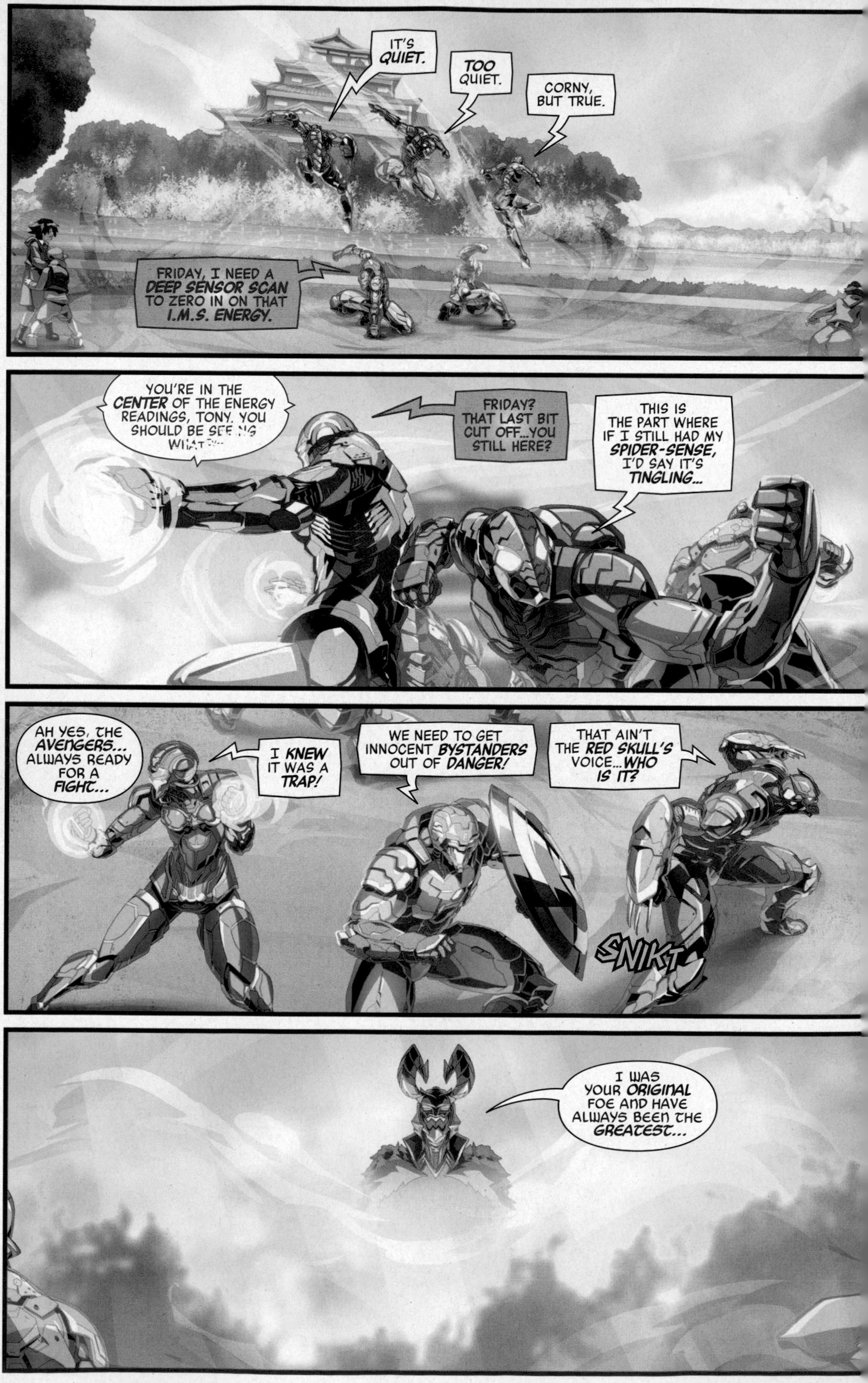
IT'S QUIET.
TOO QUIET.
CORNY, BUT TRUE.
FRIDAY, I NEED A DEEP SENSOR SCAN TO ZERO IN ON THAT I.M.S. ENERGY.
YOU'RE IN THE CENTER OF THE ENERGY READINGS, TONY. YOU SHOULD BE SEE
FRIDAY? THAT LAST BIT CUT OFF...YOU STILL HERE?
THIS IS THE PART WHERE IF I STILL HAD MY SPIDER-SENSE, I'D SAY IT'S TINGLING...
AH YES, THE AVENGERS... ALWAYS READY FOR A FIGHT...
I KNEW IT WAS A TRAP!
WE NEED TO GET INNOCENT BYSTANDERS OUT OF DANGER!
THAT AIN'T THE RED SKULL'S VOICE...WHO IS IT?
SNIKT
I WAS YOUR ORIGINAL FOE AND HAVE ALWAYS BEEN THE GREATEST...

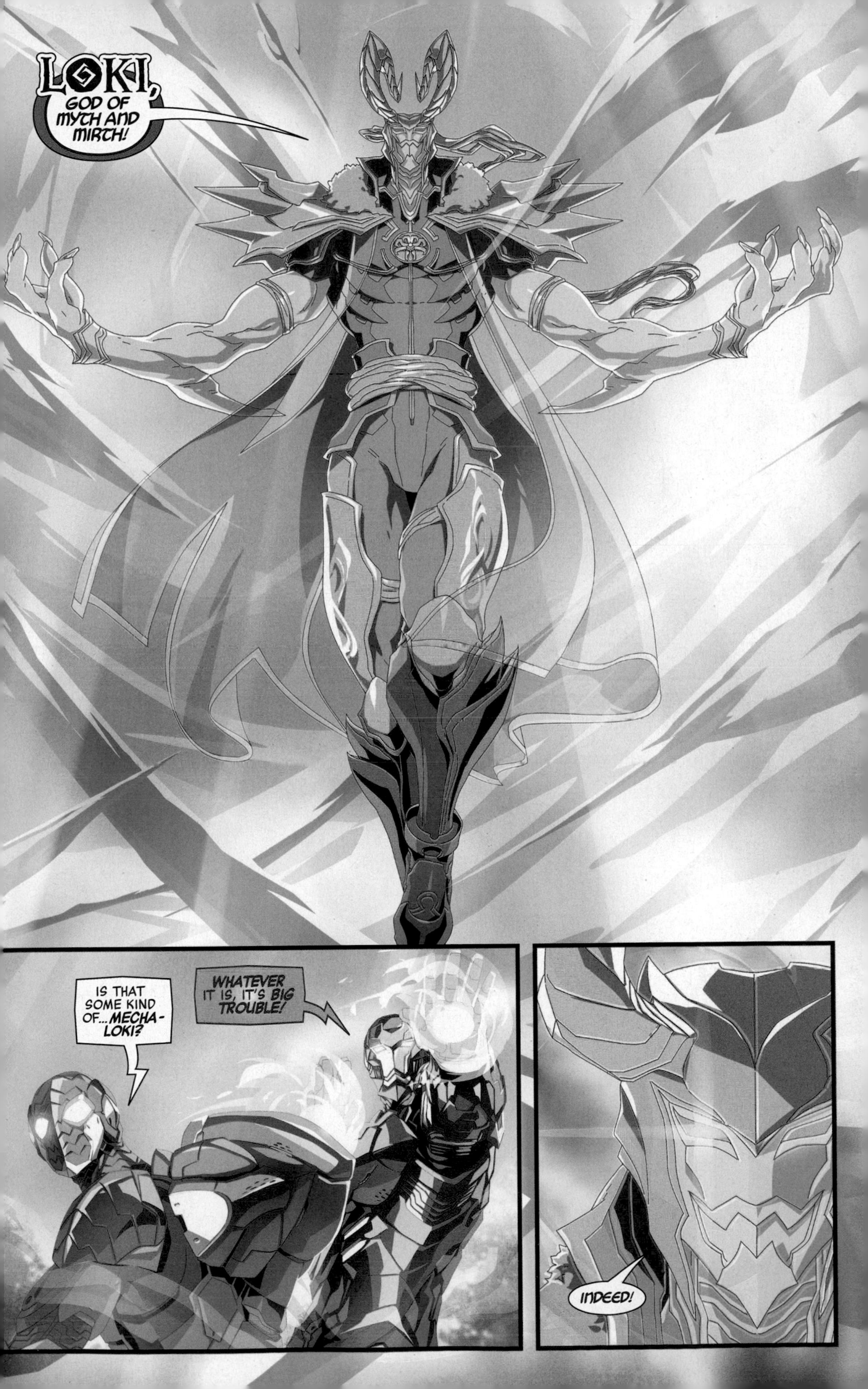
LOKI, GOD OF MYTH AND MIRTH!
IS THAT SOME KIND OF...MECHA-LOKI?
WHATEVER IT IS, IT'S BIG TROUBLE!
INDEED!

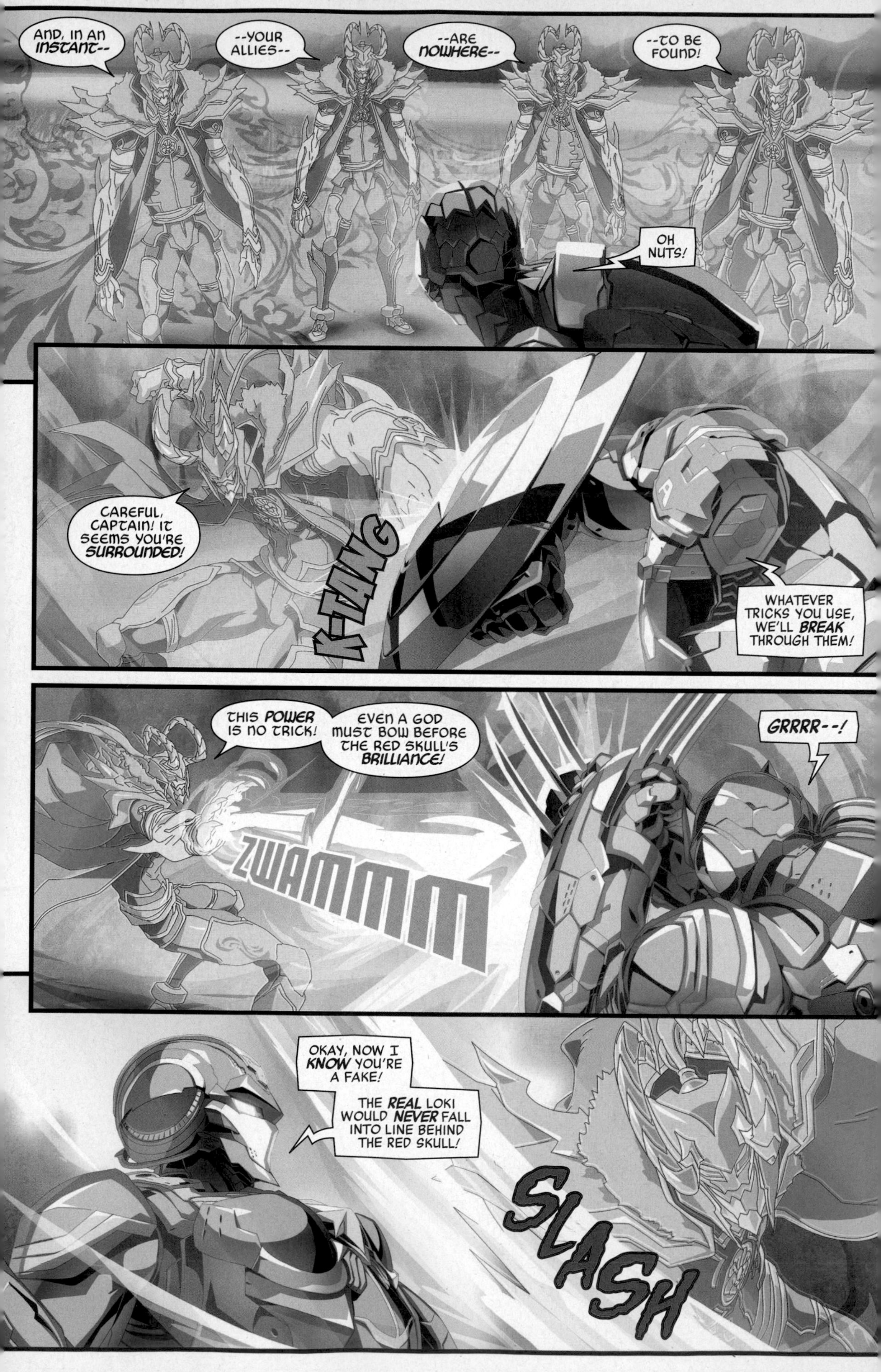

AND, IN AN INSTANT--
--YOUR ALLIES--
--ARE NOWHERE--
--TO BE FOUND!
OH NUTS!
CAREFUL, CAPTAIN! IT SEEMS YOU'RE SURROUNDED!
K-TANG
WHATEVER TRICKS YOU USE, WE'LL BREAK THROUGH THEM!
THIS POWER IS NO TRICK!
EVEN A GOD MUST BOW BEFORE THE RED SKULL'S BRILLIANCE!
GRRRR--!
ZWAMMM
OKAY, NOW I KNOW YOU'RE A FAKE!
THE REAL LOKI WOULD NEVER FALL INTO LINE BEHIND THE RED SKULL!
SLASH

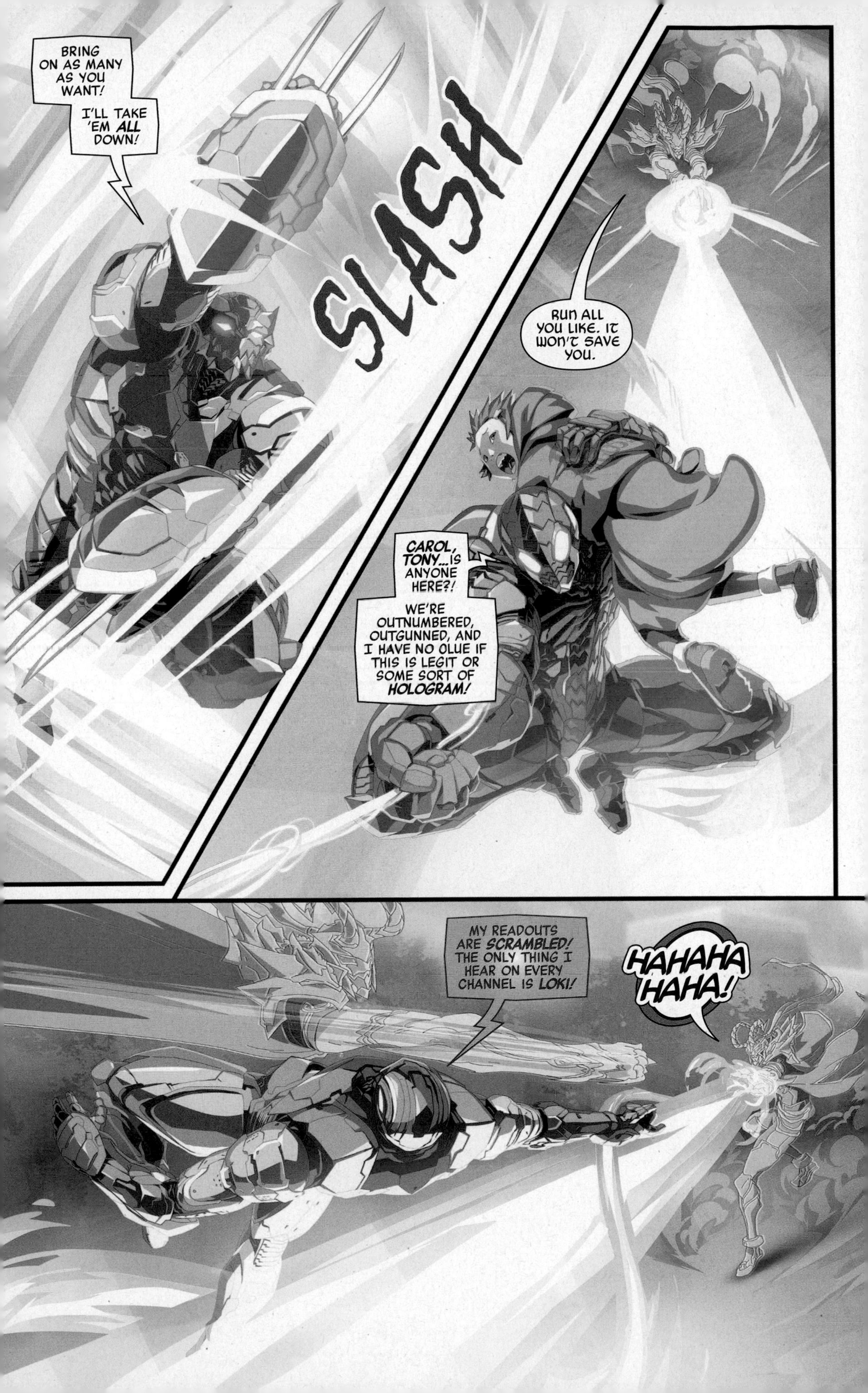
BRING ON AS MANY AS YOU WANT!
I'LL TAKE 'EM ALL DOWN!
SLASH
RUN ALL YOU LIKE. IT WON'T SAVE YOU.
CAROL, TONY... IS ANYONE HERE?!
WE'RE OUTNUMBERED, OUTGUNNED, AND I HAVE NO CLUE IF THIS IS LEGIT OR SOME SORT OF HOLOGRAM!
MY READOUTS ARE SCRAMBLED! THE ONLY THING I HEAR ON EVERY CHANNEL IS LOKI!
HAHAHA HAHA!

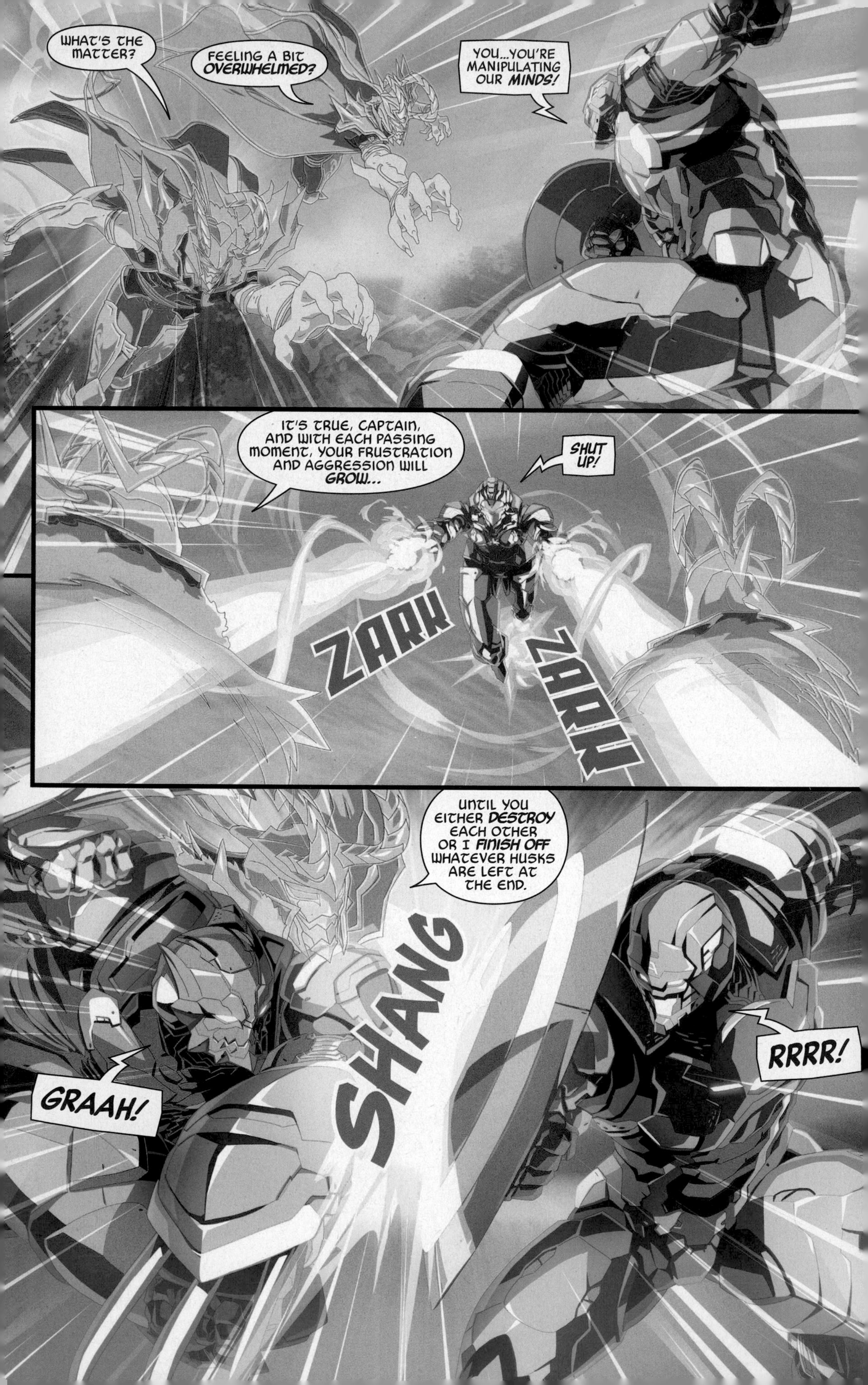
WHAT'S THE MATTER?
FEELING A BIT OVERWHELMED?
YOU...YOU'RE MANIPULATING OUR MINDS!
IT'S TRUE, CAPTAIN, AND WITH EACH PASSING MOMENT, YOUR FRUSTRATION AND AGGRESSION WILL GROW...
SHUT UP!
ZARK
ZARK
UNTIL YOU EITHER DESTROY EACH OTHER OR I FINISH OFF WHATEVER HUSKS ARE LEFT AT THE END.
SHANG
GRAAH!
RRRR!

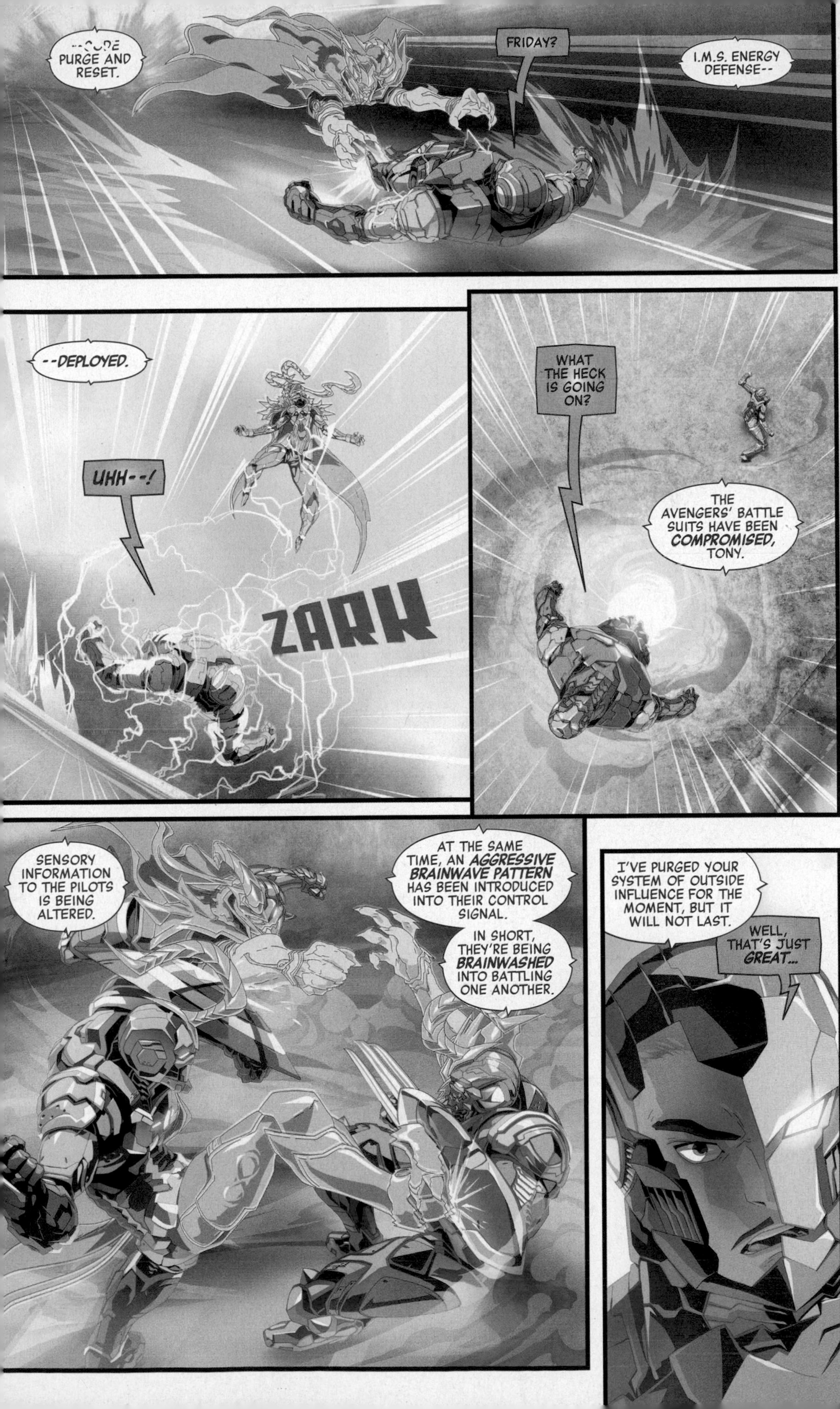
--CODE PURGE AND RESET.
FRIDAY?
I.M.S. ENERGY DEFENSE--
--DEPLOYED.
UHH--!
ZARK
WHAT THE HECK IS GOING ON?
THE AVENGERS' BATTLE SUITS HAVE BEEN *COMPROMISED,* TONY.
SENSORY INFORMATION TO THE PILOTS IS BEING ALTERED.
AT THE SAME TIME, AN *AGGRESSIVE BRAINWAVE PATTERN* HAS BEEN INTRODUCED INTO THEIR CONTROL SIGNAL.
IN SHORT, THEY'RE BEING *BRAINWASHED* INTO BATTLING ONE ANOTHER.
I'VE PURGED YOUR SYSTEM OF OUTSIDE INFLUENCE FOR THE MOMENT, BUT IT WILL NOT LAST.
WELL, THAT'S JUST *GREAT...*

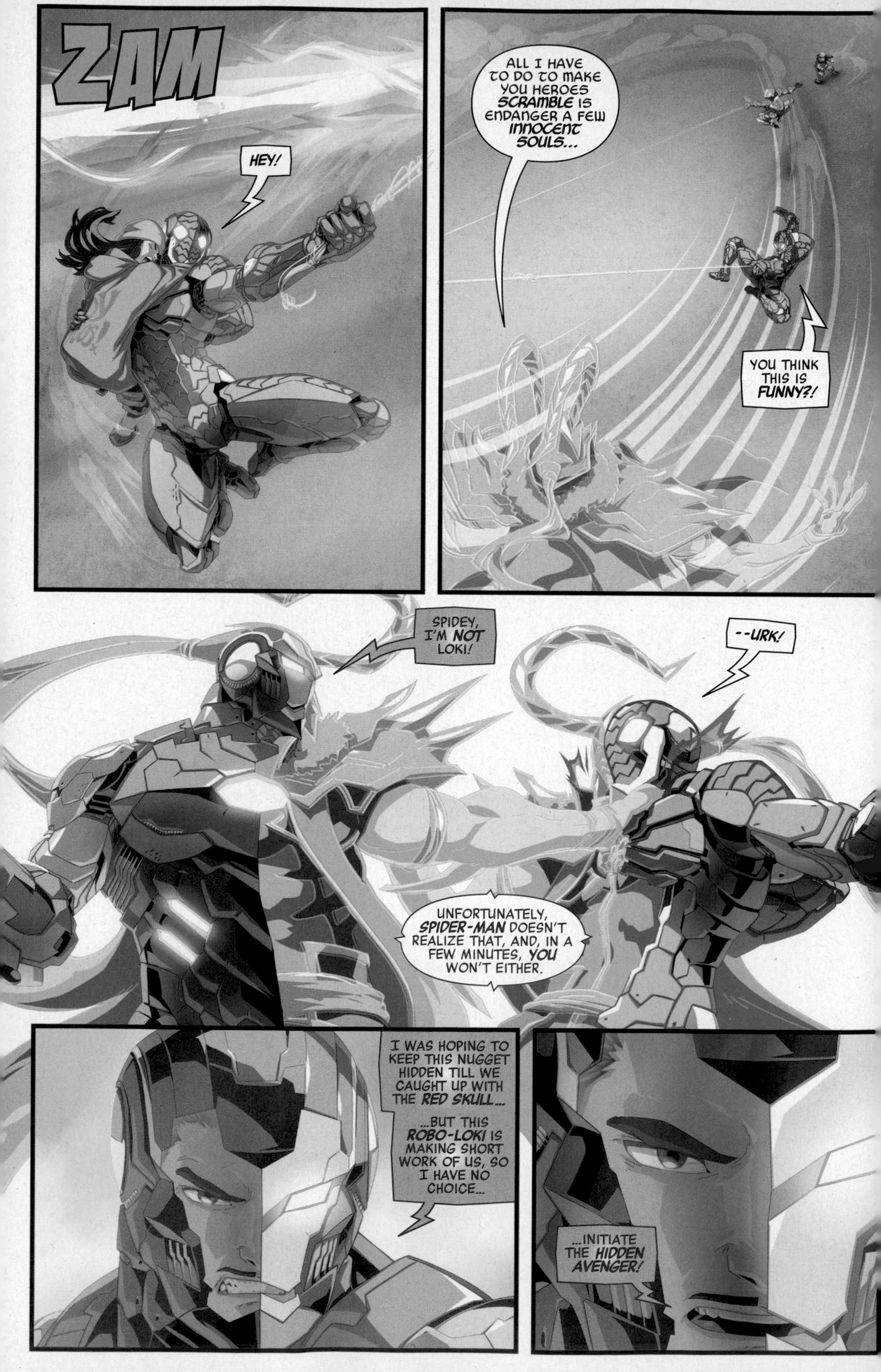
ZAM
HEY!
ALL I HAVE TO DO TO MAKE YOU HEROES SCRAMBLE IS ENDANGER A FEW INNOCENT SOULS...
YOU THINK THIS IS FUNNY?!
SPIDEY, I'M NOT LOKI!
--URK!
UNFORTUNATELY, SPIDER-MAN DOESN'T REALIZE THAT, AND, IN A FEW MINUTES, YOU WON'T EITHER.
I WAS HOPING TO KEEP THIS NUGGET HIDDEN TILL WE CAUGHT UP WITH THE RED SKULL...
...BUT THIS ROBO-LOKI IS MAKING SHORT WORK OF US, SO I HAVE NO CHOICE...
...INITIATE THE HIDDEN AVENGER!

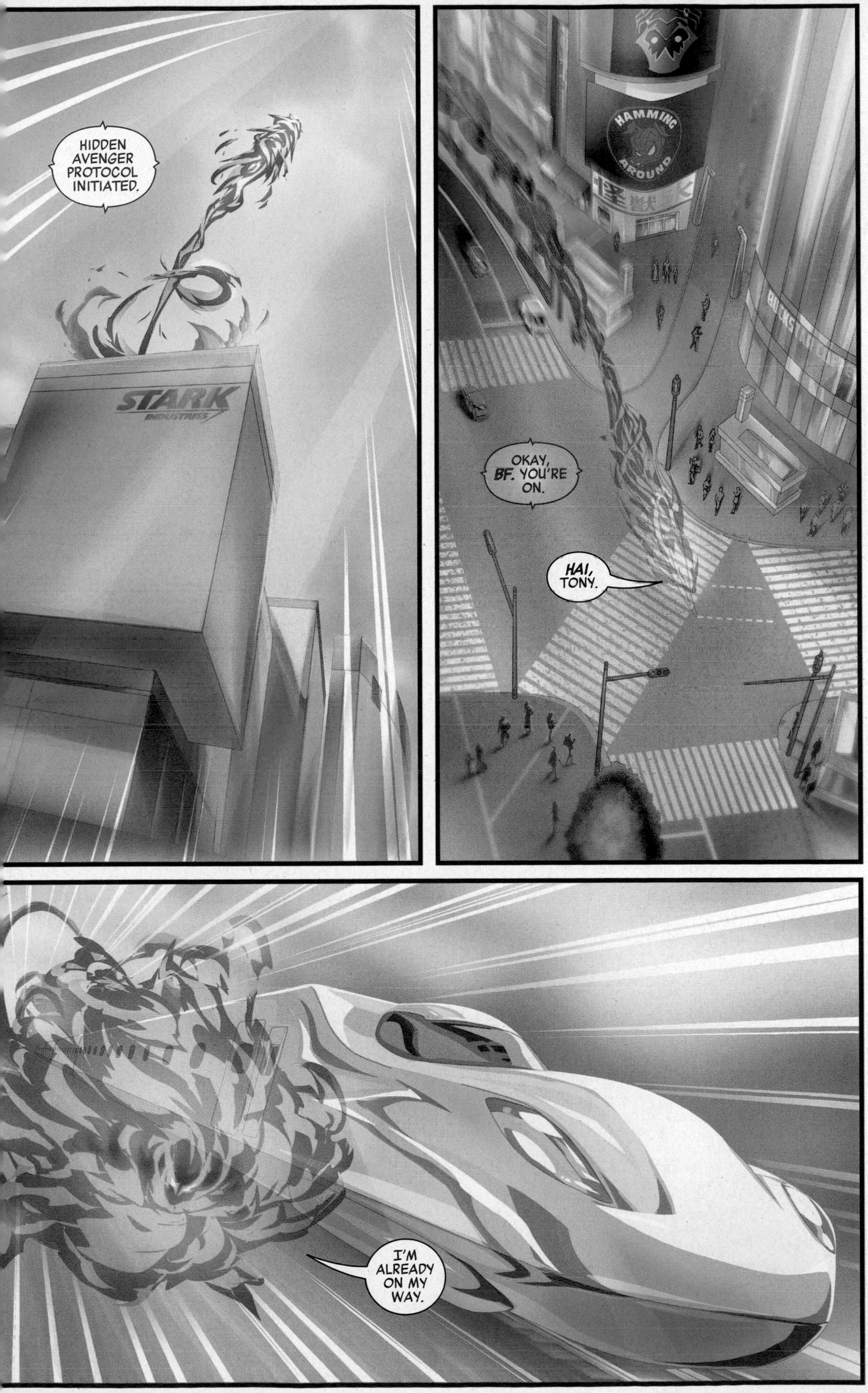
HIDDEN AVENGER PROTOCOL INITIATED.
STARK INDUSTRIES
HAMMING AROUND
OKAY, BF. YOU'RE ON.
HAI, TONY.
I'M ALREADY ON MY WAY.

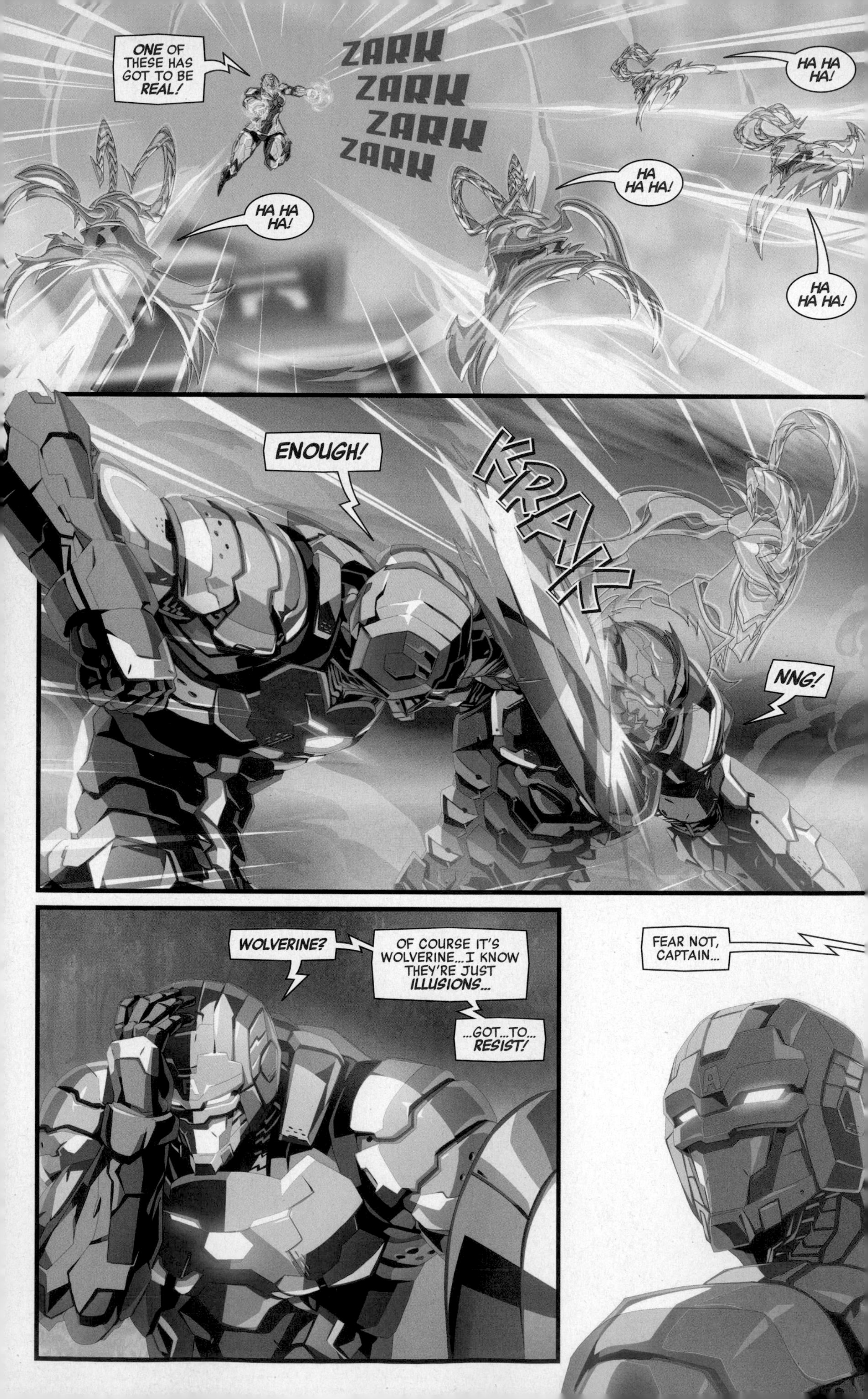
ONE OF THESE HAS GOT TO BE REAL!
ZARK ZARK ZARK ZARK
HA HA HA!
HA HA HA!
HA HA HA!
HA HA HA!
ENOUGH!
KRAK
NNG!
WOLVERINE?
OF COURSE IT'S WOLVERINE... I KNOW THEY'RE JUST ILLUSIONS...
...GOT...TO... RESIST!
FEAR NOT, CAPTAIN...

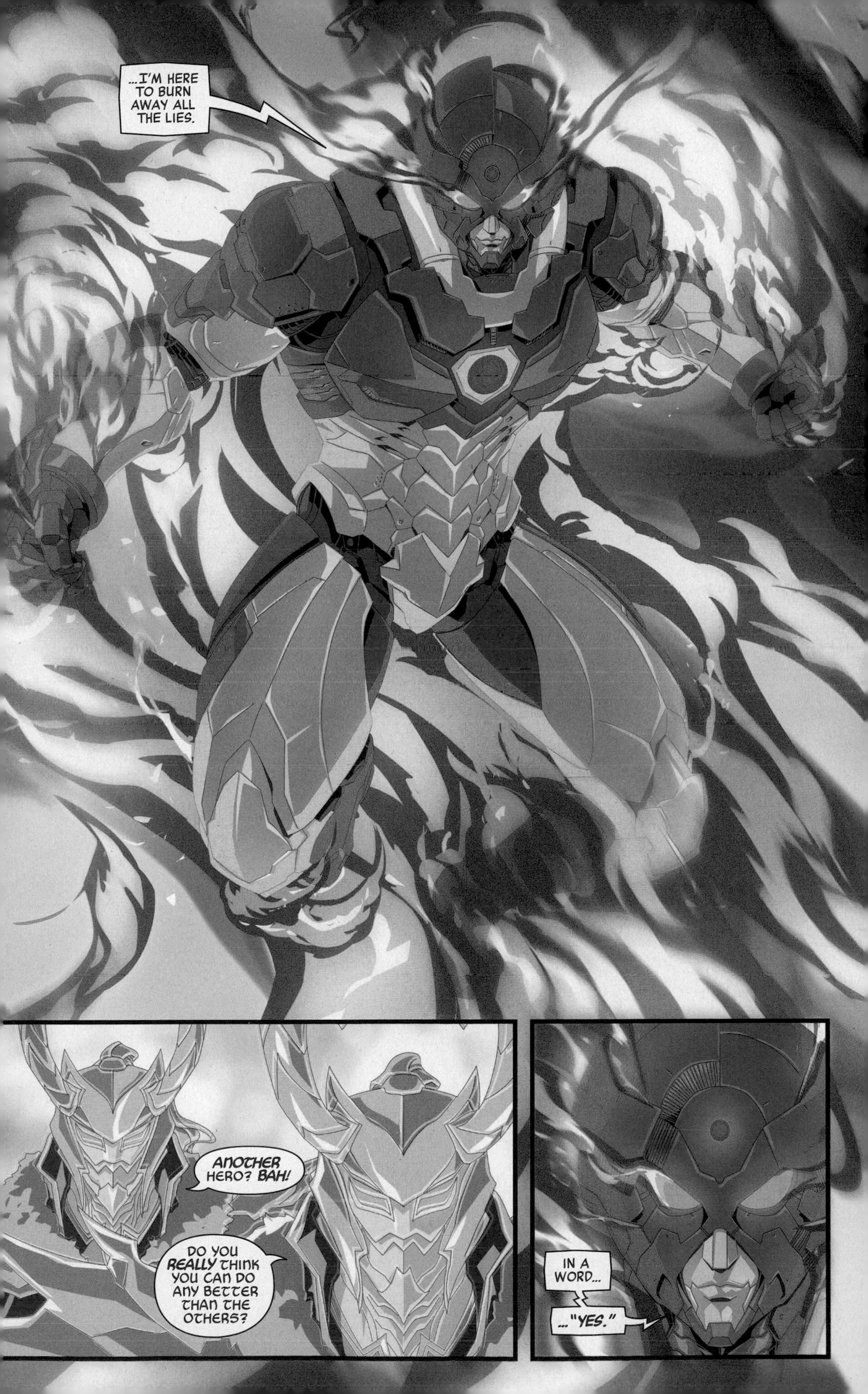
...I'M HERE TO BURN AWAY ALL THE LIES.
ANOTHER HERO? BAH!
DO YOU REALLY THINK YOU CAN DO ANY BETTER THAN THE OTHERS?
IN A WORD...
..."YES."

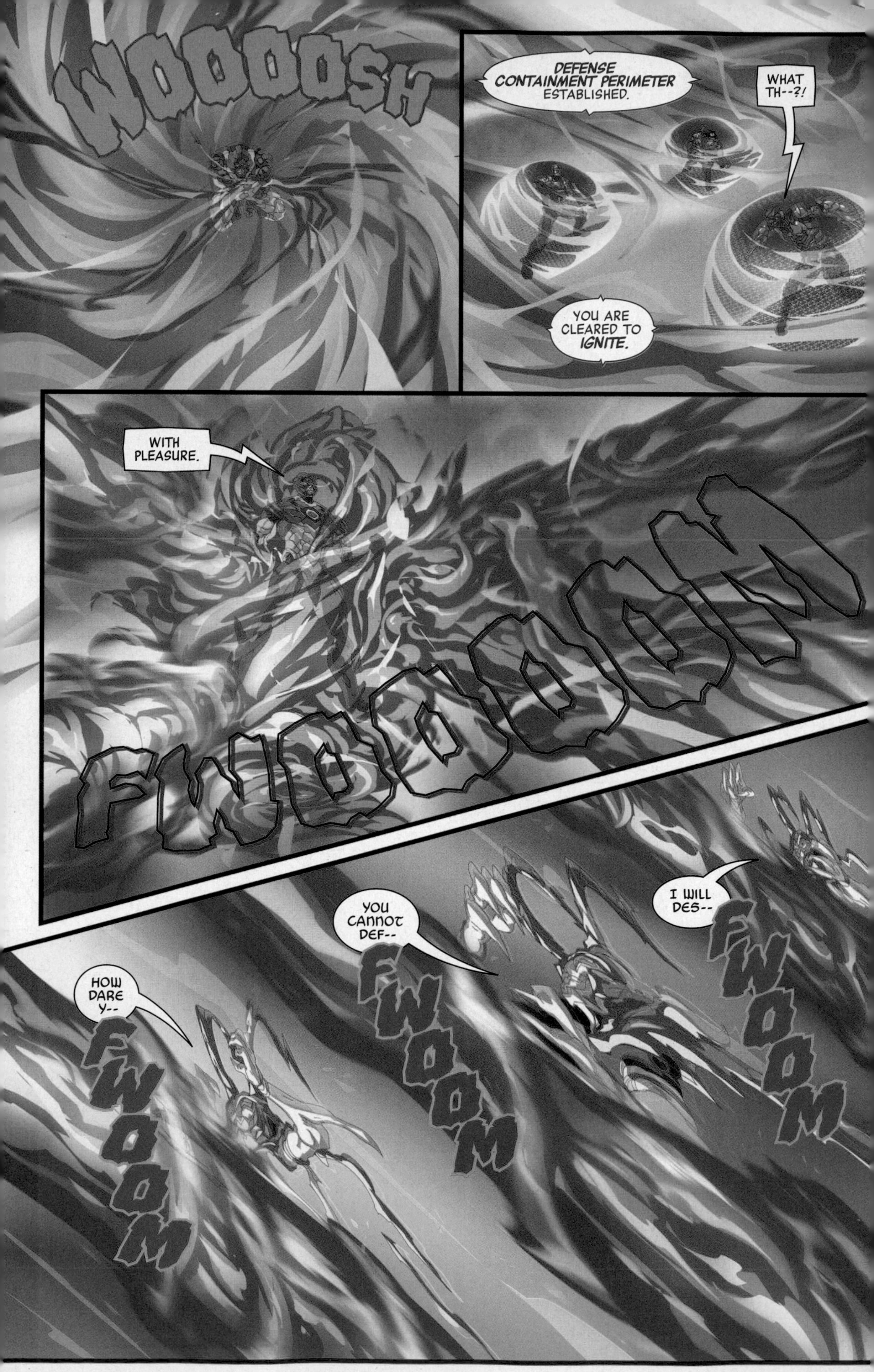
WOOOOSH
DEFENSE CONTAINMENT PERIMETER ESTABLISHED.
WHAT TH--?!
YOU ARE CLEARED TO IGNITE.
WITH PLEASURE.
FWOOOOOM
HOW DARE Y--
FWOOM
YOU CANNOT DEF--
FWOOM
I WILL DES--
FWOOM

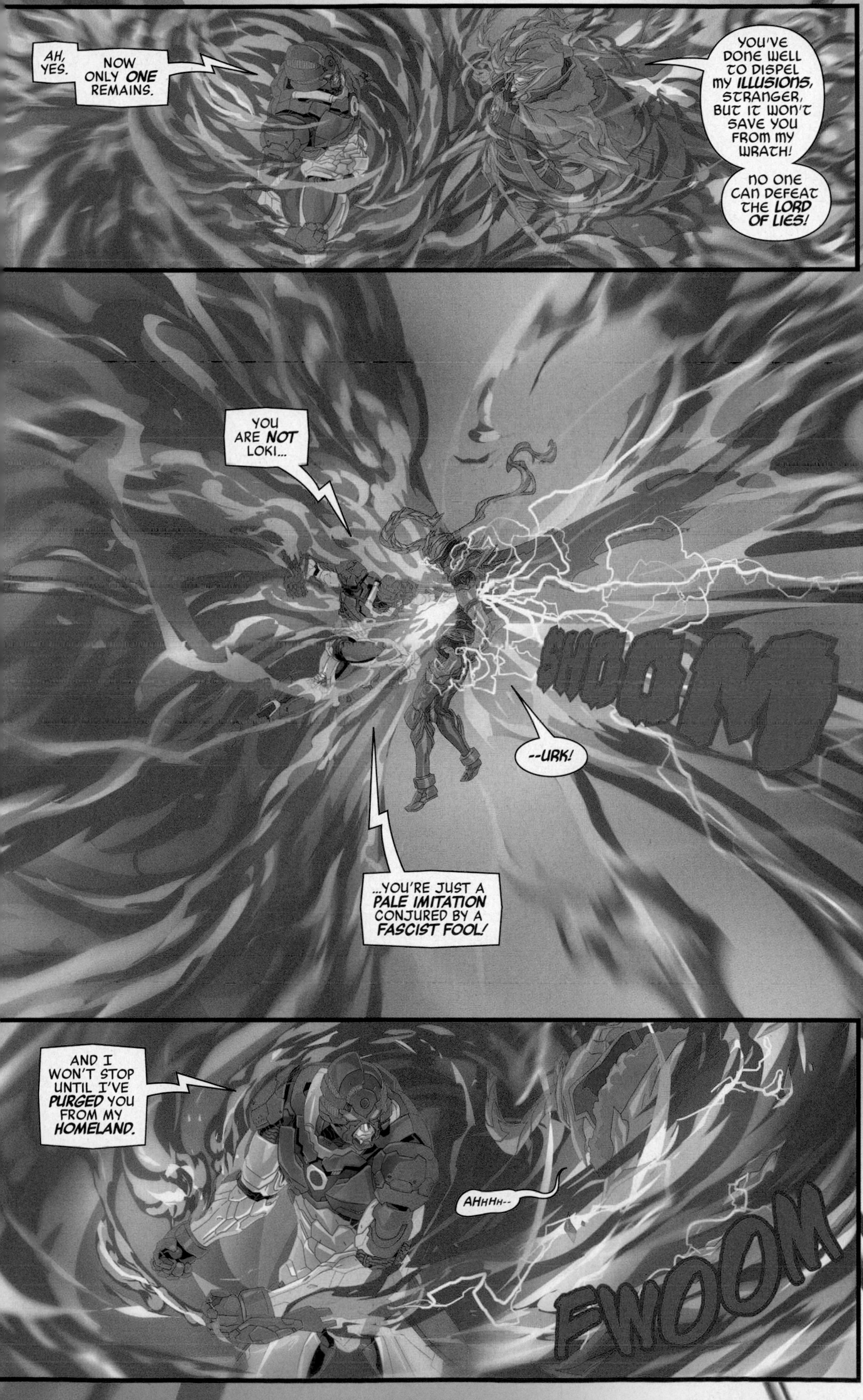
AH, YES.
NOW ONLY ONE REMAINS.
YOU'VE DONE WELL TO DISPEL MY ILLUSIONS, STRANGER, BUT IT WON'T SAVE YOU FROM MY WRATH!
NO ONE CAN DEFEAT THE LORD OF LIES!
YOU ARE NOT LOKI...
SHOOM
--URK!
...YOU'RE JUST A PALE IMITATION CONJURED BY A FASCIST FOOL!
AND I WON'T STOP UNTIL I'VE PURGED YOU FROM MY HOMELAND.
AHHHH--
FWOOM

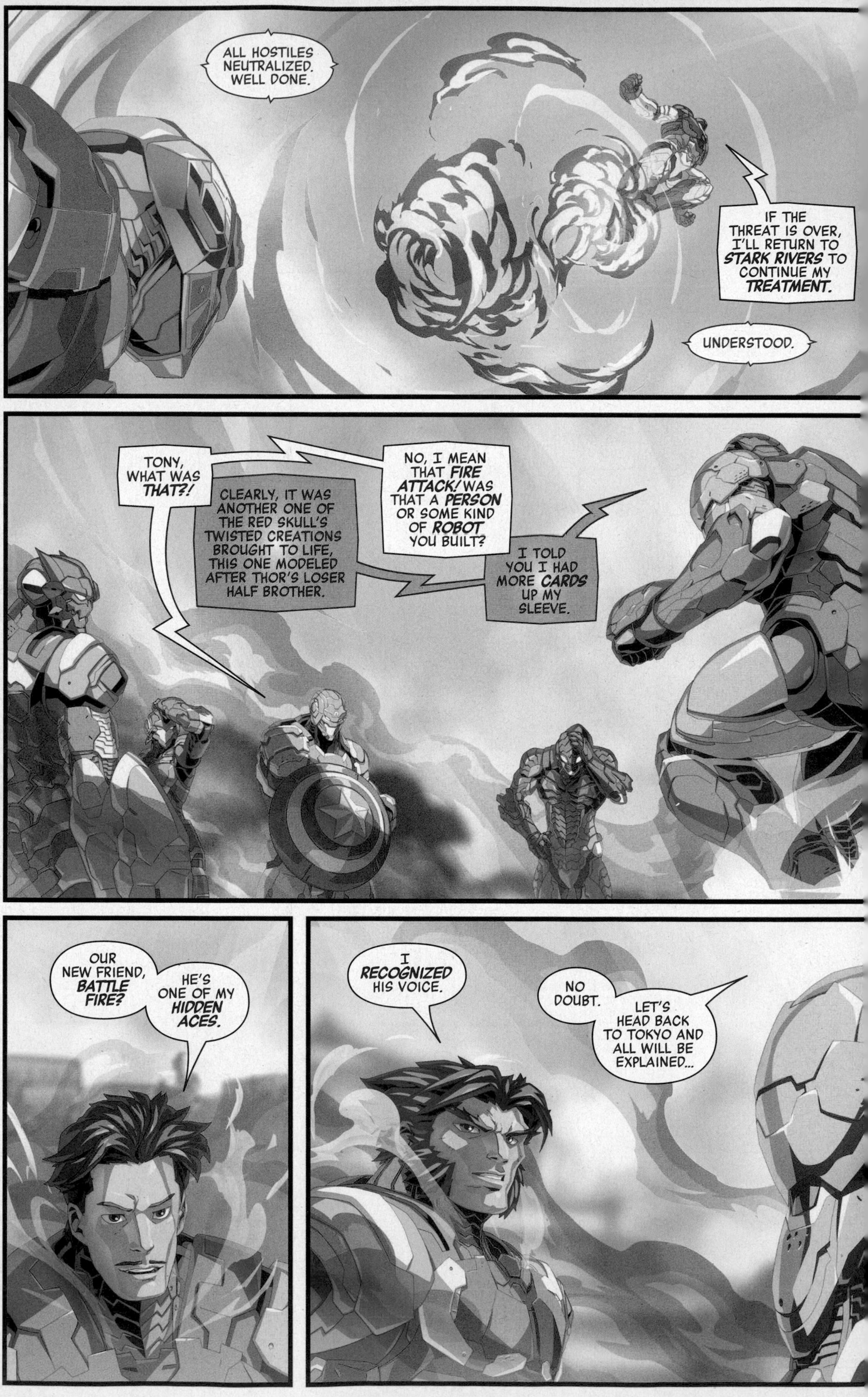
ALL HOSTILES NEUTRALIZED. WELL DONE.
IF THE THREAT IS OVER, I'LL RETURN TO STARK RIVERS TO CONTINUE MY TREATMENT.
UNDERSTOOD.
TONY, WHAT WAS THAT?!
NO, I MEAN THAT FIRE ATTACK! WAS THAT A PERSON OR SOME KIND OF ROBOT YOU BUILT?
CLEARLY, IT WAS ANOTHER ONE OF THE RED SKULL'S TWISTED CREATIONS BROUGHT TO LIFE, THIS ONE MODELED AFTER THOR'S LOSER HALF BROTHER.
I TOLD YOU I HAD MORE CARDS UP MY SLEEVE.
OUR NEW FRIEND, BATTLE FIRE?
HE'S ONE OF MY HIDDEN ACES.
I RECOGNIZED HIS VOICE.
NO DOUBT.
LET'S HEAD BACK TO TOKYO AND ALL WILL BE EXPLAINED...

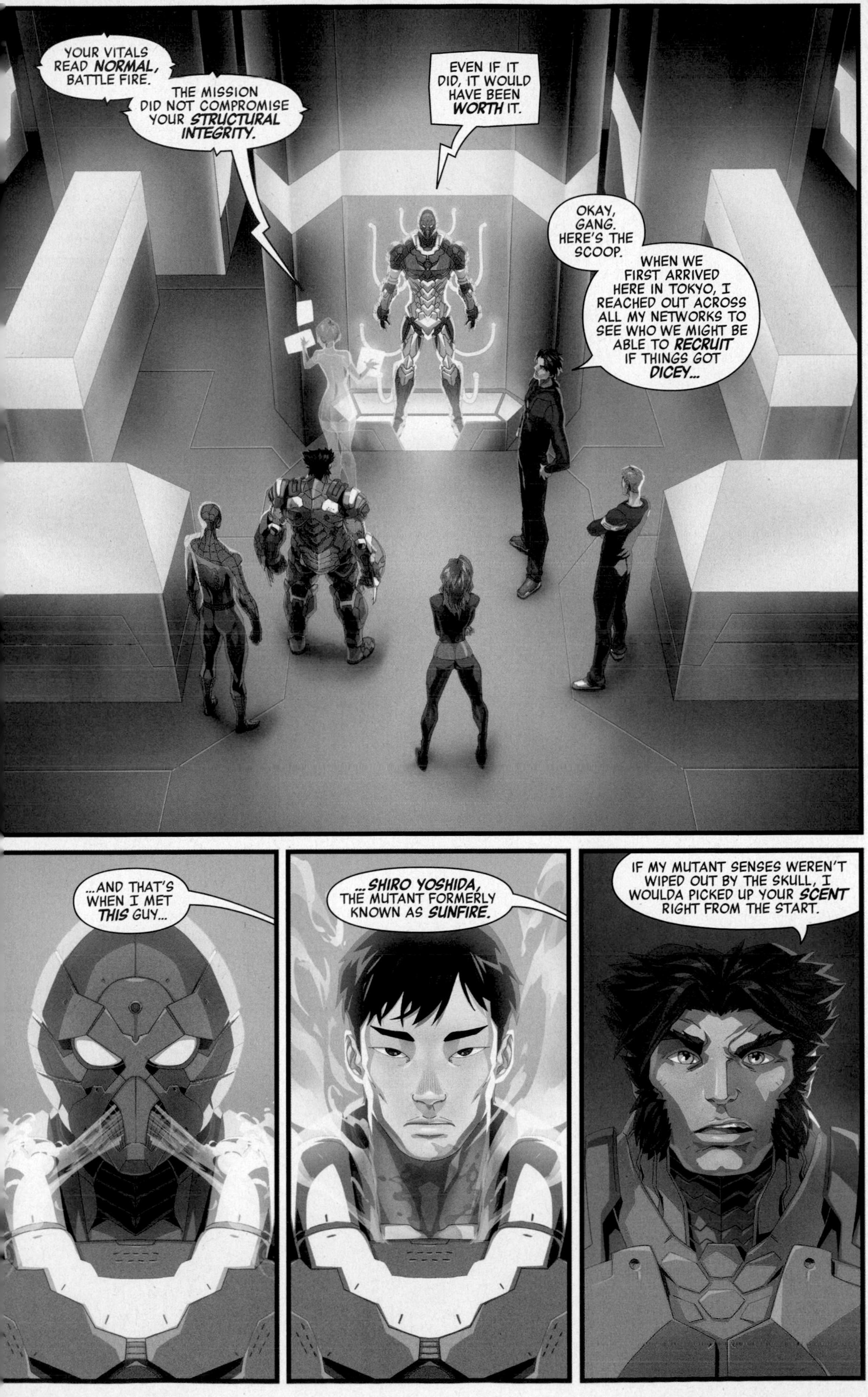
YOUR VITALS READ NORMAL, BATTLE FIRE.
THE MISSION DID NOT COMPROMISE YOUR STRUCTURAL INTEGRITY.
EVEN IF IT DID, IT WOULD HAVE BEEN WORTH IT.
OKAY, GANG. HERE'S THE SCOOP.
WHEN WE FIRST ARRIVED HERE IN TOKYO, I REACHED OUT ACROSS ALL MY NETWORKS TO SEE WHO WE MIGHT BE ABLE TO RECRUIT IF THINGS GOT DICEY...
...AND THAT'S WHEN I MET THIS GUY...
...SHIRO YOSHIDA, THE MUTANT FORMERLY KNOWN AS SUNFIRE.
IF MY MUTANT SENSES WEREN'T WIPED OUT BY THE SKULL, I WOULDA PICKED UP YOUR SCENT RIGHT FROM THE START.

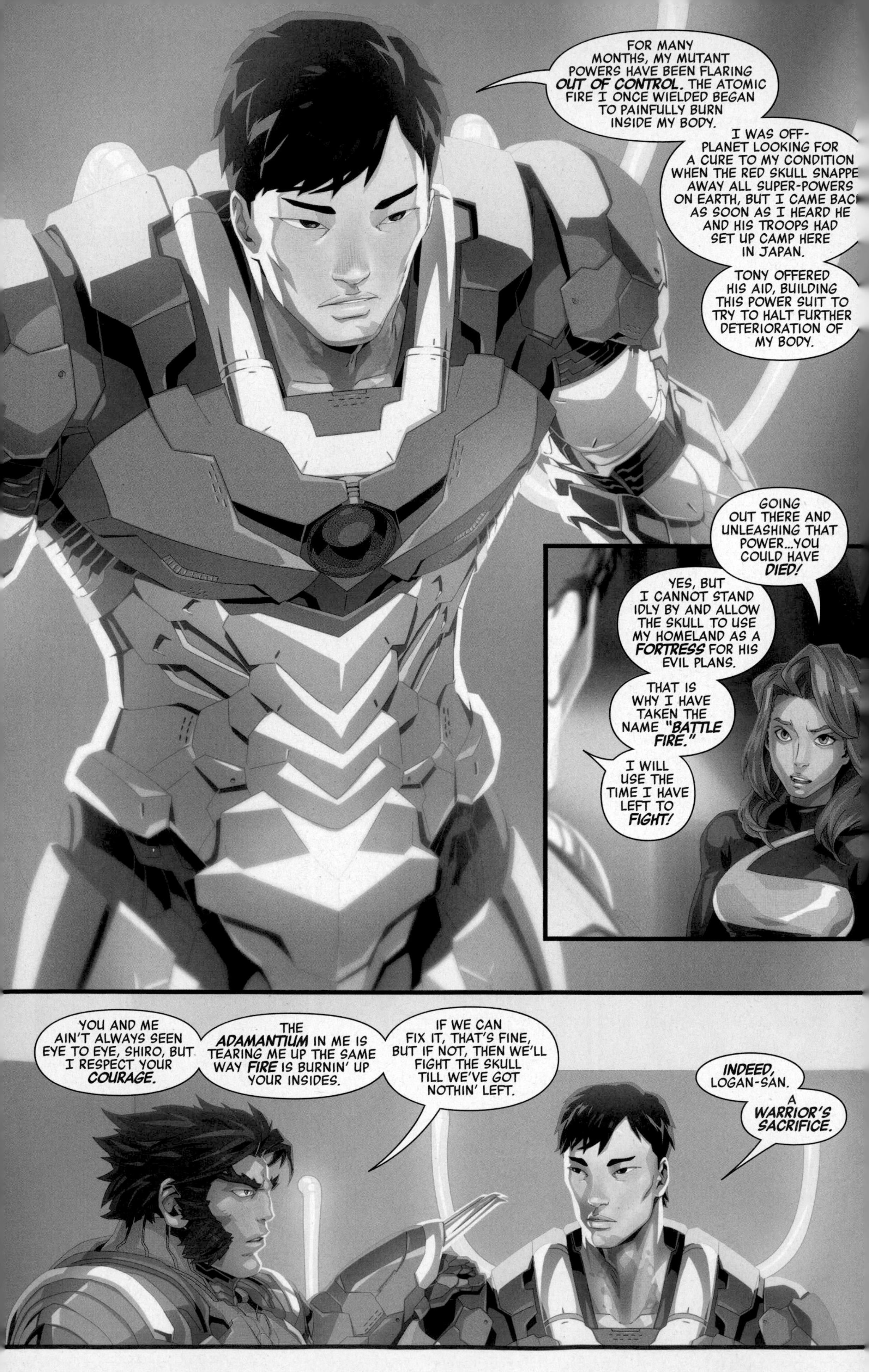
FOR MANY MONTHS, MY MUTANT POWERS HAVE BEEN FLARING OUT OF CONTROL. THE ATOMIC FIRE I ONCE WIELDED BEGAN TO PAINFULLY BURN INSIDE MY BODY.
I WAS OFF-PLANET LOOKING FOR A CURE TO MY CONDITION WHEN THE RED SKULL SNAPPE AWAY ALL SUPER-POWERS ON EARTH, BUT I CAME BAC AS SOON AS I HEARD HE AND HIS TROOPS HAD SET UP CAMP HERE IN JAPAN.
TONY OFFERED HIS AID, BUILDING THIS POWER SUIT TO TRY TO HALT FURTHER DETERIORATION OF MY BODY.
GOING OUT THERE AND UNLEASHING THAT POWER...YOU COULD HAVE DIED!
YES, BUT I CANNOT STAND IDLY BY AND ALLOW THE SKULL TO USE MY HOMELAND AS A FORTRESS FOR HIS EVIL PLANS.
THAT IS WHY I HAVE TAKEN THE NAME "BATTLE FIRE."
I WILL USE THE TIME I HAVE LEFT TO FIGHT!
YOU AND ME AIN'T ALWAYS SEEN EYE TO EYE, SHIRO, BUT I RESPECT YOUR COURAGE.
THE ADAMANTIUM IN ME IS TEARING ME UP THE SAME WAY FIRE IS BURNIN' UP YOUR INSIDES.
IF WE CAN FIX IT, THAT'S FINE, BUT IF NOT, THEN WE'LL FIGHT THE SKULL TILL WE'VE GOT NOTHIN' LEFT.
INDEED, LOGAN-SAN.
A WARRIOR'S SACRIFICE.

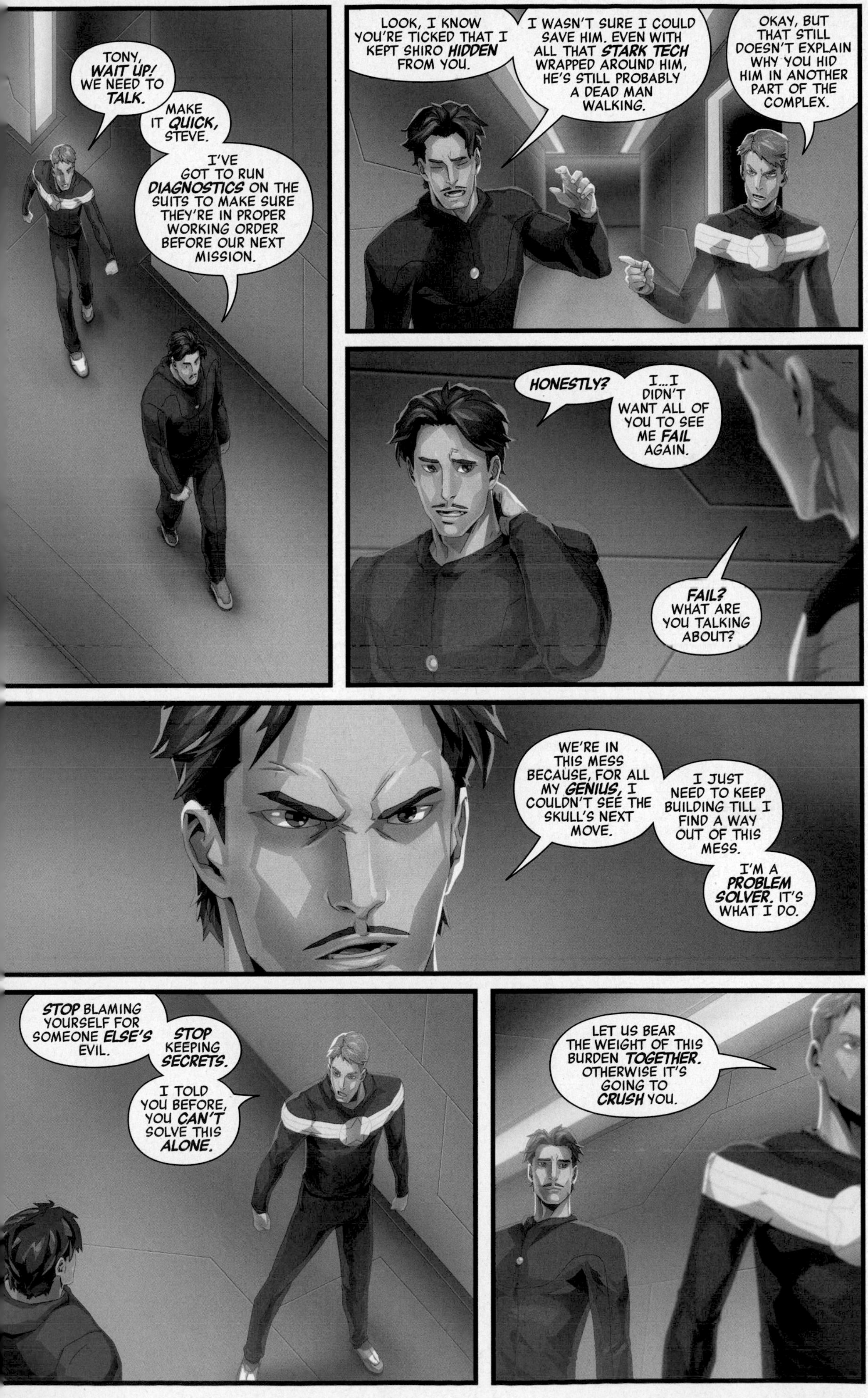
TONY, WAIT UP! WE NEED TO TALK.
MAKE IT QUICK, STEVE.
I'VE GOT TO RUN DIAGNOSTICS ON THE SUITS TO MAKE SURE THEY'RE IN PROPER WORKING ORDER BEFORE OUR NEXT MISSION.
LOOK, I KNOW YOU'RE TICKED THAT I KEPT SHIRO HIDDEN FROM YOU.
I WASN'T SURE I COULD SAVE HIM. EVEN WITH ALL THAT STARK TECH WRAPPED AROUND HIM, HE'S STILL PROBABLY A DEAD MAN WALKING.
OKAY, BUT THAT STILL DOESN'T EXPLAIN WHY YOU HID HIM IN ANOTHER PART OF THE COMPLEX.
HONESTLY?
I...I DIDN'T WANT ALL OF YOU TO SEE ME FAIL AGAIN.
FAIL? WHAT ARE YOU TALKING ABOUT?
WE'RE IN THIS MESS BECAUSE, FOR ALL MY GENIUS, I COULDN'T SEE THE SKULL'S NEXT MOVE.
I JUST NEED TO KEEP BUILDING TILL I FIND A WAY OUT OF THIS MESS.
I'M A PROBLEM SOLVER. IT'S WHAT I DO.
STOP BLAMING YOURSELF FOR SOMEONE ELSE'S EVIL.
STOP KEEPING SECRETS.
I TOLD YOU BEFORE, YOU CAN'T SOLVE THIS ALONE.
LET US BEAR THE WEIGHT OF THIS BURDEN TOGETHER. OTHERWISE IT'S GOING TO CRUSH YOU.

MIRROR *LOKI* HAS BEEN DESTROYED, RED SKULL.

AS EXPECTED.

YOU *KNEW?*

OF COURSE. I NEEDED TO PUSH THE AVENGERS TO FIND THEIR *WEAKNESSES* AND DISCOVER ANY *TRICKS* STARK HAD HIDDEN IN RESERVE.

LOKI WAS A GOOD TEST. WE GAINED VALUABLE *DATA.*

ALTHOUGH STARK'S BATTLE SUITS ARE QUITE *POWERFUL,* THEY CAN BE OVERCOME. THE PEOPLE INSIDE THOSE SHELLS ARE OH SO *VULNERABLE.*

IF INNOCENT LIVES ARE THREATENED IN *MULTIPLE* LOCATIONS, WE CAN SPREAD THEIR RESOURCES TOO THIN AND THEN SLOWLY TEAR THEM APART.

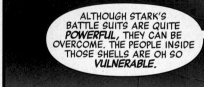

YOU HAVE THE SOLDIERS AND CREATURES OF *OROCHI* READY TO FIGHT FOR YOUR HONOR!

YES, AND IN TIME I WILL USE THEM, BUT NOT YET.

THIS NEXT STEP REQUIRES SOMETHING *FAMILIAR,* ANOTHER OLD FOE *TWISTED* BY I.M.S. ENERGY TO KEEP ROGERS AND HIS FRIENDS *OFF GUARD...*

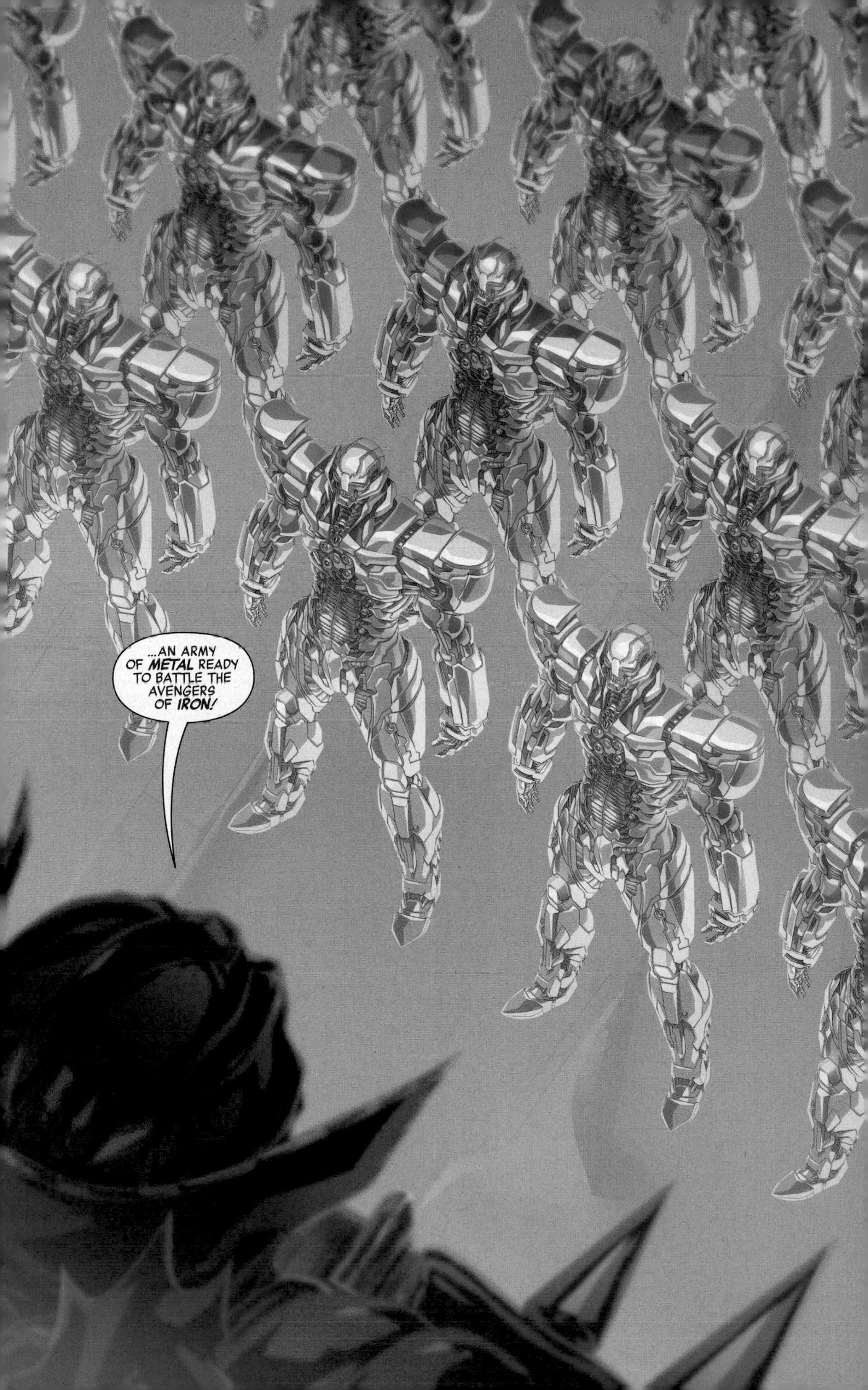
...AN ARMY OF METAL READY TO BATTLE THE AVENGERS OF IRON!

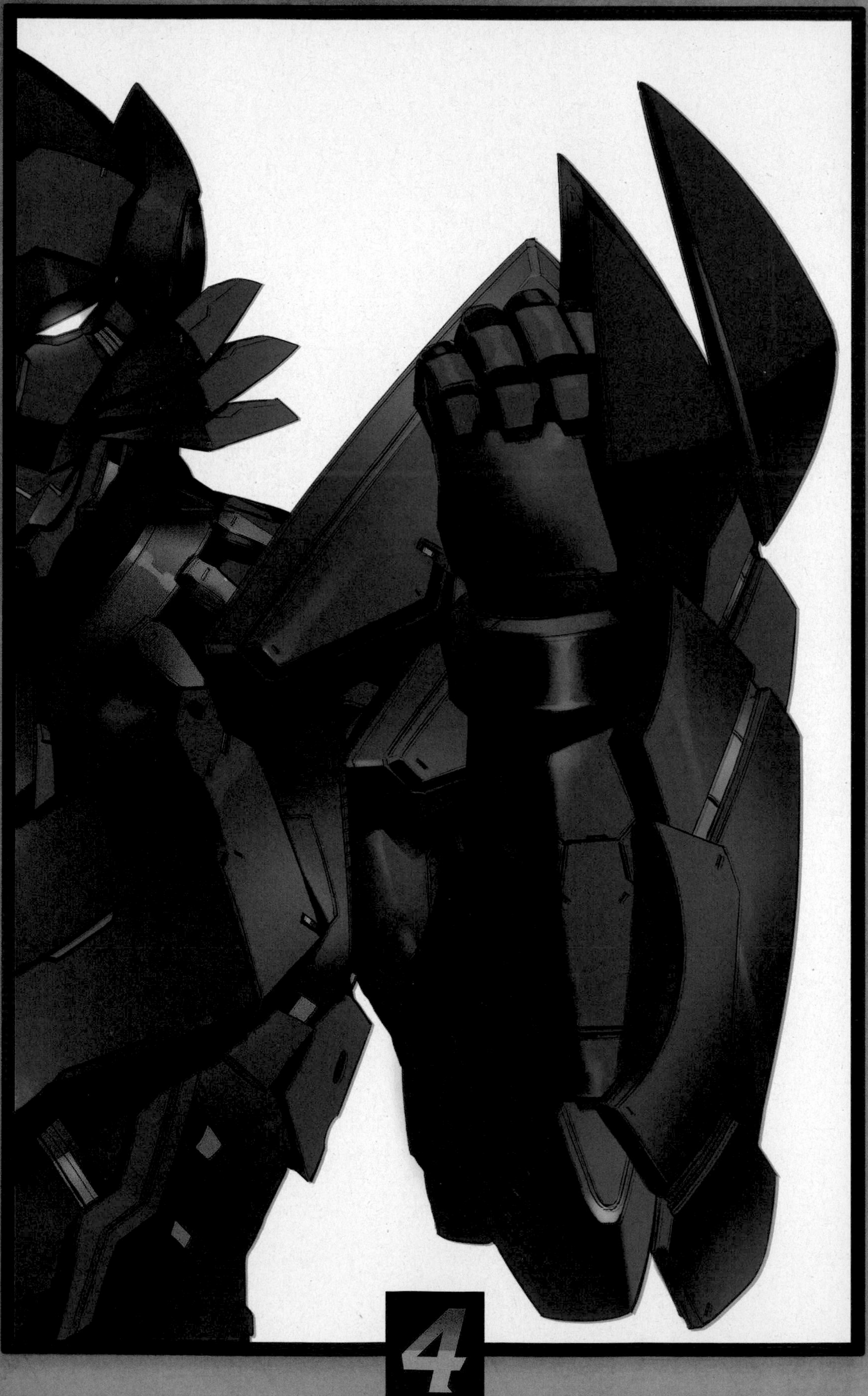

4

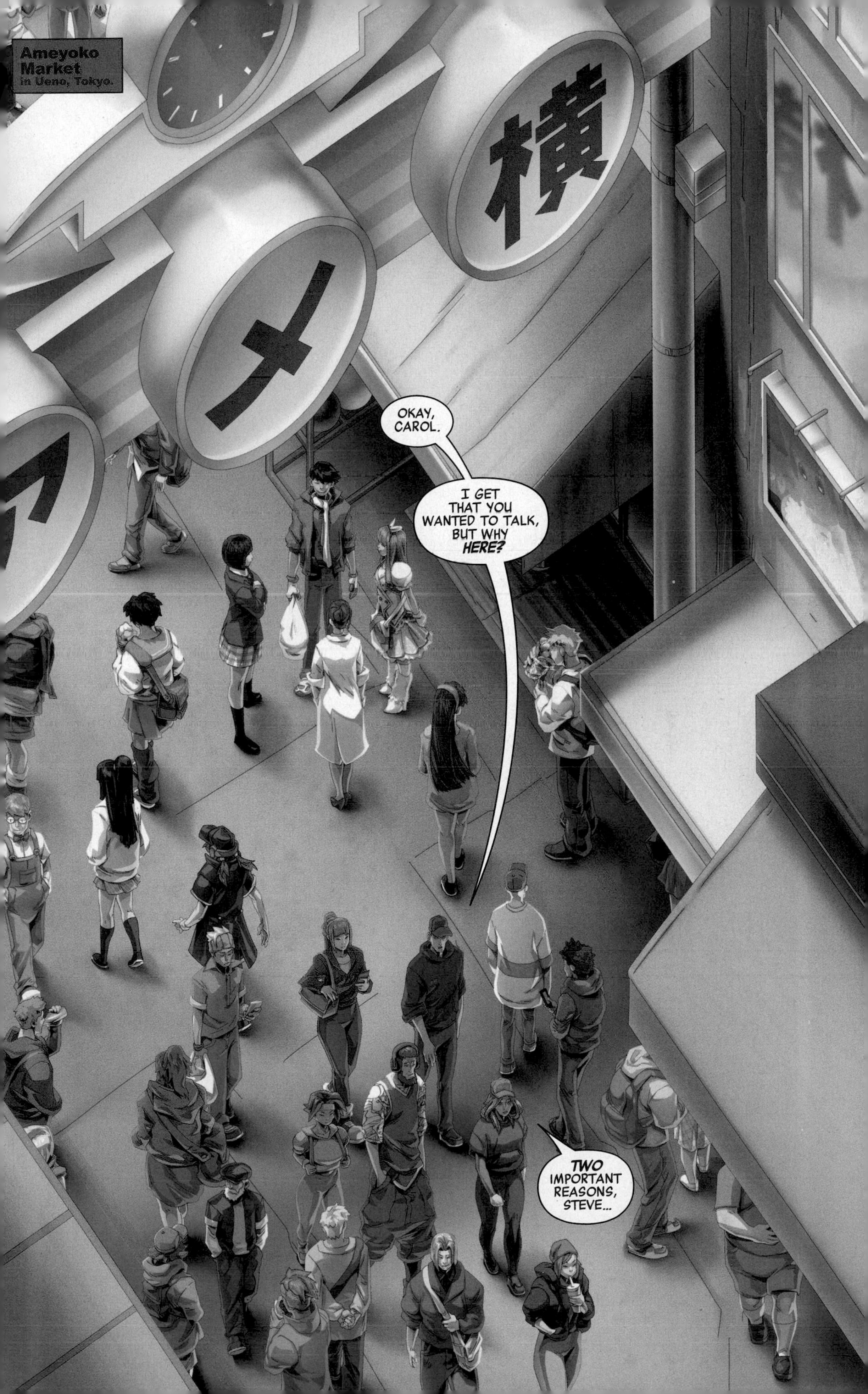
Ameyoko Market in Ueno, Tokyo.
横
OKAY, CAROL.
I GET THAT YOU WANTED TO TALK, BUT WHY HERE?
TWO IMPORTANT REASONS, STEVE...

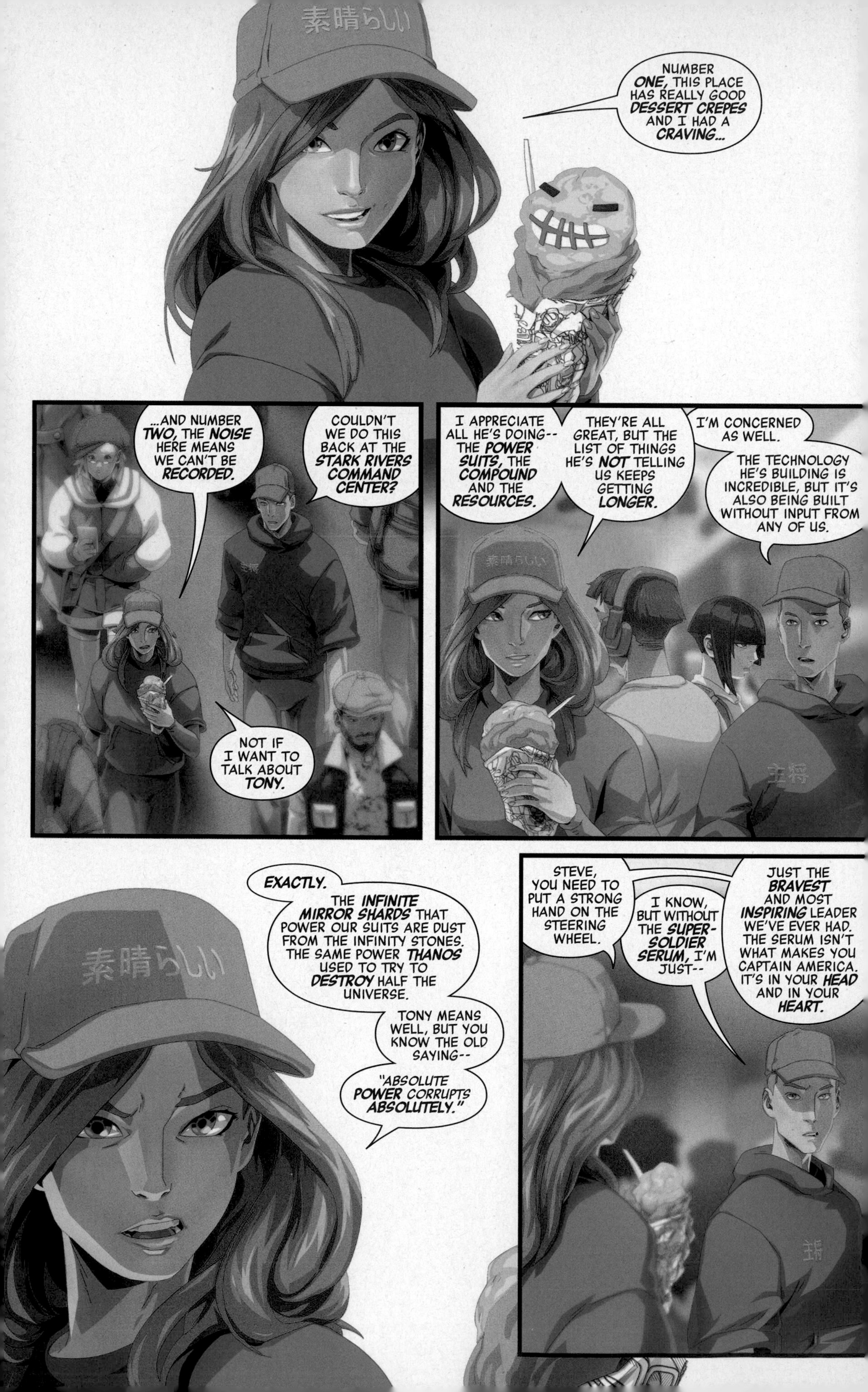

NUMBER ONE, THIS PLACE HAS REALLY GOOD DESSERT CREPES AND I HAD A CRAVING...
...AND NUMBER TWO, THE NOISE HERE MEANS WE CAN'T BE RECORDED.
COULDN'T WE DO THIS BACK AT THE STARK RIVERS COMMAND CENTER?
NOT IF I WANT TO TALK ABOUT TONY.
I APPRECIATE ALL HE'S DOING-- THE POWER SUITS, THE COMPOUND AND THE RESOURCES.
THEY'RE ALL GREAT, BUT THE LIST OF THINGS HE'S NOT TELLING US KEEPS GETTING LONGER.
I'M CONCERNED AS WELL.
THE TECHNOLOGY HE'S BUILDING IS INCREDIBLE, BUT IT'S ALSO BEING BUILT WITHOUT INPUT FROM ANY OF US.
EXACTLY.
THE INFINITE MIRROR SHARDS THAT POWER OUR SUITS ARE DUST FROM THE INFINITY STONES. THE SAME POWER THANOS USED TO TRY TO DESTROY HALF THE UNIVERSE.
TONY MEANS WELL, BUT YOU KNOW THE OLD SAYING--
"ABSOLUTE POWER CORRUPTS ABSOLUTELY."
STEVE, YOU NEED TO PUT A STRONG HAND ON THE STEERING WHEEL.
I KNOW, BUT WITHOUT THE SUPER-SOLDIER SERUM, I'M JUST--
JUST THE BRAVEST AND MOST INSPIRING LEADER WE'VE EVER HAD. THE SERUM ISN'T WHAT MAKES YOU CAPTAIN AMERICA. IT'S IN YOUR HEAD AND IN YOUR HEART.

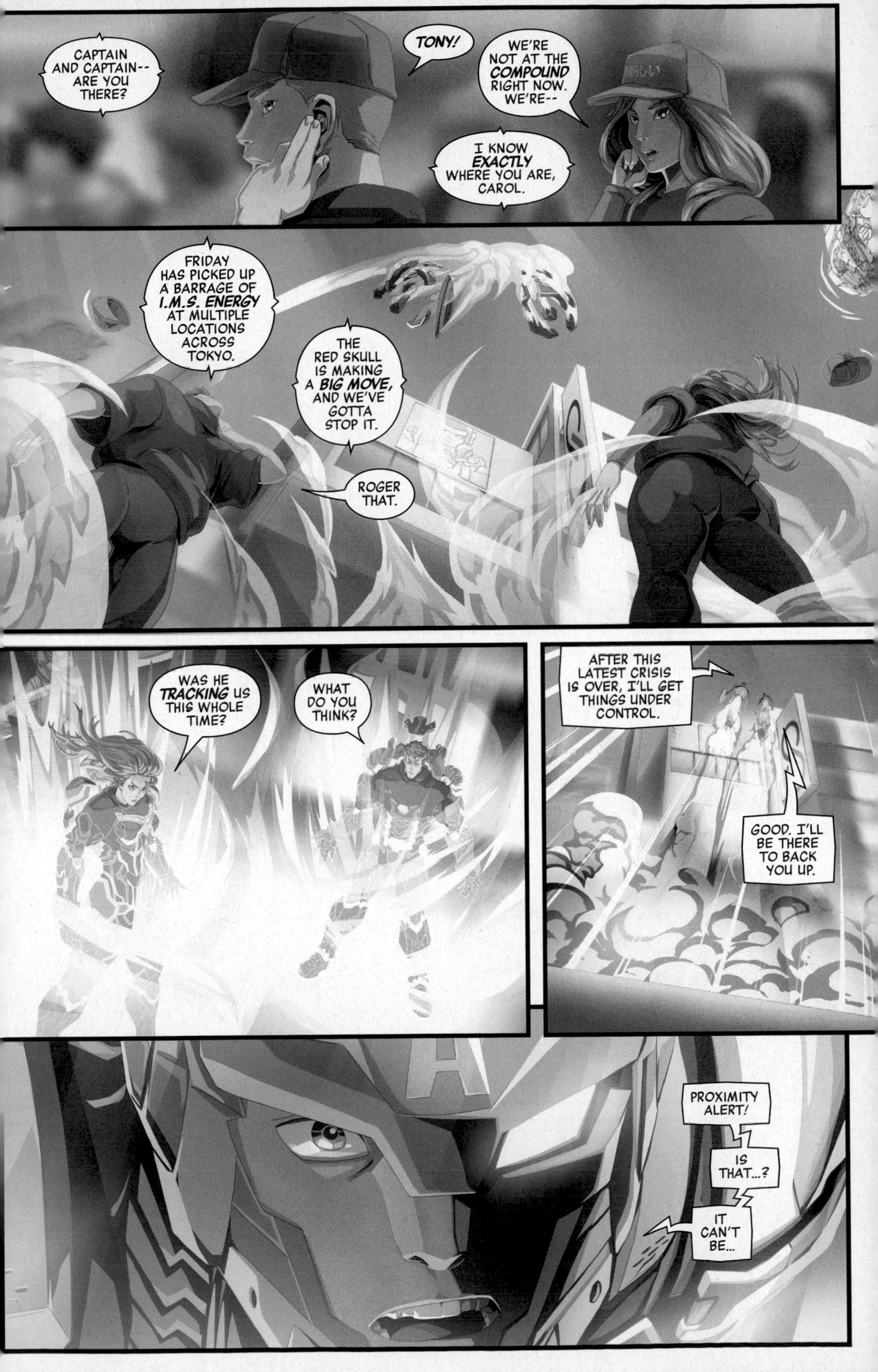
CAPTAIN AND CAPTAIN-- ARE YOU THERE?
TONY!
WE'RE NOT AT THE COMPOUND RIGHT NOW. WE'RE--
I KNOW EXACTLY WHERE YOU ARE, CAROL.
FRIDAY HAS PICKED UP A BARRAGE OF I.M.S. ENERGY AT MULTIPLE LOCATIONS ACROSS TOKYO.
THE RED SKULL IS MAKING A BIG MOVE, AND WE'VE GOTTA STOP IT.
ROGER THAT.
WAS HE TRACKING US THIS WHOLE TIME?
WHAT DO YOU THINK?
AFTER THIS LATEST CRISIS IS OVER, I'LL GET THINGS UNDER CONTROL.
GOOD. I'LL BE THERE TO BACK YOU UP.
PROXIMITY ALERT!
IS THAT...?
IT CAN'T BE...

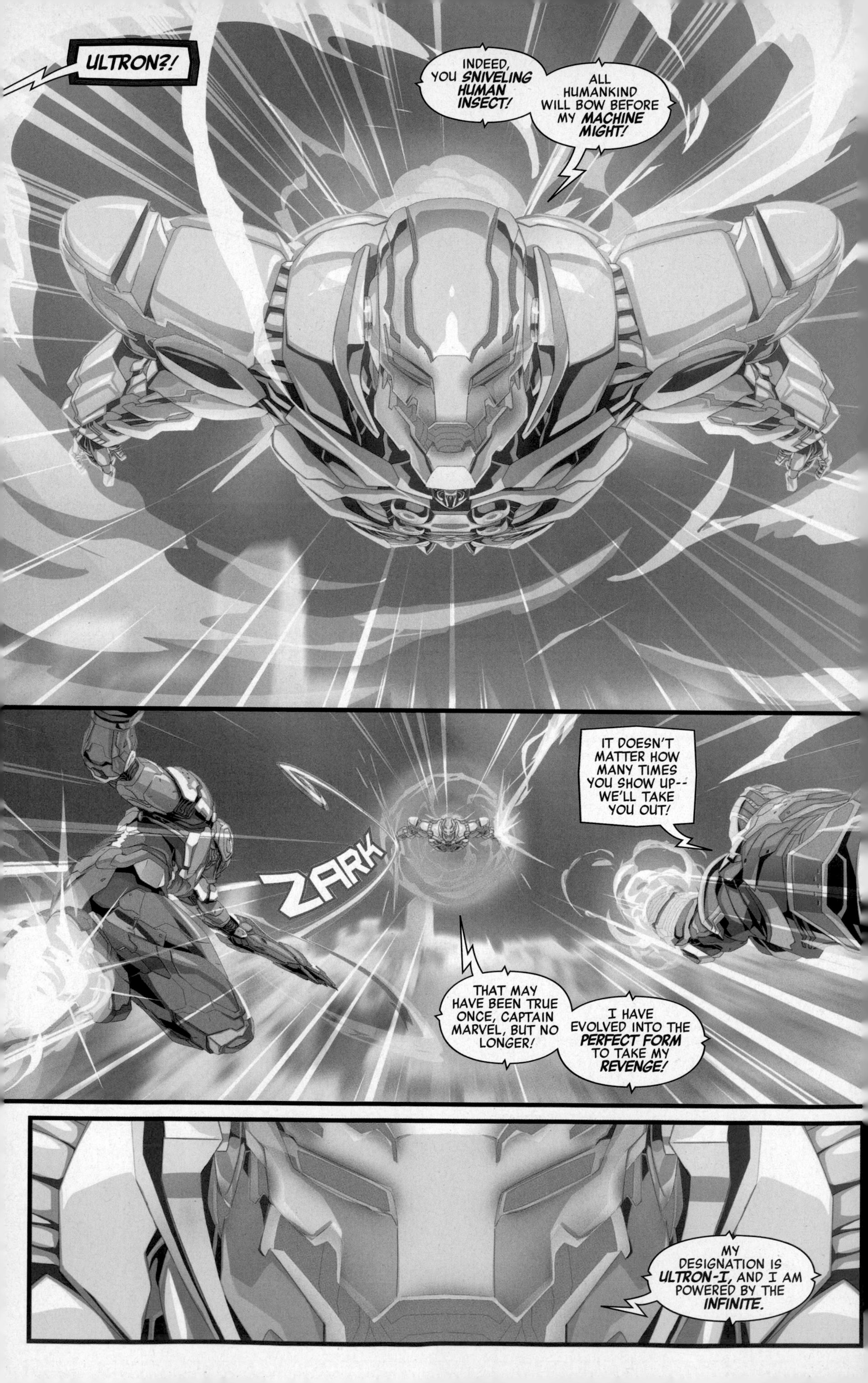
ULTRON?!
INDEED, YOU SNIVELING HUMAN INSECT!
ALL HUMANKIND WILL BOW BEFORE MY MACHINE MIGHT!
IT DOESN'T MATTER HOW MANY TIMES YOU SHOW UP-- WE'LL TAKE YOU OUT!
ZARK
THAT MAY HAVE BEEN TRUE ONCE, CAPTAIN MARVEL, BUT NO LONGER!
I HAVE EVOLVED INTO THE PERFECT FORM TO TAKE MY REVENGE!
MY DESIGNATION IS ULTRON-I, AND I AM POWERED BY THE INFINITE.

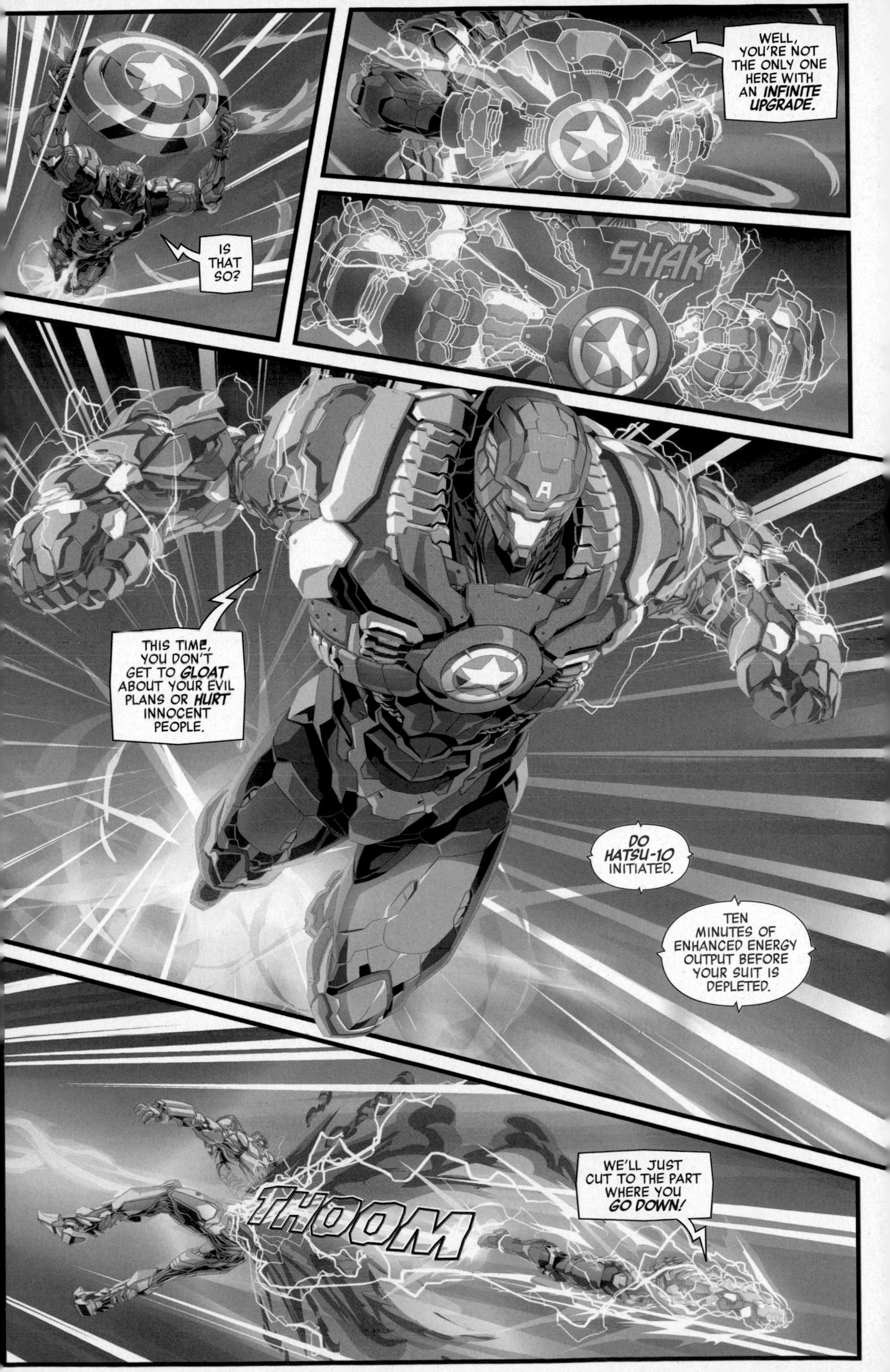
WELL, YOU'RE NOT THE ONLY ONE HERE WITH AN INFINITE UPGRADE.
IS THAT SO?
SHAK
THIS TIME, YOU DON'T GET TO GLOAT ABOUT YOUR EVIL PLANS OR HURT INNOCENT PEOPLE.
DO HATSU-10 INITIATED.
TEN MINUTES OF ENHANCED ENERGY OUTPUT BEFORE YOUR SUIT IS DEPLETED.
THOOM
WE'LL JUST CUT TO THE PART WHERE YOU GO DOWN!

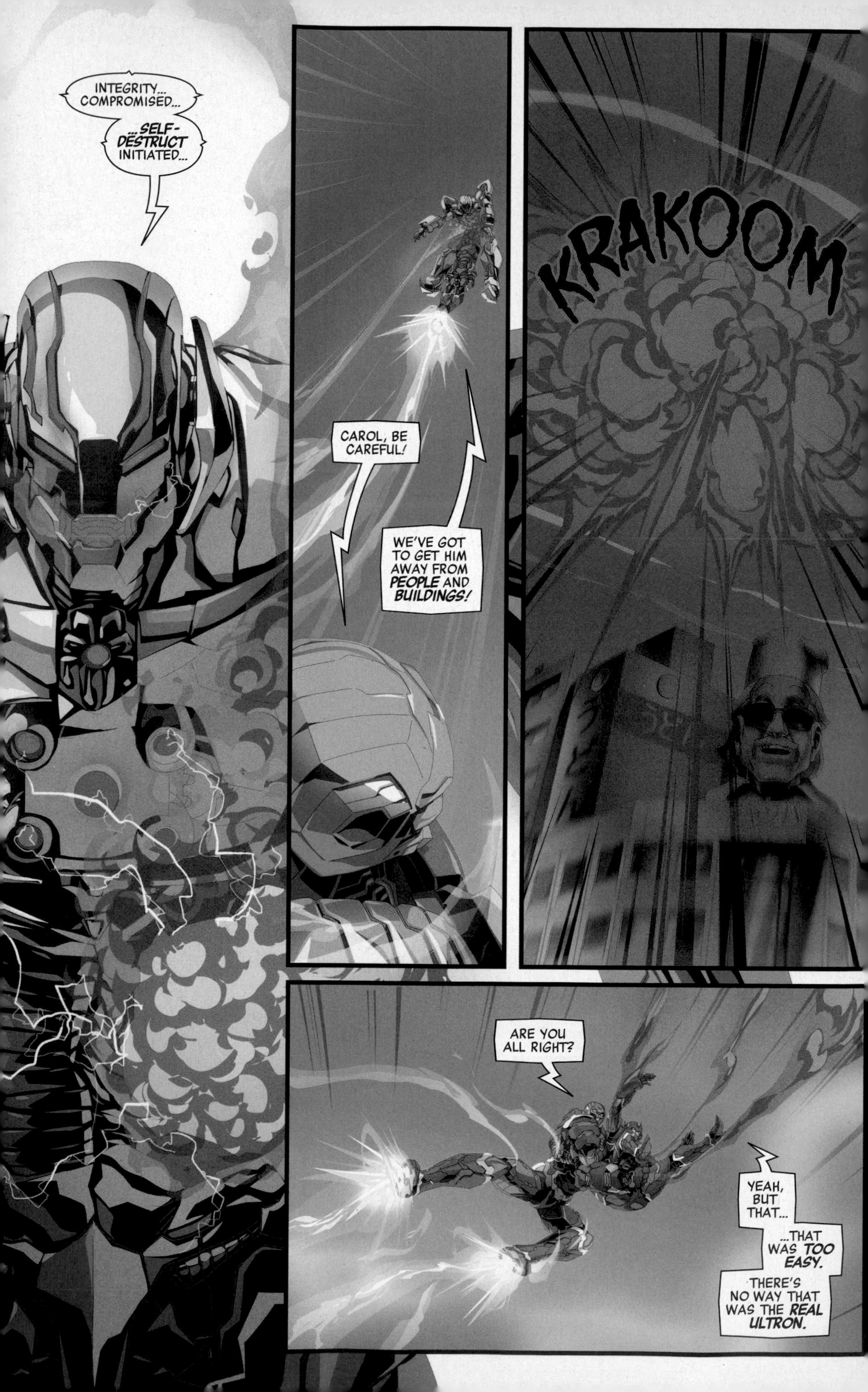
INTEGRITY... COMPROMISED...
...SELF-DESTRUCT INITIATED...
CAROL, BE CAREFUL!
WE'VE GOT TO GET HIM AWAY FROM PEOPLE AND BUILDINGS!
KRAKOOM
ARE YOU ALL RIGHT?
YEAH, BUT THAT...
...THAT WAS TOO EASY.
THERE'S NO WAY THAT WAS THE REAL ULTRON.

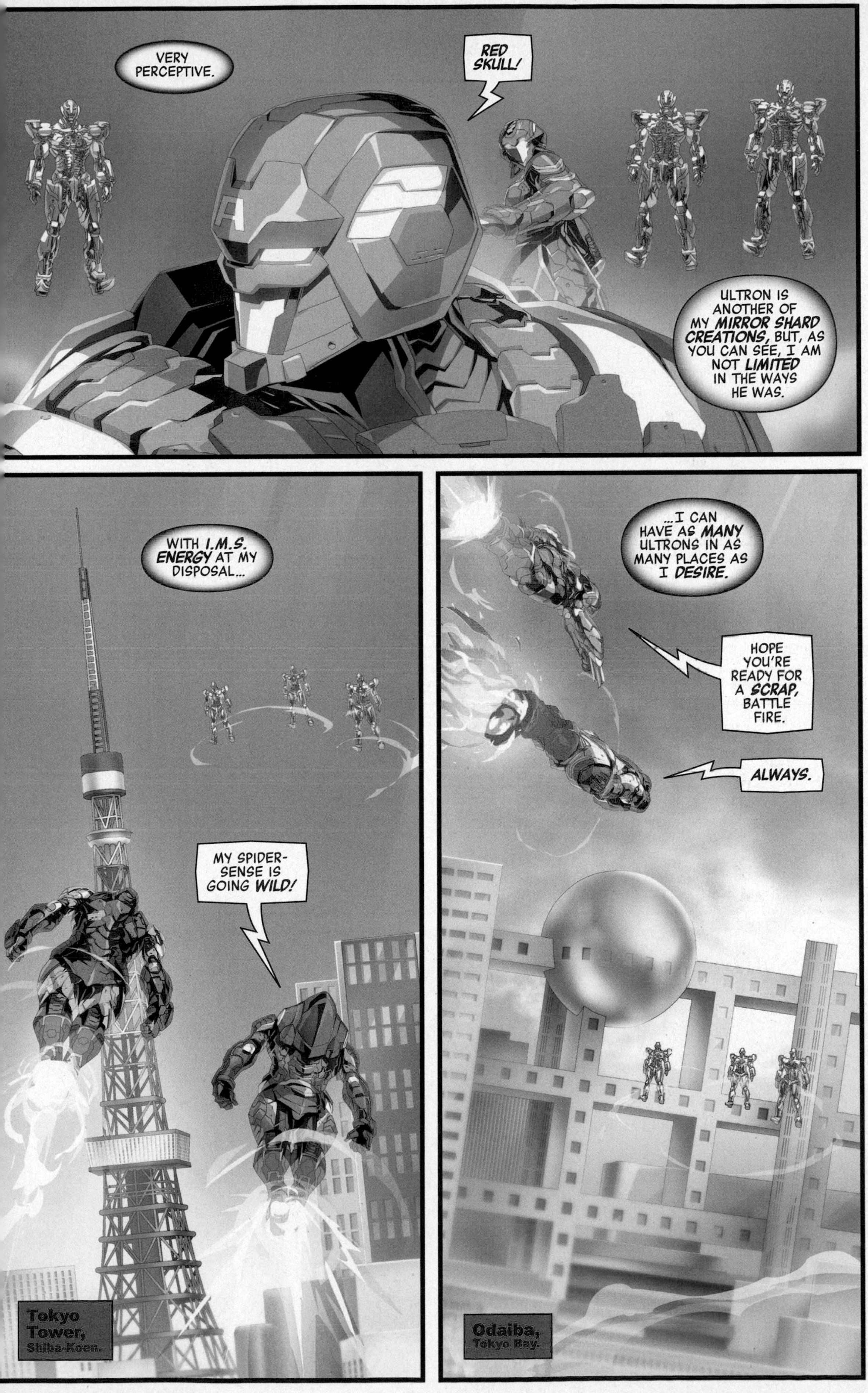
VERY PERCEPTIVE.
RED SKULL!
ULTRON IS ANOTHER OF MY MIRROR SHARD CREATIONS, BUT, AS YOU CAN SEE, I AM NOT LIMITED IN THE WAYS HE WAS.
WITH I.M.S. ENERGY AT MY DISPOSAL...
MY SPIDER-SENSE IS GOING WILD!
Tokyo Tower, Shiba-Koen.
...I CAN HAVE AS MANY ULTRONS IN AS MANY PLACES AS I DESIRE.
HOPE YOU'RE READY FOR A SCRAP, BATTLE FIRE.
ALWAYS.
Odaiba, Tokyo Bay.

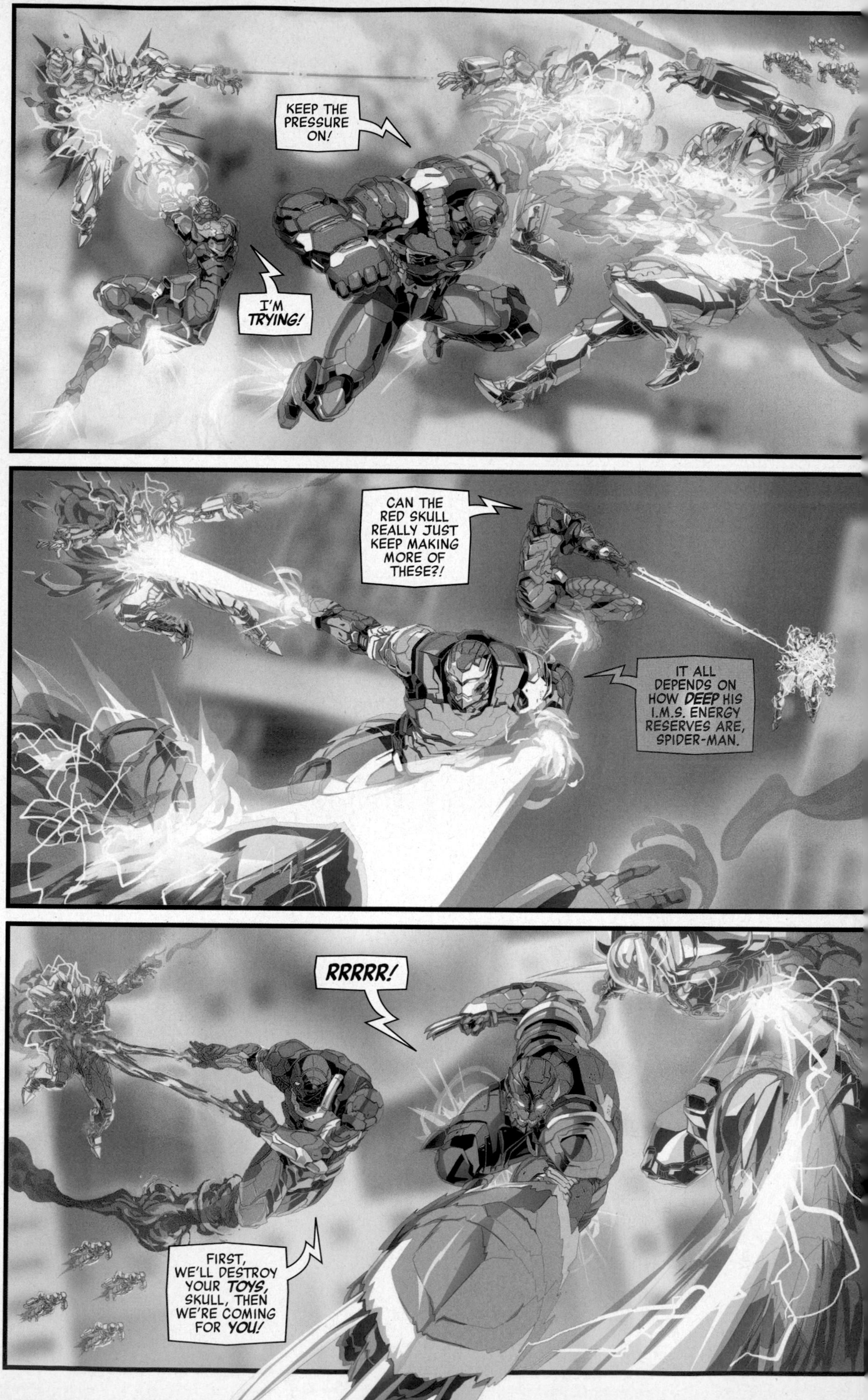
KEEP THE PRESSURE ON!
I'M TRYING!
CAN THE RED SKULL REALLY JUST KEEP MAKING MORE OF THESE?!
IT ALL DEPENDS ON HOW DEEP HIS I.M.S. ENERGY RESERVES ARE, SPIDER-MAN.
RRRRR!
FIRST, WE'LL DESTROY YOUR TOYS, SKULL, THEN WE'RE COMING FOR YOU!

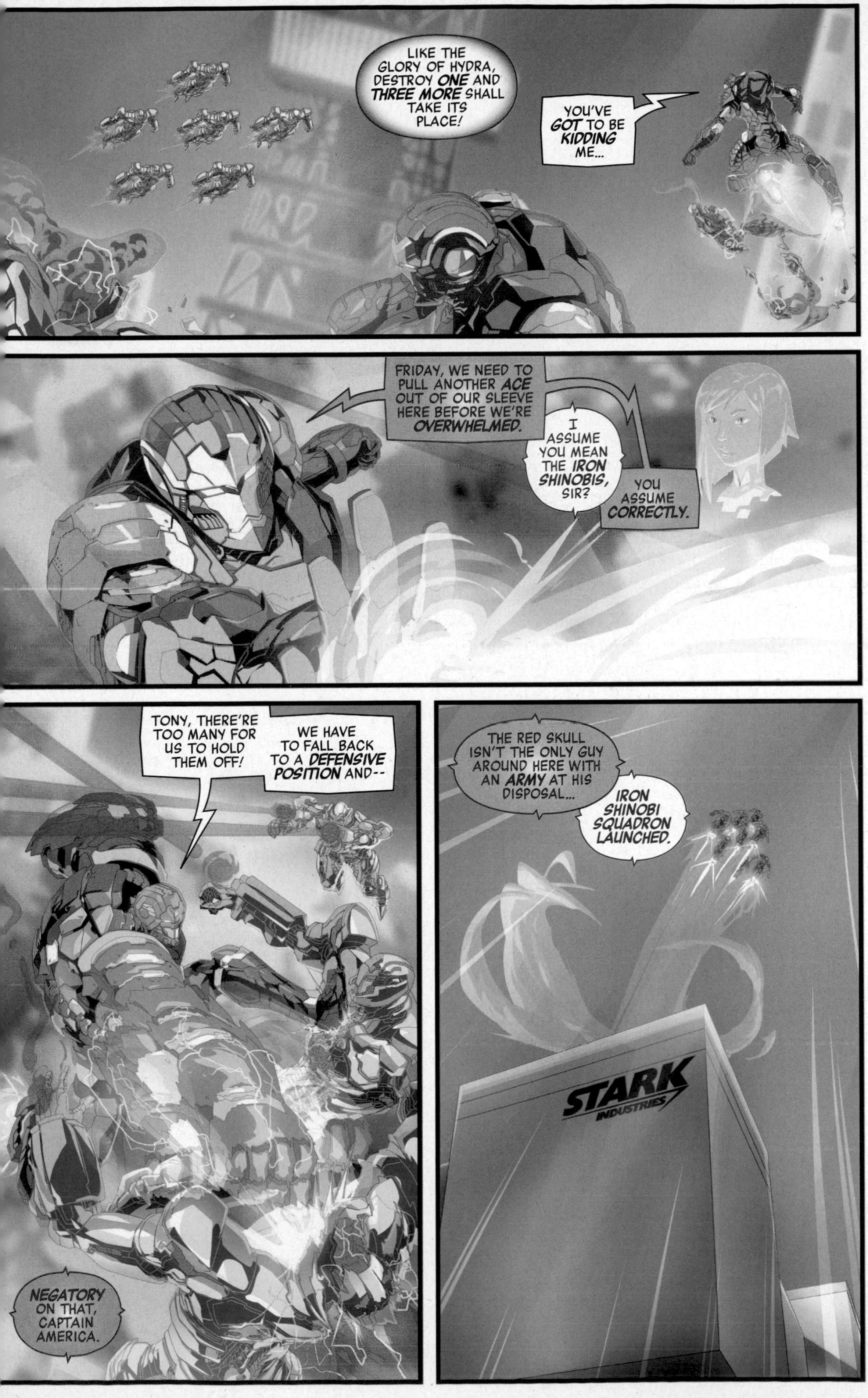

LIKE THE GLORY OF HYDRA, DESTROY ONE AND THREE MORE SHALL TAKE ITS PLACE!
YOU'VE GOT TO BE KIDDING ME...
FRIDAY, WE NEED TO PULL ANOTHER ACE OUT OF OUR SLEEVE HERE BEFORE WE'RE OVERWHELMED.
I ASSUME YOU MEAN THE IRON SHINOBIS, SIR?
YOU ASSUME CORRECTLY.
TONY, THERE'RE TOO MANY FOR US TO HOLD THEM OFF!
WE HAVE TO FALL BACK TO A DEFENSIVE POSITION AND--
NEGATORY ON THAT, CAPTAIN AMERICA.
THE RED SKULL ISN'T THE ONLY GUY AROUND HERE WITH AN ARMY AT HIS DISPOSAL...
IRON SHINOBI SQUADRON LAUNCHED.
STARK INDUSTRIES

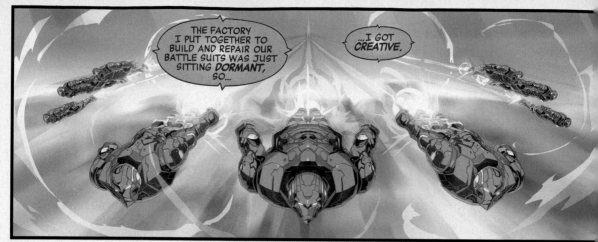

THE FACTORY I PUT TOGETHER TO BUILD AND REPAIR OUR BATTLE SUITS WAS JUST SITTING *DORMANT,* SO...

...I GOT *CREATIVE.*

WHAT THE HELL?!

THE *IRON SHINOBIS* ARE REMOTE-CONTROLLED IRON MEN PROGRAMMED TO *ASSIST* OR *ATTACK* AS NEEDED AGAINST LARGE FORCES.

THEY'RE NOT AS GOOD AS A *HUMAN* IN COMBAT OR AS *SUAVE* AS ME, BUT IN A PINCH, THEY'RE PRETTY SOLID *BACKUP.*

REALLY? MORE *SECRETS,* TONY?

NOT AT ALL, CAROL! IF YOU'D WANDERED THROUGH MY FACTORY, YOU WOULD HAVE SEEN THEM IN *PRODUCTION,* BUT I GUESS YOU WERE TOO *BUSY* VISITING TOURIST SITES HERE IN *JAPAN.*

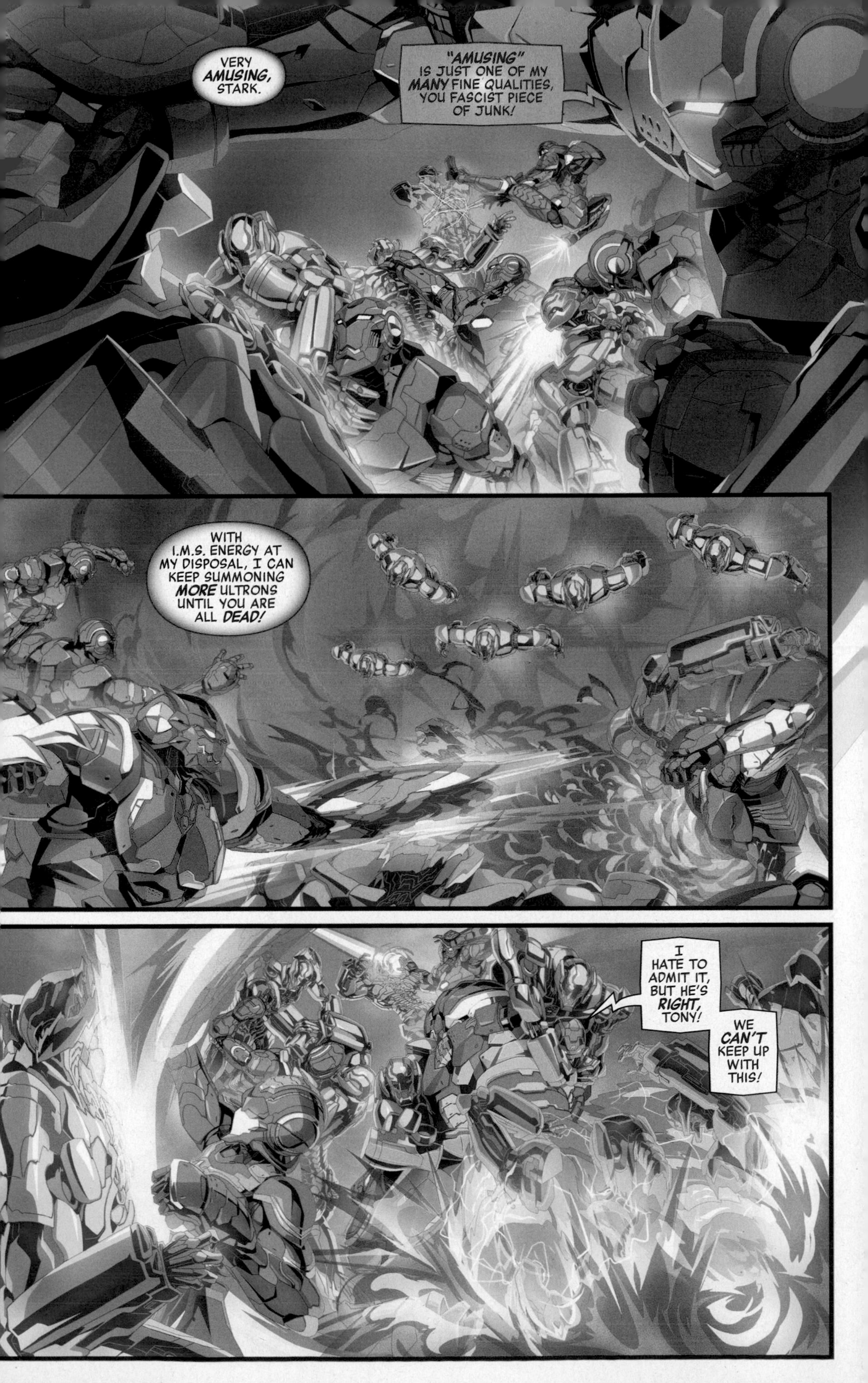
VERY AMUSING, STARK.
"AMUSING" IS JUST ONE OF MY MANY FINE QUALITIES, YOU FASCIST PIECE OF JUNK!
WITH I.M.S. ENERGY AT MY DISPOSAL, I CAN KEEP SUMMONING MORE ULTRONS UNTIL YOU ARE ALL DEAD!
I HATE TO ADMIT IT, BUT HE'S RIGHT, TONY!
WE CAN'T KEEP UP WITH THIS!

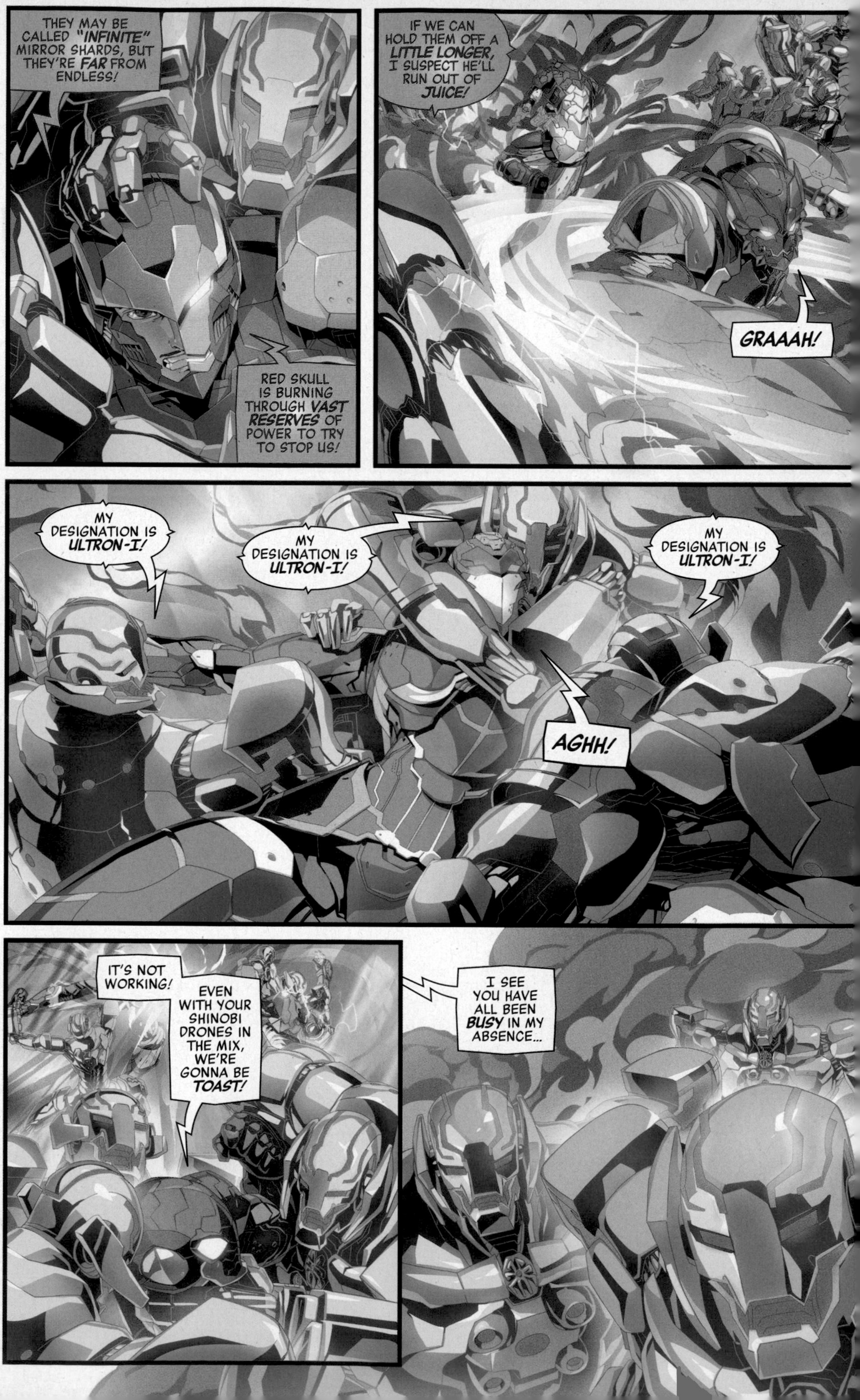
THEY MAY BE CALLED "INFINITE" MIRROR SHARDS, BUT THEY'RE FAR FROM ENDLESS!
RED SKULL IS BURNING THROUGH VAST RESERVES OF POWER TO TRY TO STOP US!
IF WE CAN HOLD THEM OFF A LITTLE LONGER, I SUSPECT HE'LL RUN OUT OF JUICE!
GRAAAH!
MY DESIGNATION IS ULTRON-I!
MY DESIGNATION IS ULTRON-I!
MY DESIGNATION IS ULTRON-I!
AGHH!
IT'S NOT WORKING!
EVEN WITH YOUR SHINOBI DRONES IN THE MIX, WE'RE GONNA BE TOAST!
I SEE YOU HAVE ALL BEEN BUSY IN MY ABSENCE...

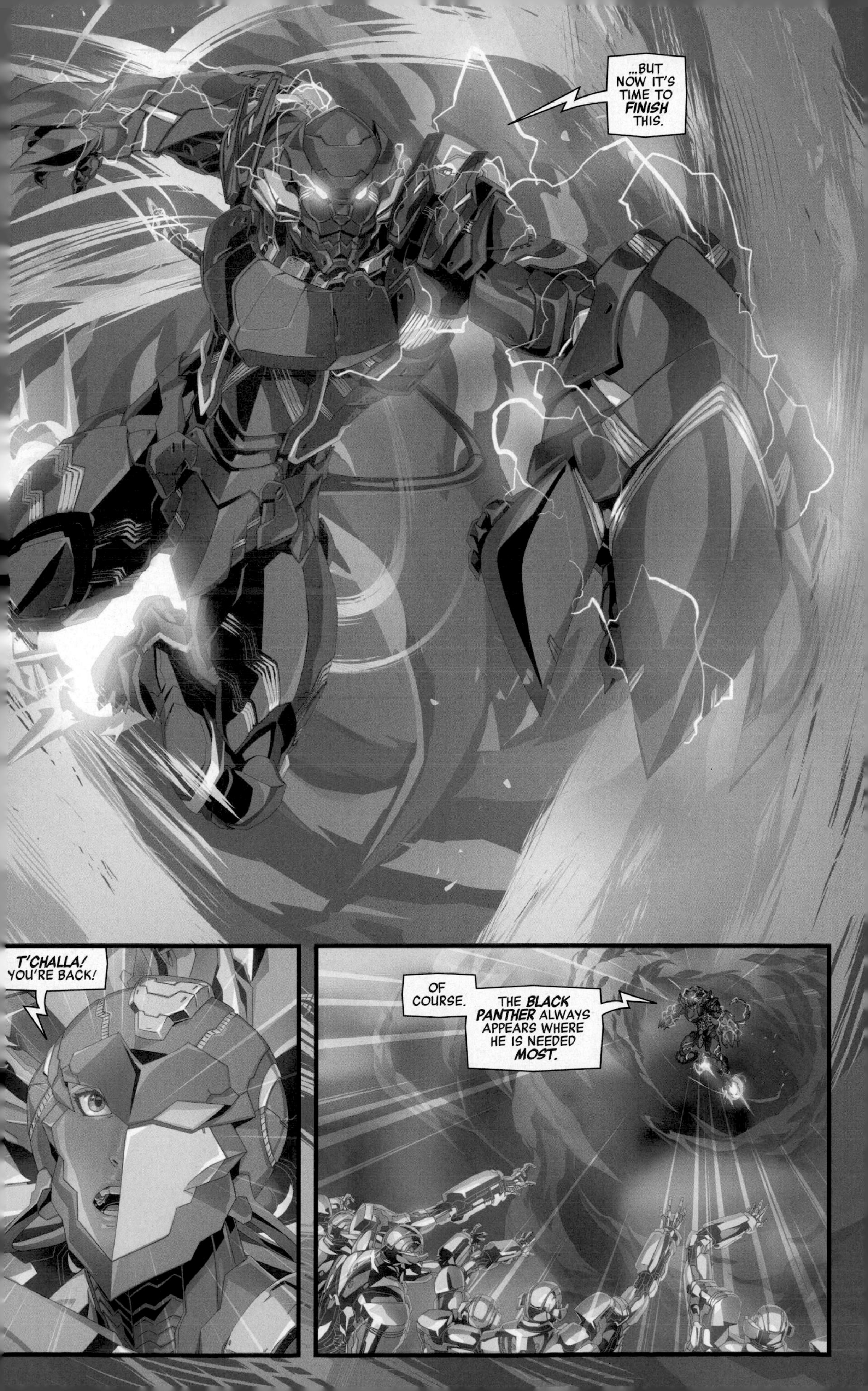
...BUT NOW IT'S TIME TO FINISH THIS.
T'CHALLA! YOU'RE BACK!
OF COURSE.
THE BLACK PANTHER ALWAYS APPEARS WHERE HE IS NEEDED MOST.

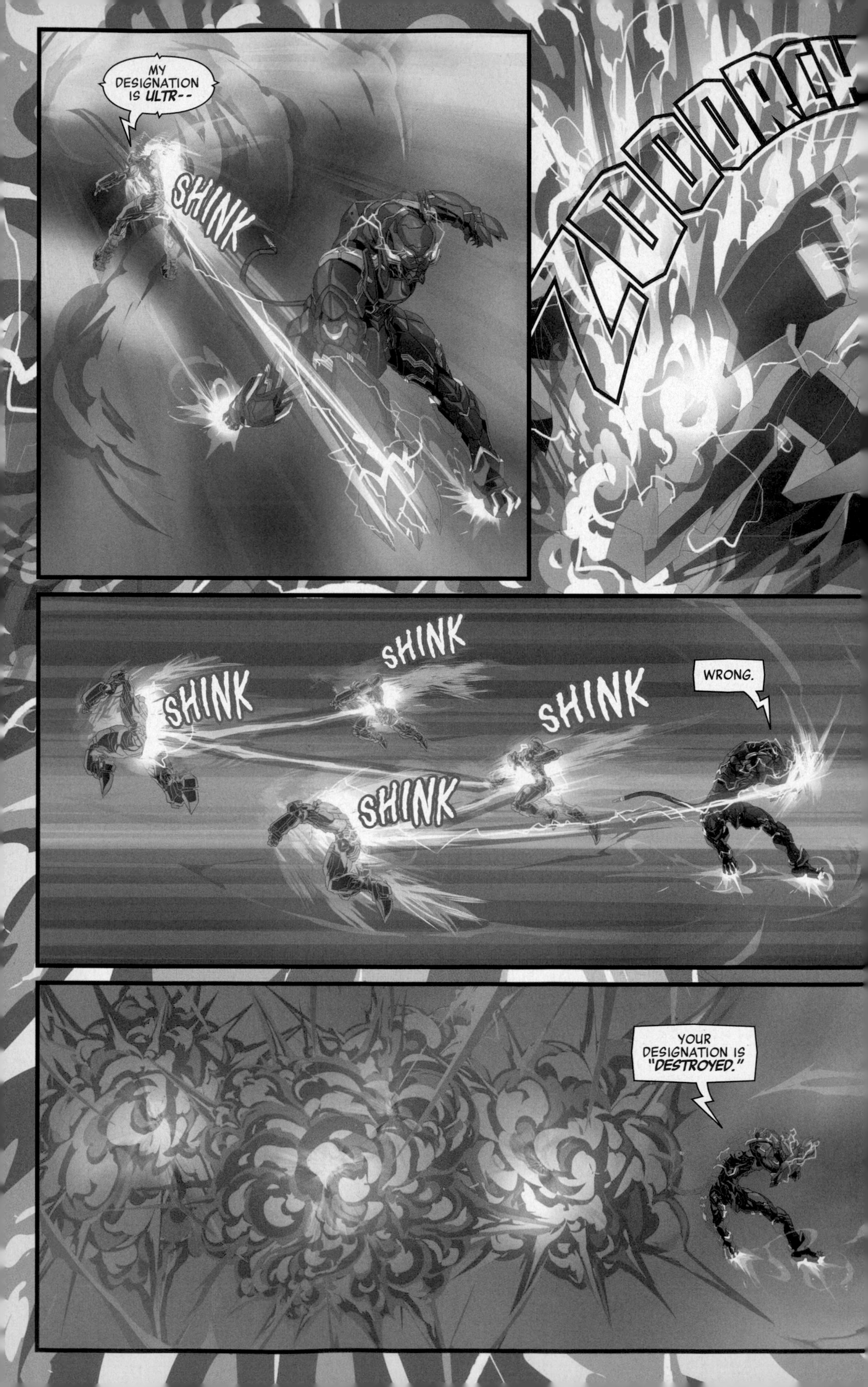
MY DESIGNATION IS ULTR--
SHINK
SHINK
SHINK
SHINK
SHINK
WRONG.
YOUR DESIGNATION IS "DESTROYED."

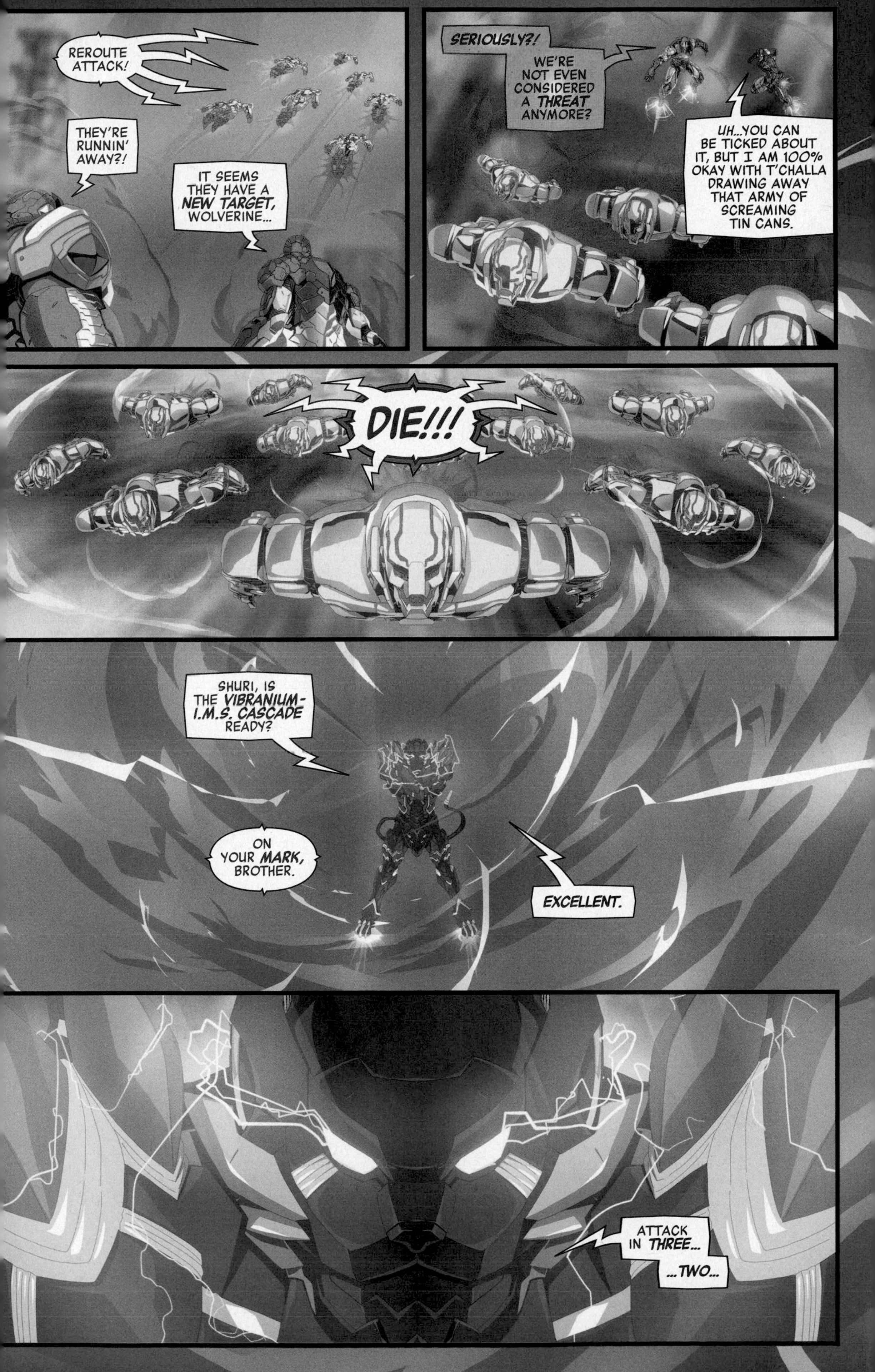
REROUTE ATTACK!
THEY'RE RUNNIN' AWAY?!
IT SEEMS THEY HAVE A NEW TARGET, WOLVERINE...
SERIOUSLY?!
WE'RE NOT EVEN CONSIDERED A THREAT ANYMORE?
UH...YOU CAN BE TICKED ABOUT IT, BUT I AM 100% OKAY WITH T'CHALLA DRAWING AWAY THAT ARMY OF SCREAMING TIN CANS.
DIE!!!
SHURI, IS THE VIBRANIUM-I.M.S. CASCADE READY?
ON YOUR MARK, BROTHER.
EXCELLENT.
ATTACK IN THREE...
...TWO...

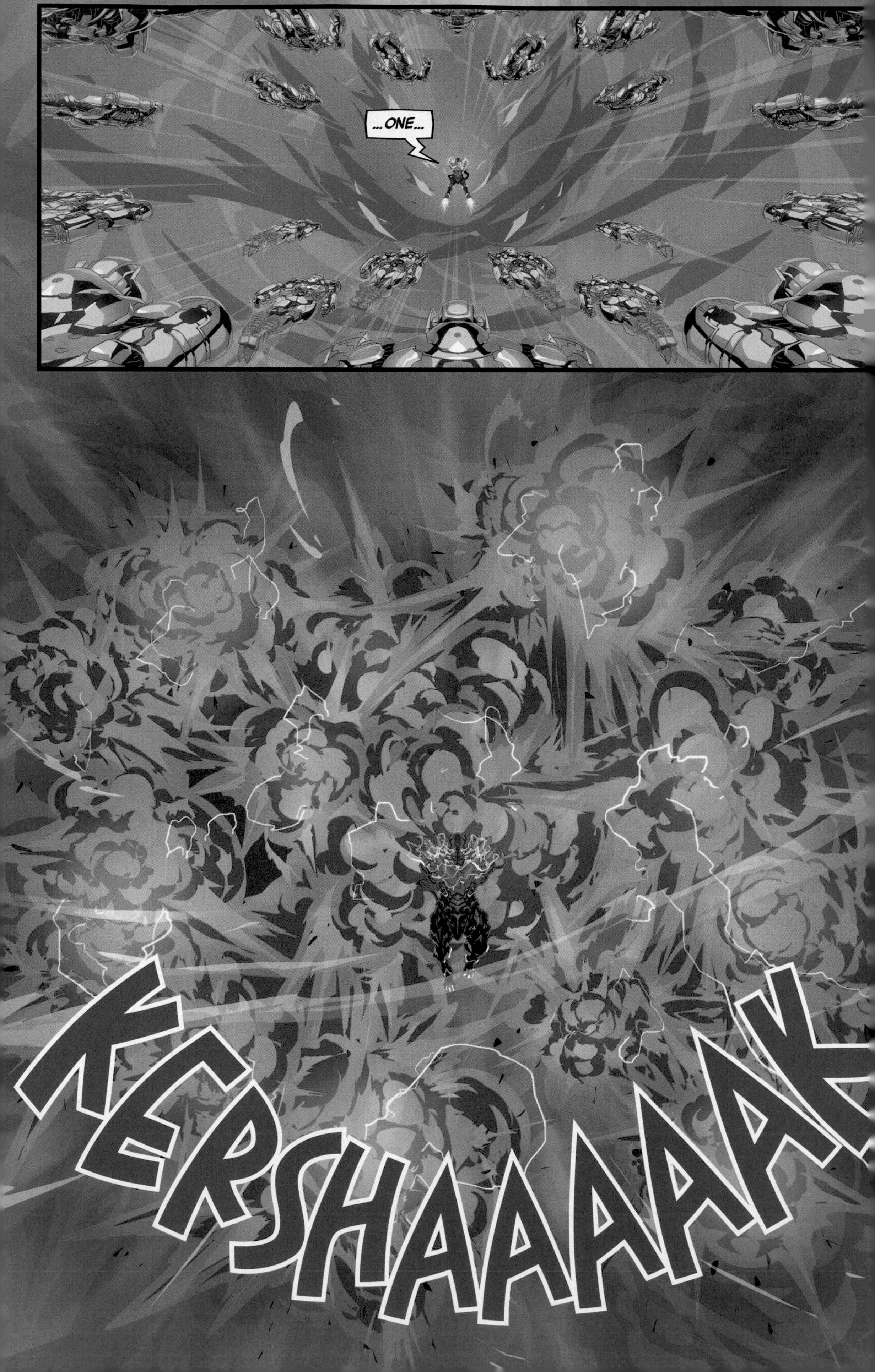
...ONE...
KERSHAAAAK

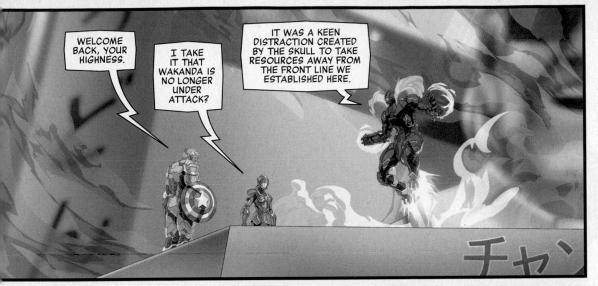

WELCOME BACK, YOUR HIGHNESS.

I TAKE IT THAT WAKANDA IS NO LONGER UNDER ATTACK?

IT WAS A KEEN DISTRACTION CREATED BY THE SKULL TO TAKE RESOURCES AWAY FROM THE FRONT LINE WE ESTABLISHED HERE.

チャン

BUT IT ALSO GAVE ME TIME TO *UPGRADE* STARK'S PANTHER ARMOR TO INCORPORATE A FULL ARRAY OF WAKANDAN *IMPROVEMENTS*.

I APPRECIATE THE STYLE, BUT THAT'S *PATENTED* STARK TECHNOLOGY YOU'RE MESSING WITH.

I'LL BE SURE TO ASK FOR *PERMISSION* ONCE WE'RE NO LONGER FIGHTING A WAR.

OBVIOUSLY.

HERE'S THE *IMPORTANT* PART--SHURI HAS DISCOVERED THE *SECRET* BEHIND RED SKULL'S *INFINITE MIRROR SHARD* TECHNOLOGY.

WITH IT, WE CAN FINALLY TURN THE TIDE AND BRING THIS *EVIL* TO AN END.

ARE YOU SURE?

ABSOLUTELY...

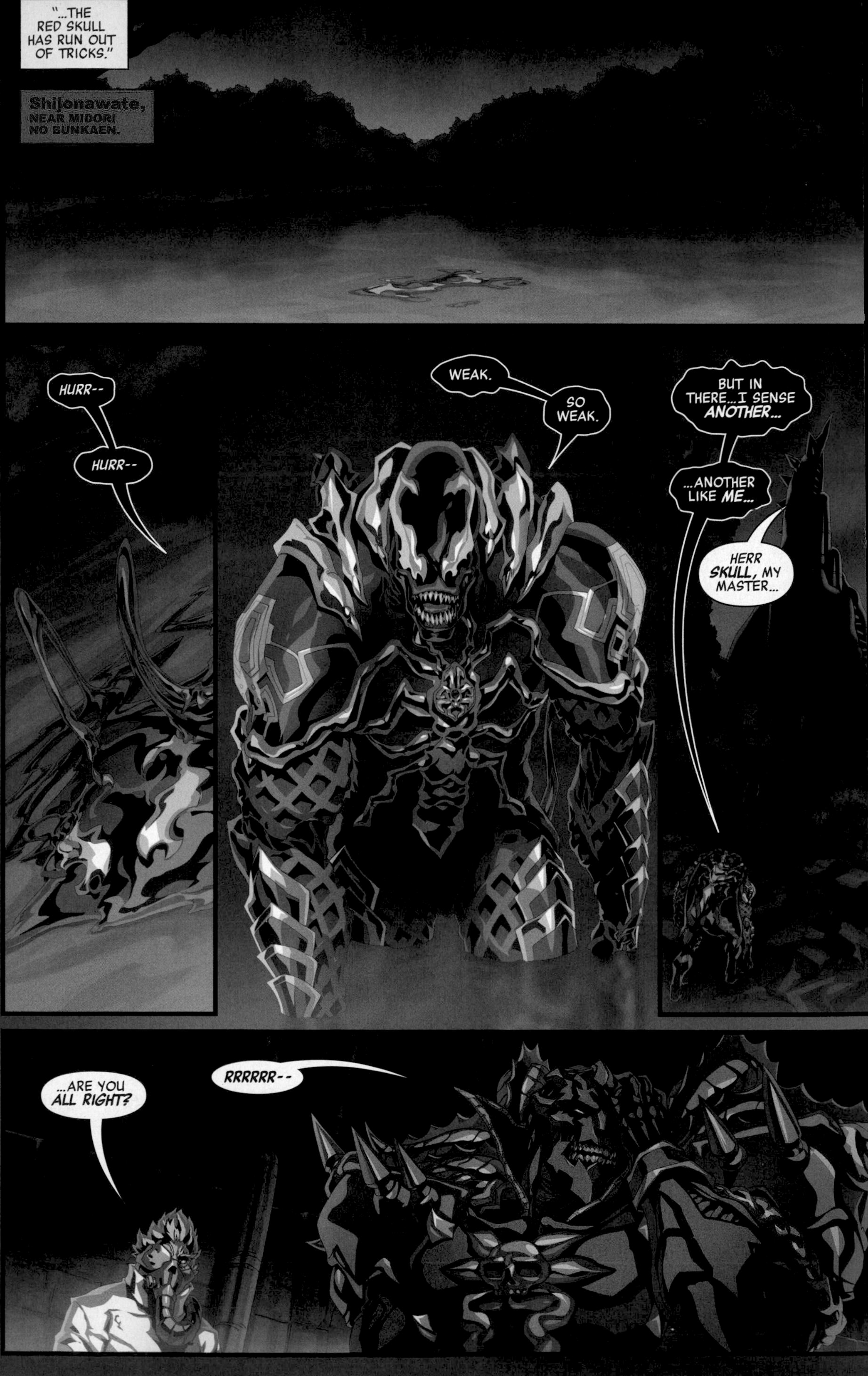
"...THE RED SKULL HAS RUN OUT OF TRICKS."
Shijonawate, NEAR MIDORI NO BUNKAEN.
HURR--
HURR--
WEAK.
SO WEAK.
BUT IN THERE...I SENSE ANOTHER...
...ANOTHER LIKE ME...
HERR SKULL, MY MASTER...
...ARE YOU ALL RIGHT?
RRRRRR--

NO!

I AM NOT "ALL RIGHT," YOU FOOL!

UHH!

ALL THAT ENERGY... WASTED!

WHATEVER THE PANTHER DID TO MY ULTRON ARMY, IT VAPORIZED THE I.M.S. I INVESTED IN IT!

THE ENERGY IS GONE-- TORN AWAY FROM ME!

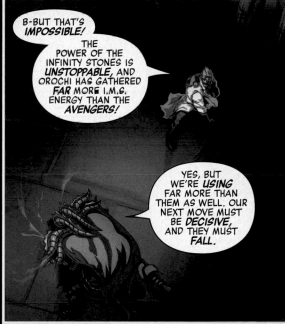

B-BUT THAT'S IMPOSSIBLE!

THE POWER OF THE INFINITY STONES IS UNSTOPPABLE, AND OROCHI HAS GATHERED FAR MORE I.M.S. ENERGY THAN THE AVENGERS!

YES, BUT WE'RE USING FAR MORE THAN THEM AS WELL. OUR NEXT MOVE MUST BE DECISIVE, AND THEY MUST FALL.

IS THE ADVANCED SYMBIOTE PROJECT COMPLETE?

THE CREATURE GROWS AT AN INCREDIBLE RATE, THAT IS CERTAIN, BUT I'M NOT SURE IF IT'S FIELD READY...

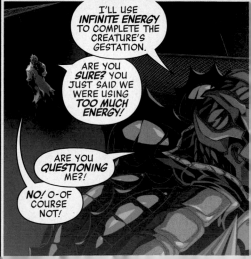

I'LL USE INFINITE ENERGY TO COMPLETE THE CREATURE'S GESTATION.

ARE YOU SURE? YOU JUST SAID WE WERE USING TOO MUCH ENERGY!

ARE YOU QUESTIONING ME?!

NO! O-OF COURSE NOT!

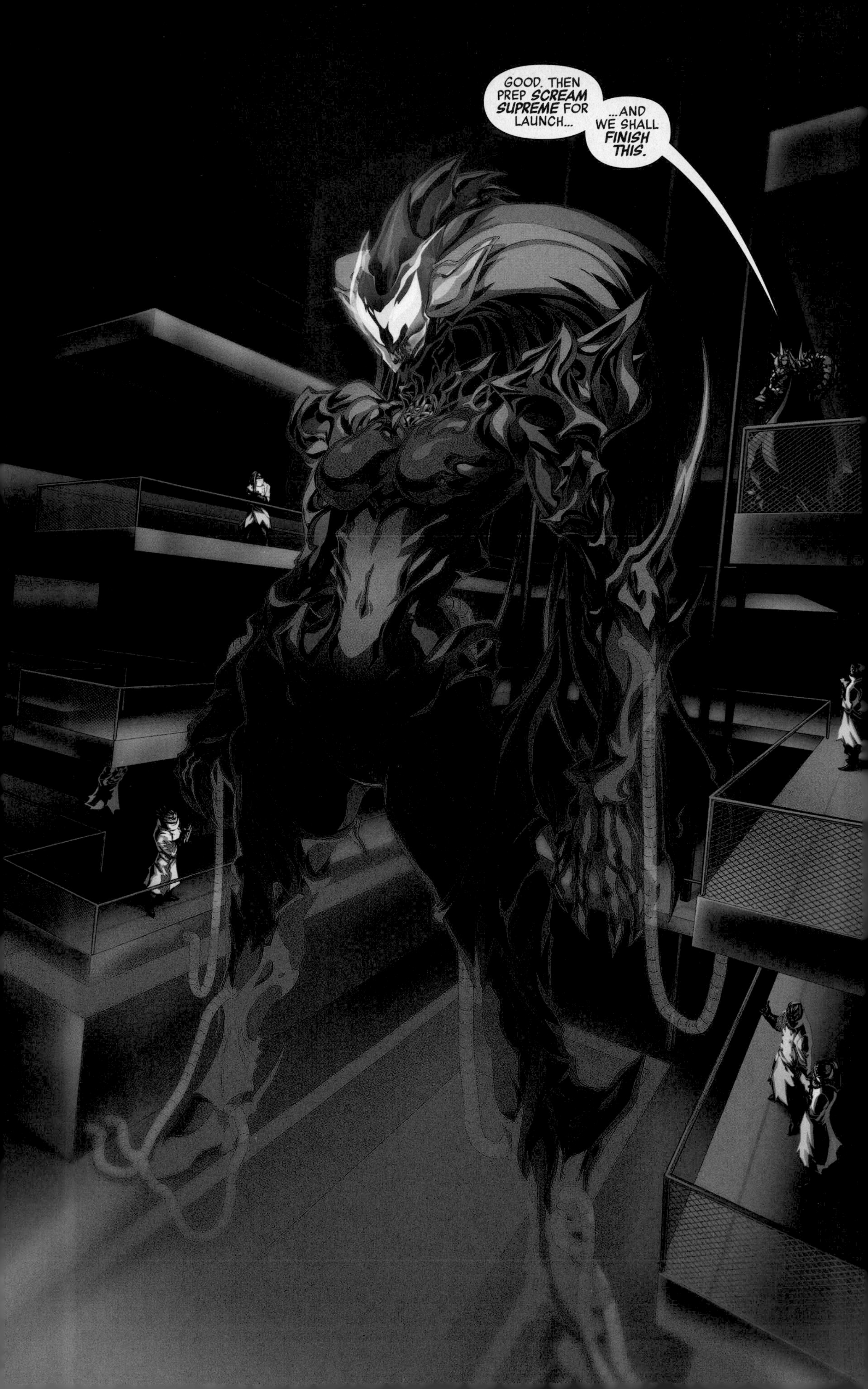
GOOD. THEN PREP SCREAM SUPREME FOR LAUNCH...
...AND WE SHALL FINISH THIS.

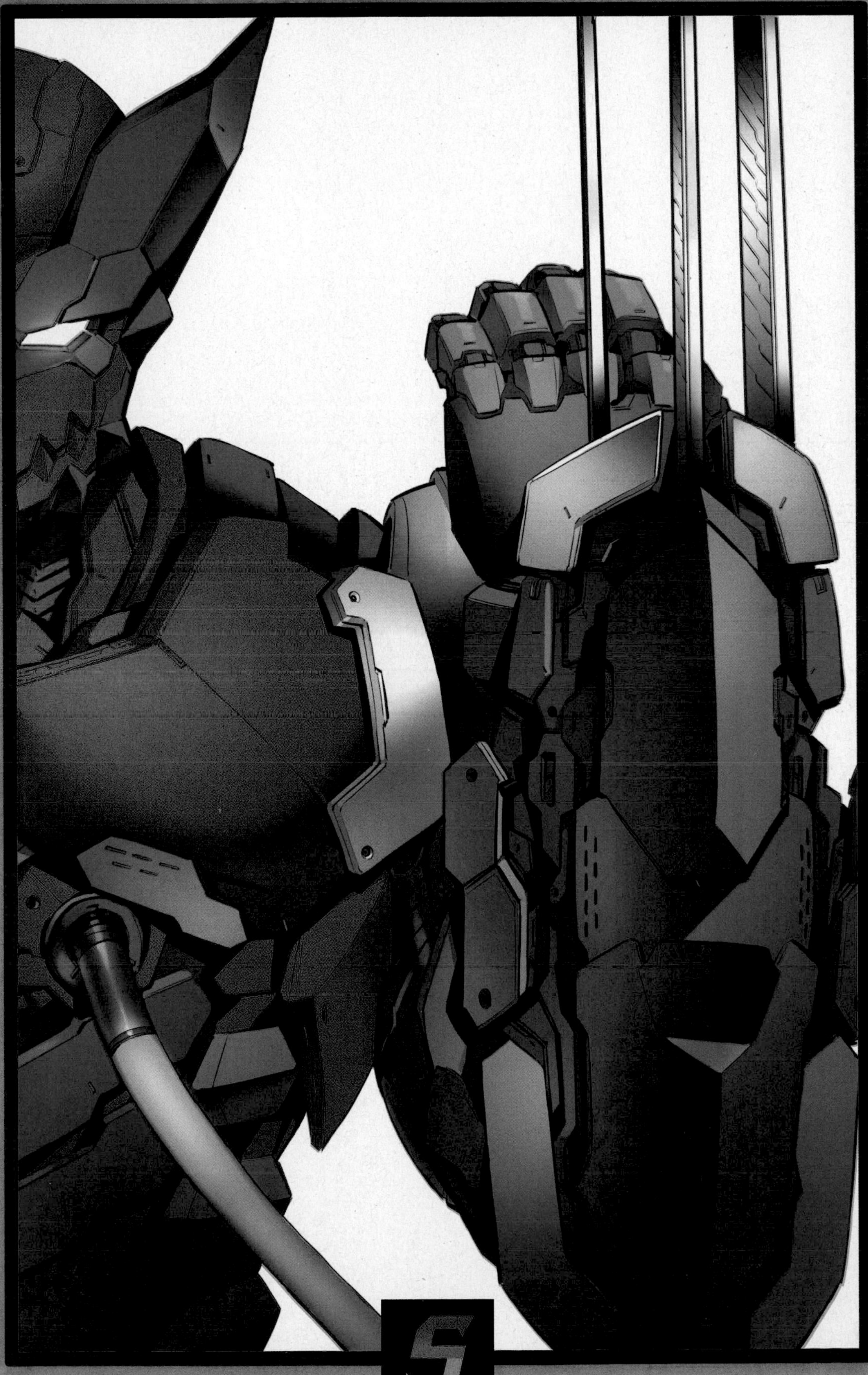

5

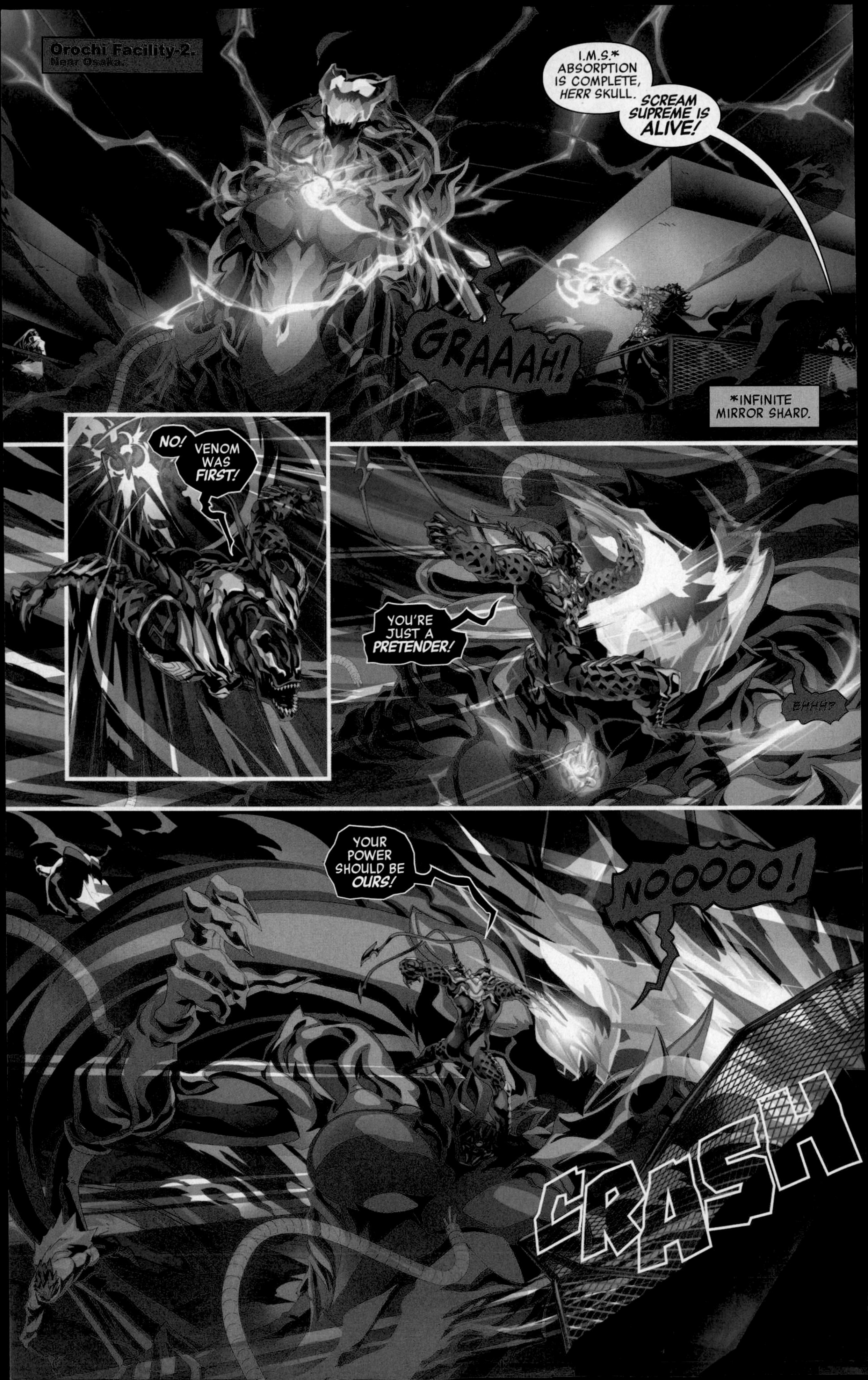

Orochi Facility-2.
Near Osaka.
I.M.S.* ABSORPTION IS COMPLETE, HERR SKULL.
SCREAM SUPREME IS ALIVE!
GRAAAH!
*INFINITE MIRROR SHARD.
NO!
VENOM WAS FIRST!
YOU'RE JUST A PRETENDER!
EHHH?
YOUR POWER SHOULD BE OURS!
NOOOOO!
CRASH

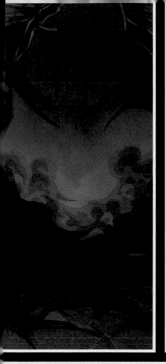

WHAT. WAS. THAT?!

KROOM

YOU TOLD ME VENOM HAD BEEN *UTTERLY DESTROYED* BY IRON MAN!*

I--I THOUGHT HE *WAS!*

TH-THERE'S NO WAY I COULD HAVE ANTICIPATED SUCH *REGROWTH* FROM *ATOMIZED PARTICLES!*

*BACK IN *AVENGERS TECH-ON* #2. --TOM

NOW MY NEW CREATION IS RUNNING *AMUCK.* THIS LOCATION AND OUR PLAN WILL BE *COMPROMISED!*

YOU WERE *SLOPPY,* PROFESSOR KURICHA...

PLEASE, HERR SKULL! I WILL *PROVE* MY *WORTH!*

BWIP BWIP BWIP

HMM? WHAT'S THIS?

A NEW SOURCE OF *I.M.S.* ENERGY?

YES. THIS COULD CHANGE... ...EVERYTHING.

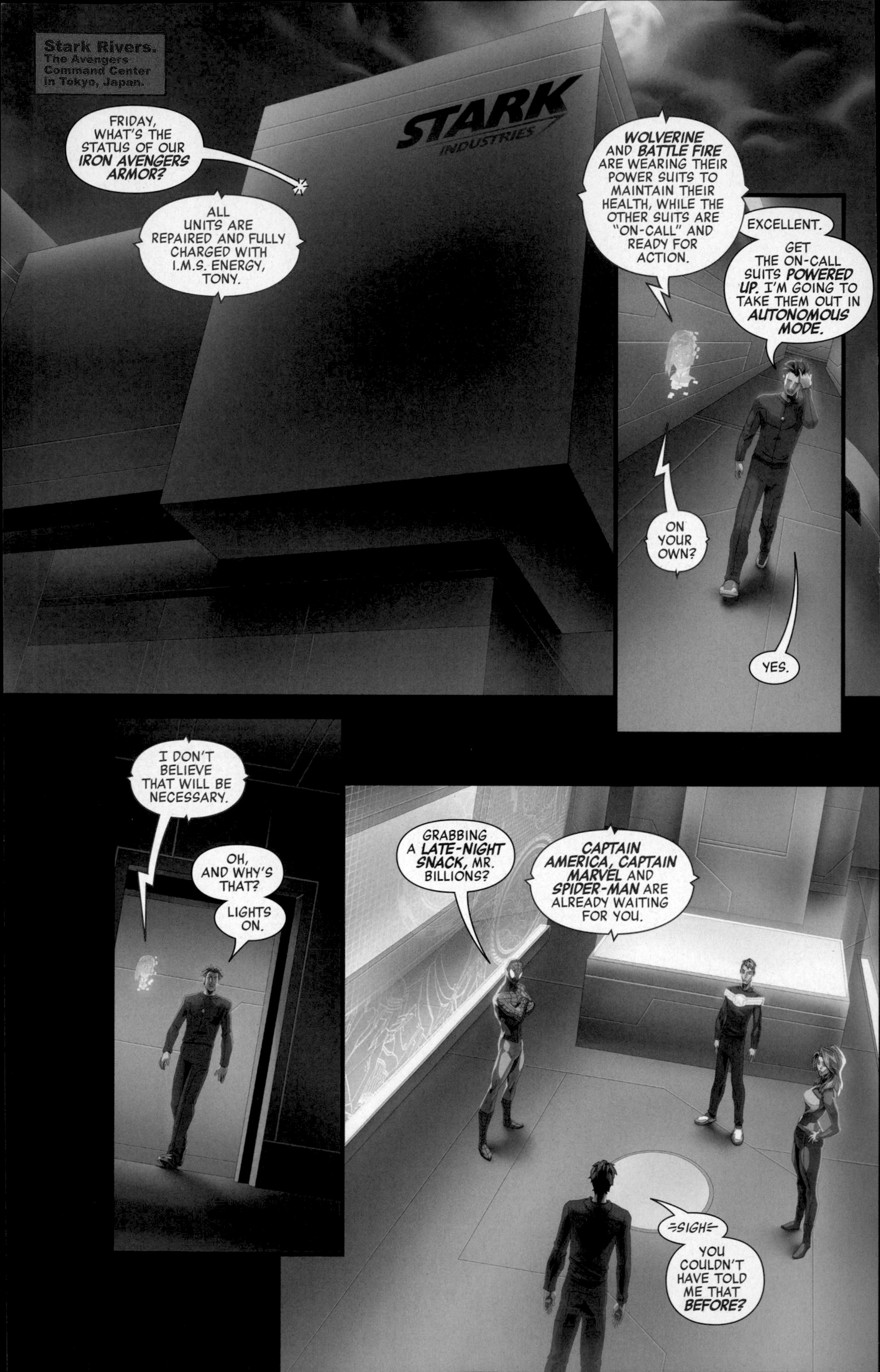
Stark Rivers. The Avengers Command Center in Tokyo, Japan.
STARK INDUSTRIES
FRIDAY, WHAT'S THE STATUS OF OUR IRON AVENGERS ARMOR?
ALL UNITS ARE REPAIRED AND FULLY CHARGED WITH I.M.S. ENERGY, TONY.
WOLVERINE AND BATTLE FIRE ARE WEARING THEIR POWER SUITS TO MAINTAIN THEIR HEALTH, WHILE THE OTHER SUITS ARE "ON-CALL" AND READY FOR ACTION.
EXCELLENT.
GET THE ON-CALL SUITS POWERED UP. I'M GOING TO TAKE THEM OUT IN AUTONOMOUS MODE.
ON YOUR OWN?
YES.
I DON'T BELIEVE THAT WILL BE NECESSARY.
OH, AND WHY'S THAT?
LIGHTS ON.
GRABBING A LATE-NIGHT SNACK, MR. BILLIONS?
CAPTAIN AMERICA, CAPTAIN MARVEL AND SPIDER-MAN ARE ALREADY WAITING FOR YOU.
=SIGH=
YOU COULDN'T HAVE TOLD ME THAT BEFORE?

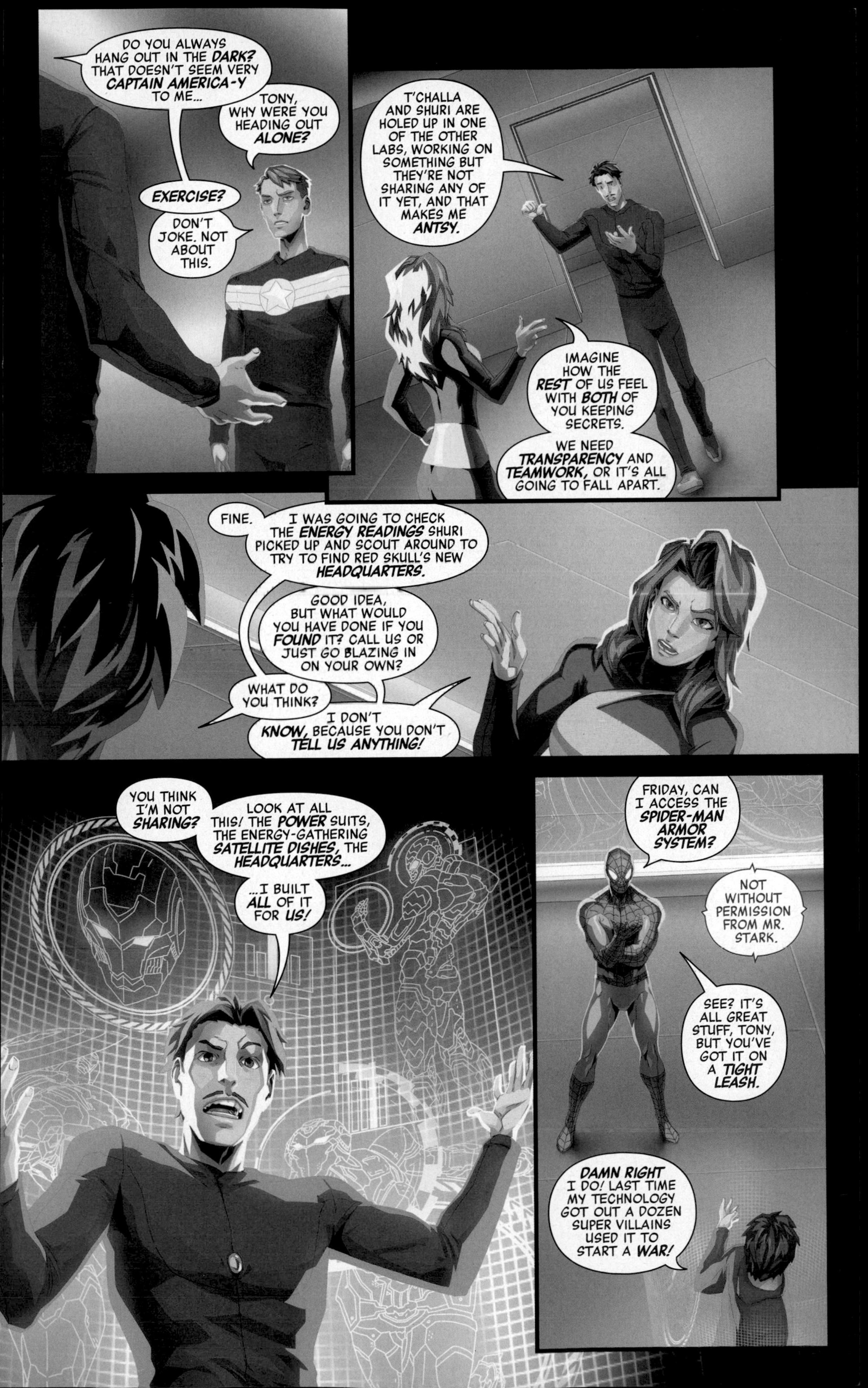

DO YOU ALWAYS HANG OUT IN THE DARK? THAT DOESN'T SEEM VERY CAPTAIN AMERICA-Y TO ME...
TONY, WHY WERE YOU HEADING OUT ALONE?
EXERCISE?
DON'T JOKE. NOT ABOUT THIS.
T'CHALLA AND SHURI ARE HOLED UP IN ONE OF THE OTHER LABS, WORKING ON SOMETHING BUT THEY'RE NOT SHARING ANY OF IT YET, AND THAT MAKES ME ANTSY.
IMAGINE HOW THE REST OF US FEEL WITH BOTH OF YOU KEEPING SECRETS.
WE NEED TRANSPARENCY AND TEAMWORK, OR IT'S ALL GOING TO FALL APART.
FINE.
I WAS GOING TO CHECK THE ENERGY READINGS SHURI PICKED UP AND SCOUT AROUND TO TRY TO FIND RED SKULL'S NEW HEADQUARTERS.
GOOD IDEA, BUT WHAT WOULD YOU HAVE DONE IF YOU FOUND IT? CALL US OR JUST GO BLAZING IN ON YOUR OWN?
WHAT DO YOU THINK?
I DON'T KNOW, BECAUSE YOU DON'T TELL US ANYTHING!
YOU THINK I'M NOT SHARING?
LOOK AT ALL THIS! THE POWER SUITS, THE ENERGY-GATHERING SATELLITE DISHES, THE HEADQUARTERS...
...I BUILT ALL OF IT FOR US!
FRIDAY, CAN I ACCESS THE SPIDER-MAN ARMOR SYSTEM?
NOT WITHOUT PERMISSION FROM MR. STARK.
SEE? IT'S ALL GREAT STUFF, TONY, BUT YOU'VE GOT IT ON A TIGHT LEASH.
DAMN RIGHT I DO! LAST TIME MY TECHNOLOGY GOT OUT A DOZEN SUPER VILLAINS USED IT TO START A WAR!

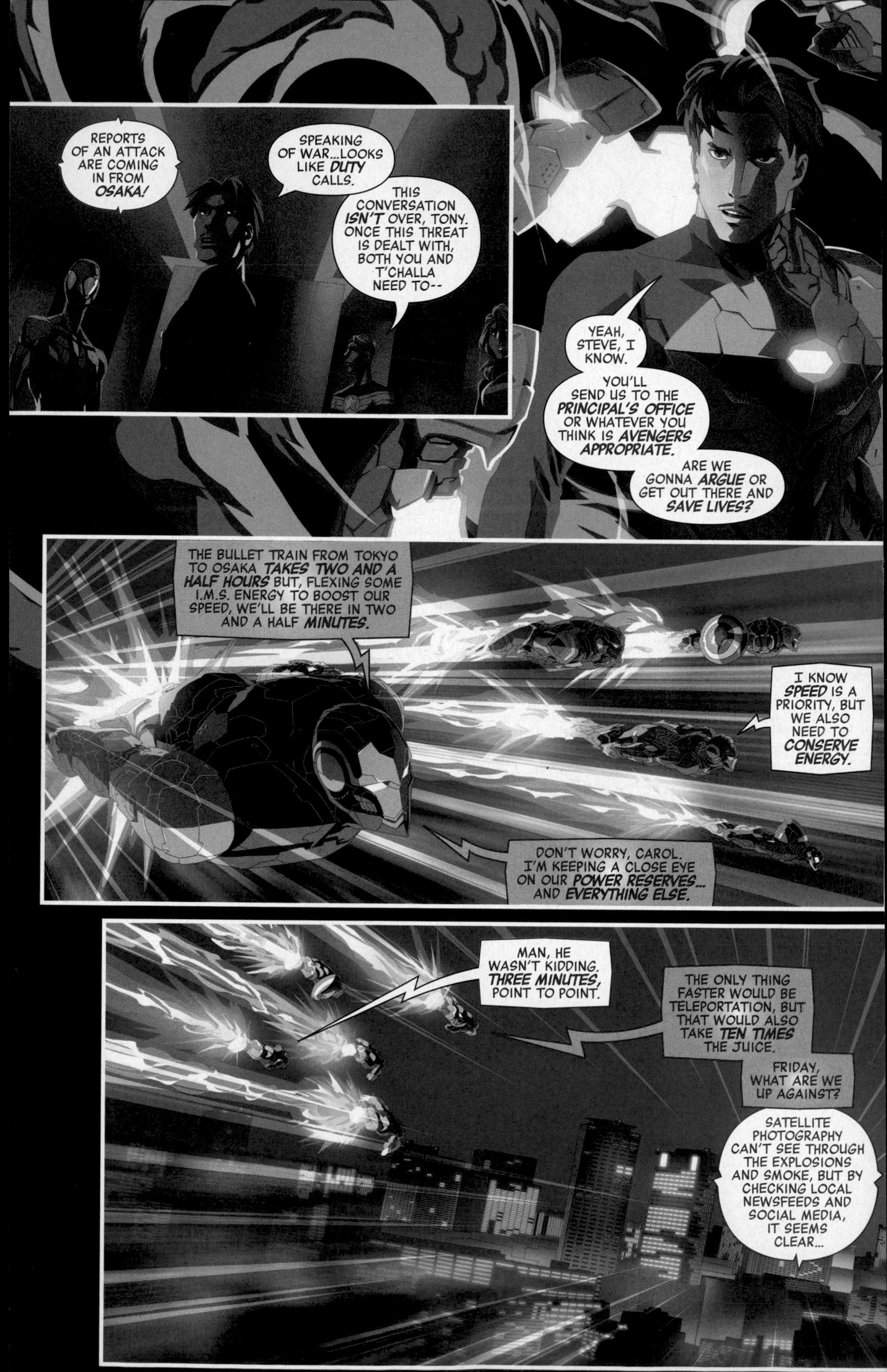

REPORTS OF AN ATTACK ARE COMING IN FROM OSAKA!
SPEAKING OF WAR...LOOKS LIKE DUTY CALLS.
THIS CONVERSATION ISN'T OVER, TONY. ONCE THIS THREAT IS DEALT WITH, BOTH YOU AND T'CHALLA NEED TO--
YEAH, STEVE, I KNOW.
YOU'LL SEND US TO THE PRINCIPAL'S OFFICE OR WHATEVER YOU THINK IS AVENGERS APPROPRIATE.
ARE WE GONNA ARGUE OR GET OUT THERE AND SAVE LIVES?
THE BULLET TRAIN FROM TOKYO TO OSAKA TAKES TWO AND A HALF HOURS BUT, FLEXING SOME I.M.S. ENERGY TO BOOST OUR SPEED, WE'LL BE THERE IN TWO AND A HALF MINUTES.
I KNOW SPEED IS A PRIORITY, BUT WE ALSO NEED TO CONSERVE ENERGY.
DON'T WORRY, CAROL. I'M KEEPING A CLOSE EYE ON OUR POWER RESERVES... AND EVERYTHING ELSE.
MAN, HE WASN'T KIDDING. THREE MINUTES, POINT TO POINT.
THE ONLY THING FASTER WOULD BE TELEPORTATION, BUT THAT WOULD ALSO TAKE TEN TIMES THE JUICE.
FRIDAY, WHAT ARE WE UP AGAINST?
SATELLITE PHOTOGRAPHY CAN'T SEE THROUGH THE EXPLOSIONS AND SMOKE, BUT BY CHECKING LOCAL NEWSFEEDS AND SOCIAL MEDIA, IT SEEMS CLEAR...

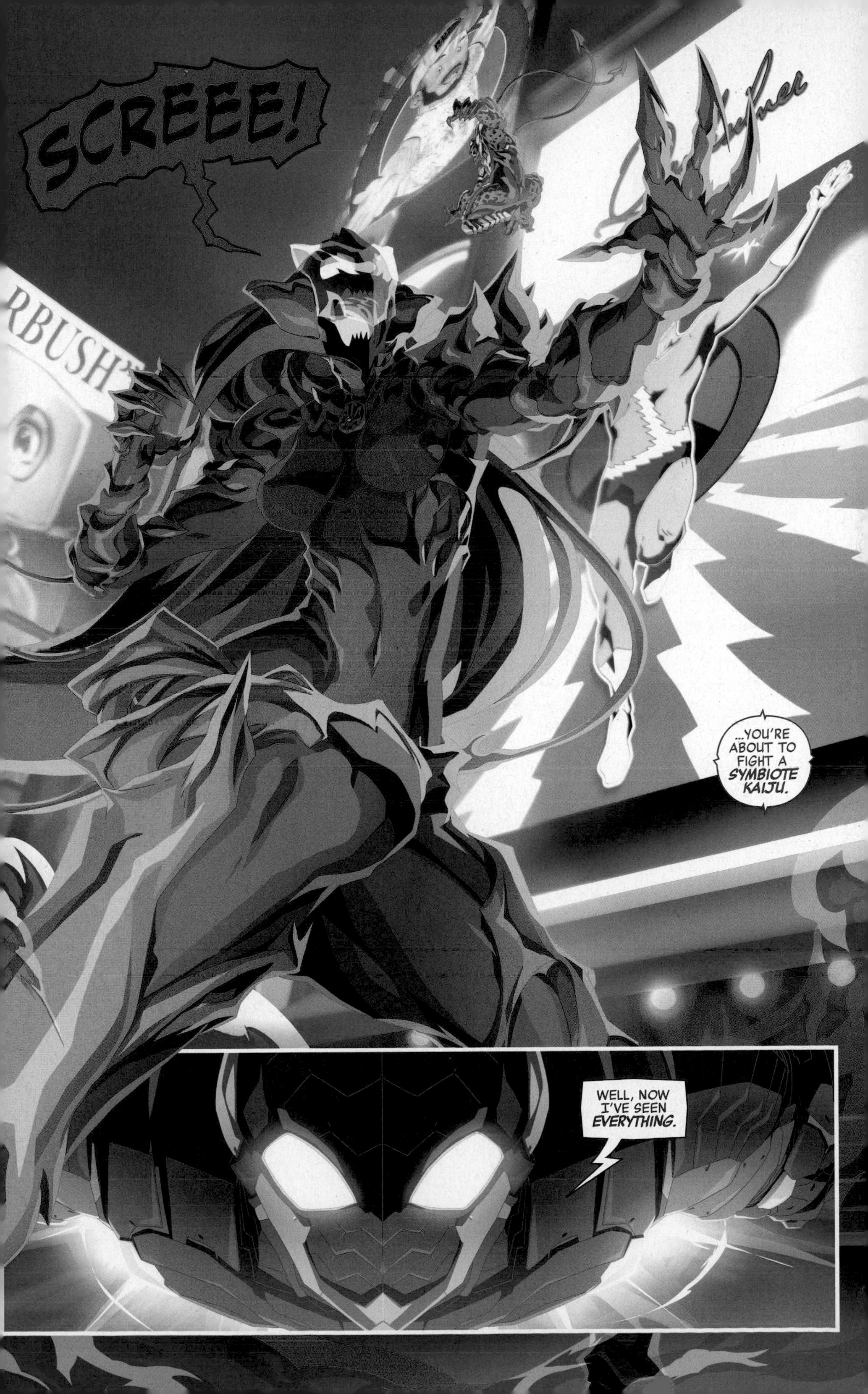
SCREEEE!
RBUSH'
...YOU'RE ABOUT TO FIGHT A SYMBIOTE KAIJU.
WELL, NOW I'VE SEEN EVERYTHING.

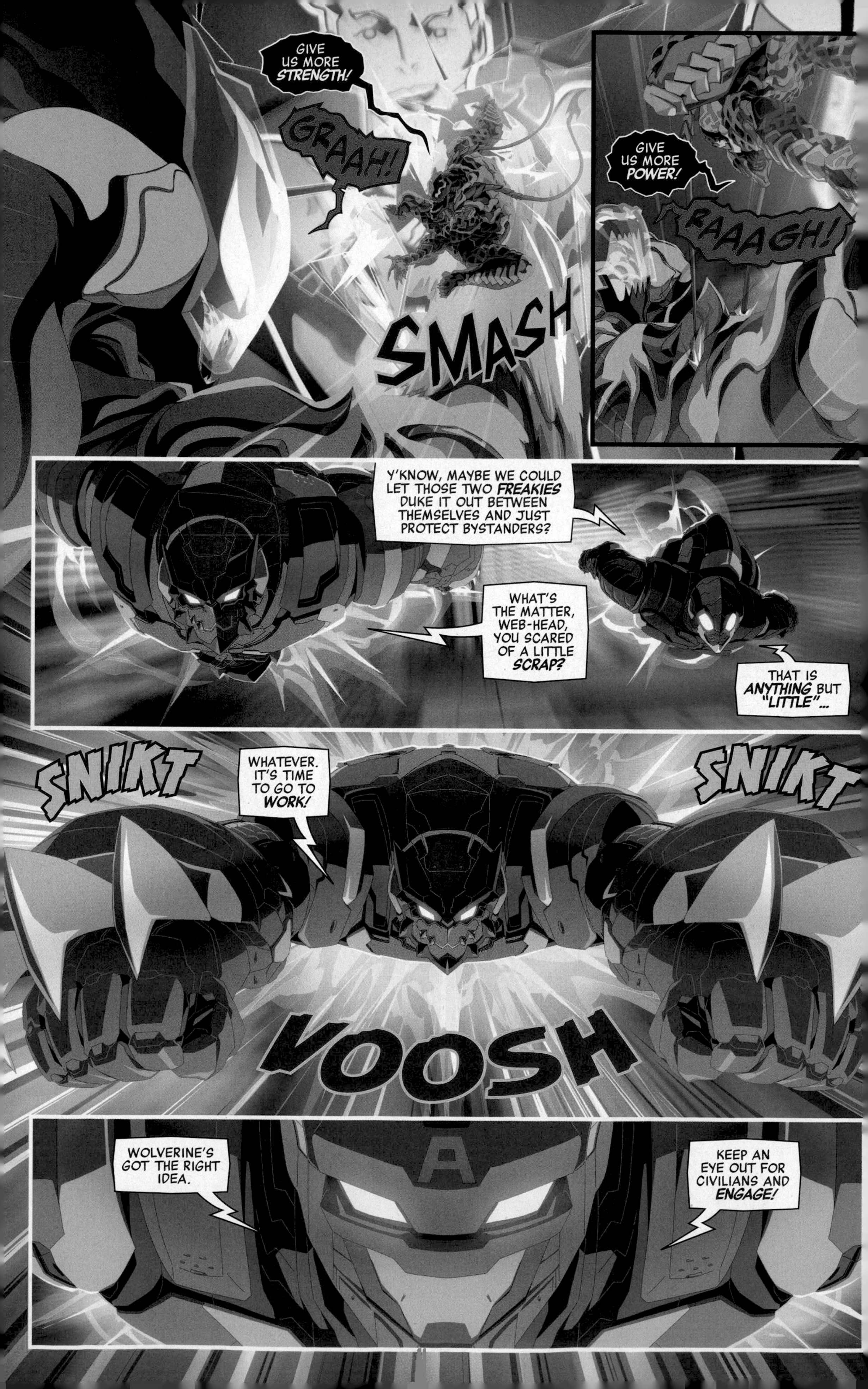
GIVE US MORE STRENGTH!
GRAAH!
SMASH
GIVE US MORE POWER!
RAAAGH!
Y'KNOW, MAYBE WE COULD LET THOSE TWO FREAKIES DUKE IT OUT BETWEEN THEMSELVES AND JUST PROTECT BYSTANDERS?
WHAT'S THE MATTER, WEB-HEAD, YOU SCARED OF A LITTLE SCRAP?
THAT IS ANYTHING BUT "LITTLE"...
SNIKT
WHATEVER. IT'S TIME TO GO TO WORK!
SNIKT
VOOSH
WOLVERINE'S GOT THE RIGHT IDEA.
KEEP AN EYE OUT FOR CIVILIANS AND ENGAGE!

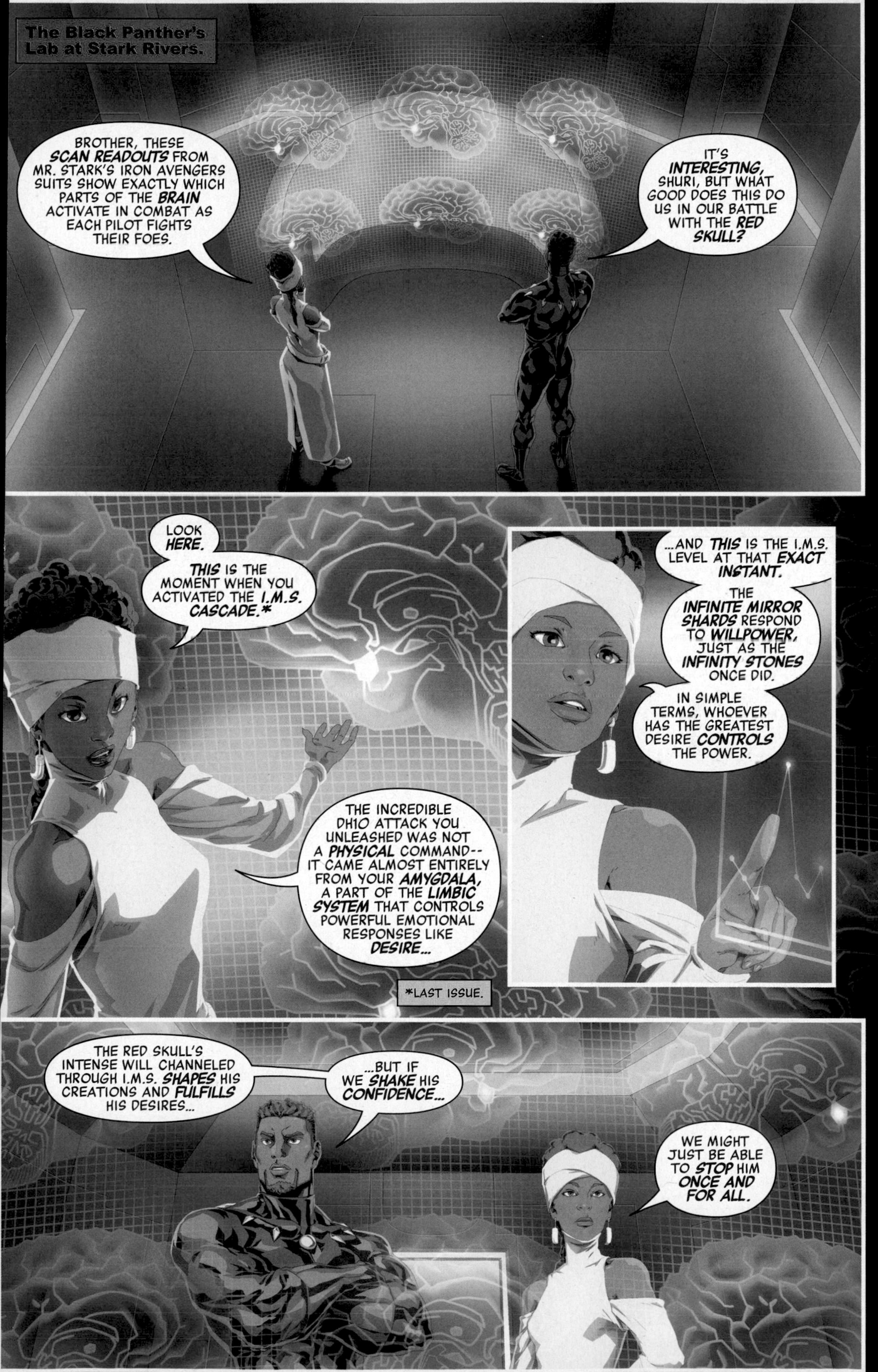
The Black Panther's Lab at Stark Rivers.
BROTHER, THESE SCAN READOUTS FROM MR. STARK'S IRON AVENGERS SUITS SHOW EXACTLY WHICH PARTS OF THE BRAIN ACTIVATE IN COMBAT AS EACH PILOT FIGHTS THEIR FOES.
IT'S INTERESTING, SHURI, BUT WHAT GOOD DOES THIS DO US IN OUR BATTLE WITH THE RED SKULL?
LOOK HERE.
THIS IS THE MOMENT WHEN YOU ACTIVATED THE I.M.S. CASCADE.*
THE INCREDIBLE DH10 ATTACK YOU UNLEASHED WAS NOT A PHYSICAL COMMAND-- IT CAME ALMOST ENTIRELY FROM YOUR AMYGDALA, A PART OF THE LIMBIC SYSTEM THAT CONTROLS POWERFUL EMOTIONAL RESPONSES LIKE DESIRE...
...AND THIS IS THE I.M.S. LEVEL AT THAT EXACT INSTANT.
THE INFINITE MIRROR SHARDS RESPOND TO WILLPOWER, JUST AS THE INFINITY STONES ONCE DID.
IN SIMPLE TERMS, WHOEVER HAS THE GREATEST DESIRE CONTROLS THE POWER.
*LAST ISSUE.
THE RED SKULL'S INTENSE WILL CHANNELED THROUGH I.M.S. SHAPES HIS CREATIONS AND FULFILLS HIS DESIRES...
...BUT IF WE SHAKE HIS CONFIDENCE...
WE MIGHT JUST BE ABLE TO STOP HIM ONCE AND FOR ALL.

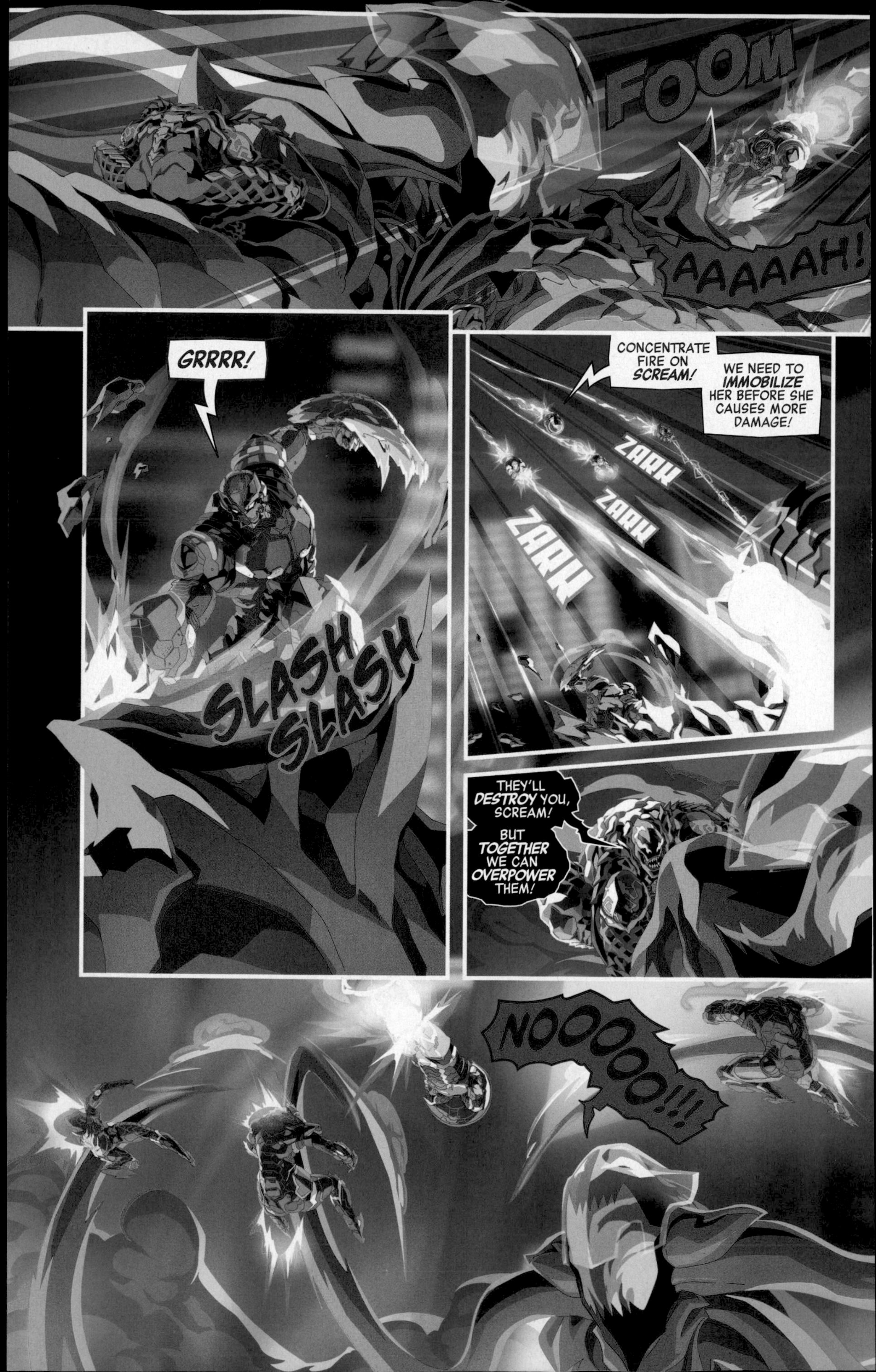
FOOM
AAAAAH!
GRRRR!
SLASH SLASH
CONCENTRATE FIRE ON SCREAM!
WE NEED TO IMMOBILIZE HER BEFORE SHE CAUSES MORE DAMAGE!
ZARK
ZARK
ZARK
THEY'LL DESTROY YOU, SCREAM!
BUT TOGETHER WE CAN OVERPOWER THEM!
NOOOOO!!!

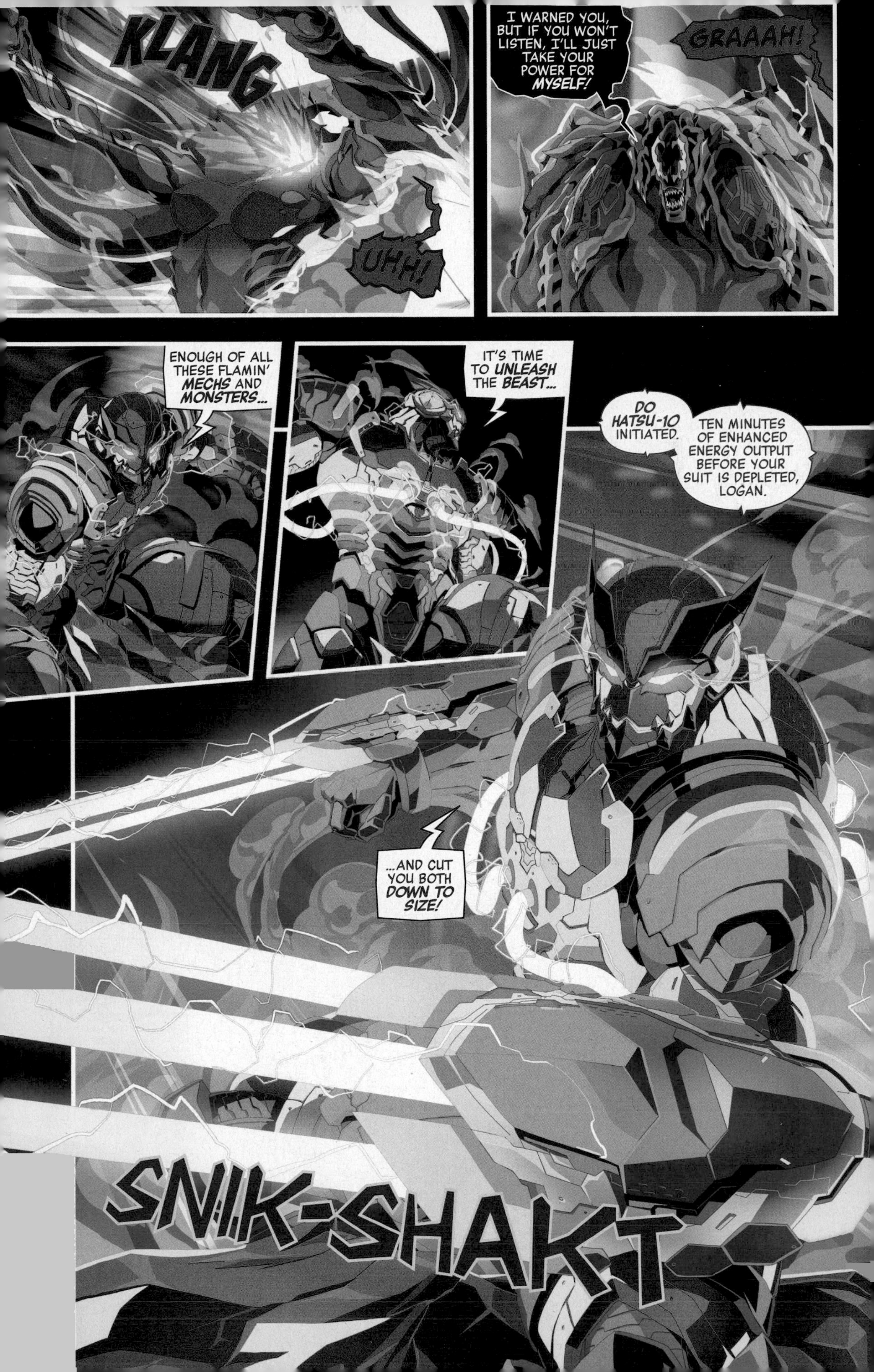
KLANG
UHH!
I WARNED YOU, BUT IF YOU WON'T LISTEN, I'LL JUST TAKE YOUR POWER FOR MYSELF!
GRAAAH!
ENOUGH OF ALL THESE FLAMIN' MECHS AND MONSTERS...
IT'S TIME TO UNLEASH THE BEAST...
DO HATSU-10 INITIATED.
TEN MINUTES OF ENHANCED ENERGY OUTPUT BEFORE YOUR SUIT IS DEPLETED, LOGAN.
...AND CUT YOU BOTH DOWN TO SIZE!
SNIK-SHAKT

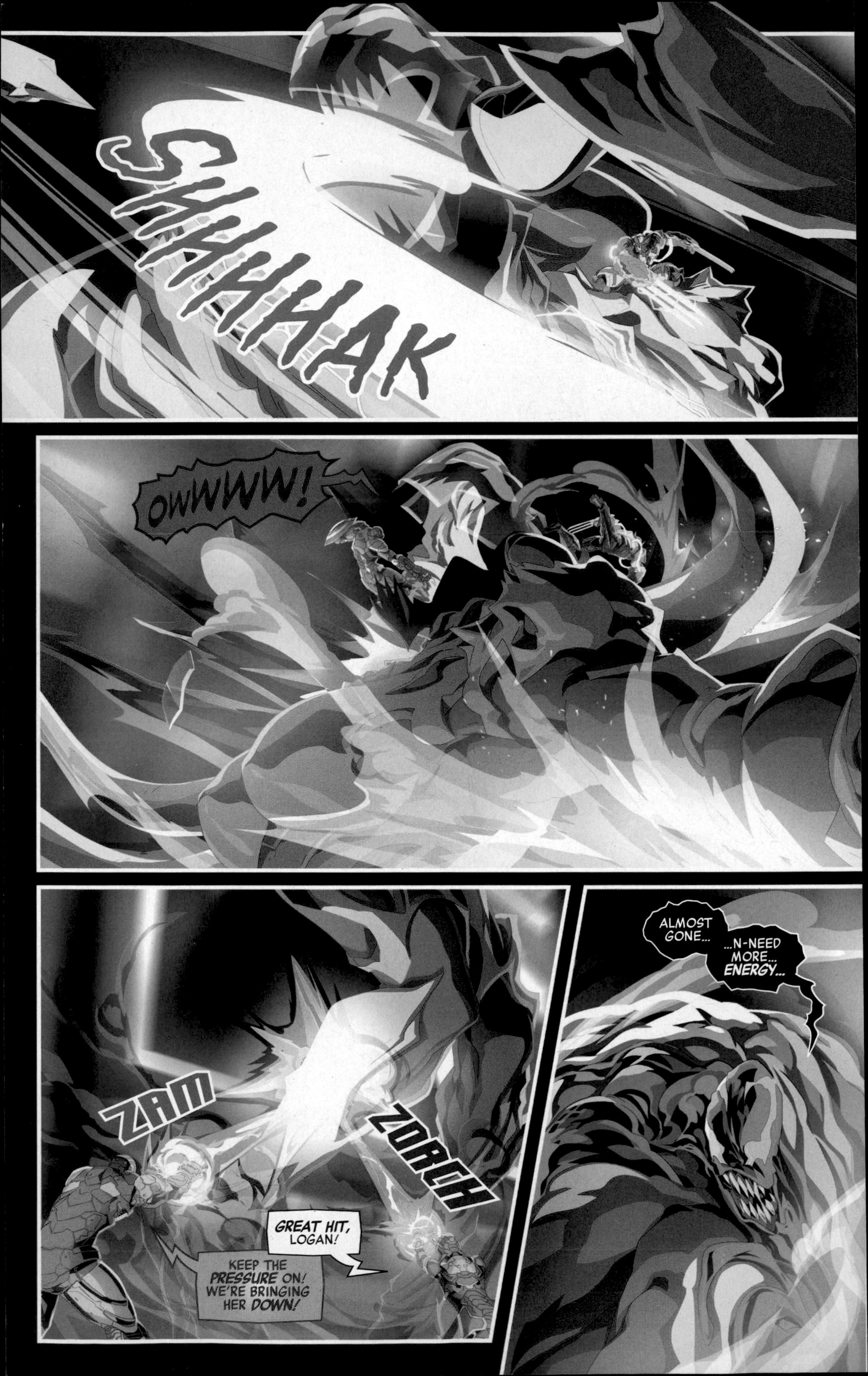
SHHHHAK
OWWWW!
ZAM
ZORCH
GREAT HIT, LOGAN!
KEEP THE PRESSURE ON! WE'RE BRINGING HER DOWN!
ALMOST GONE...
...N-NEED MORE... ENERGY...

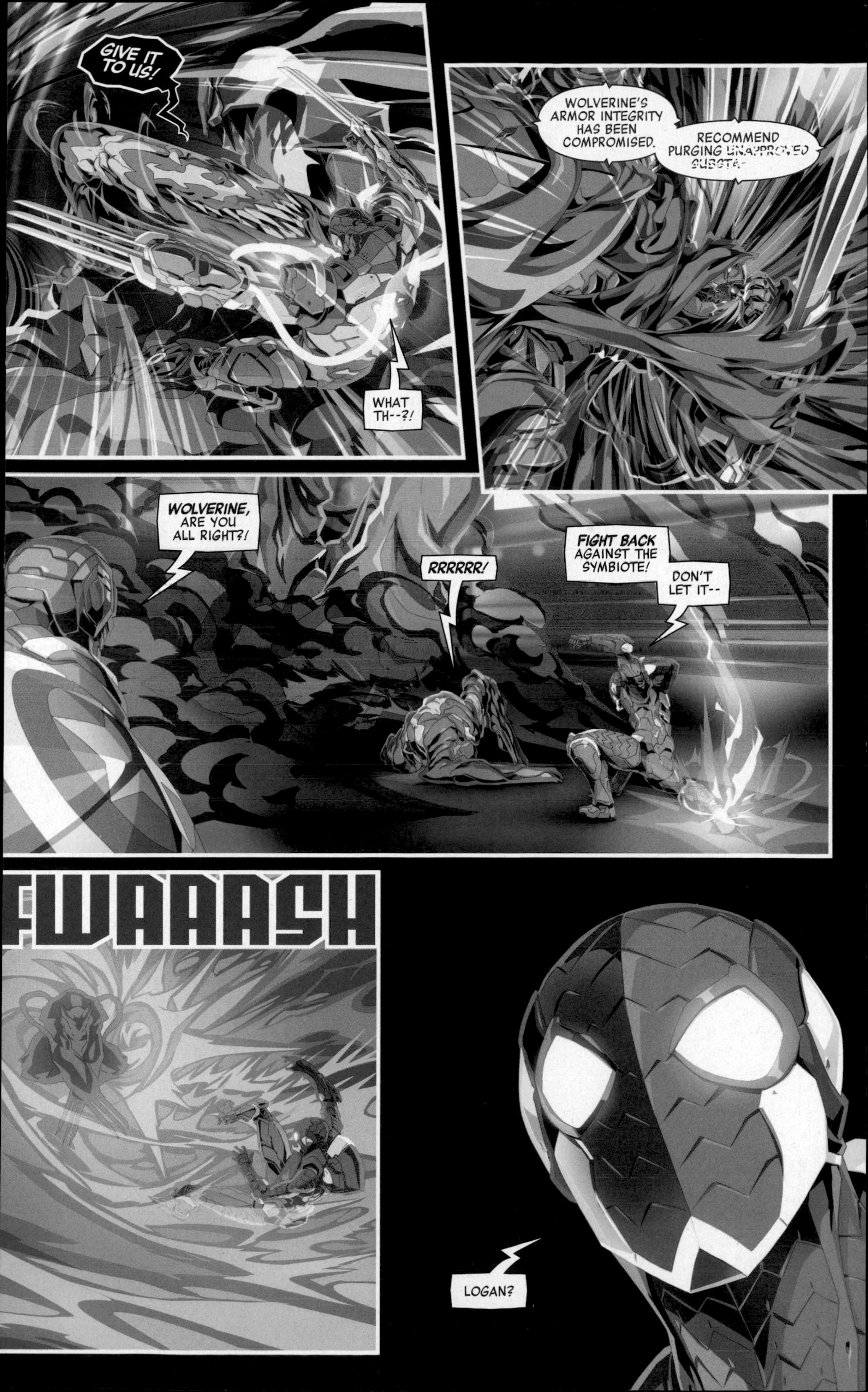
GIVE IT TO US!
WHAT TH--?!
WOLVERINE'S ARMOR INTEGRITY HAS BEEN COMPROMISED.
RECOMMEND PURGING UNAPPROVED SUBSTA--
WOLVERINE, ARE YOU ALL RIGHT?!
RRRRRR!
FIGHT BACK AGAINST THE SYMBIOTE!
DON'T LET IT--
FWAAASH
LOGAN?

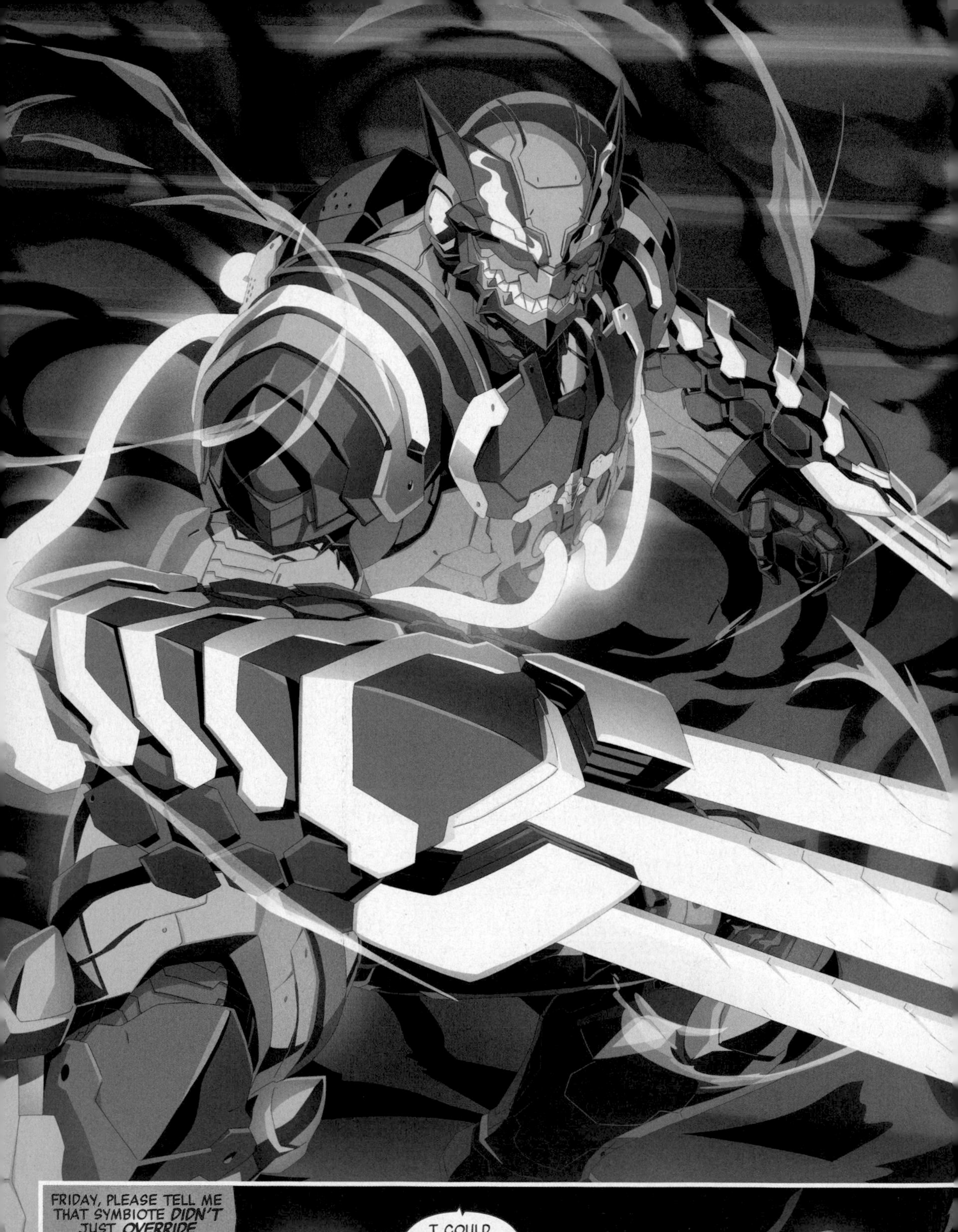

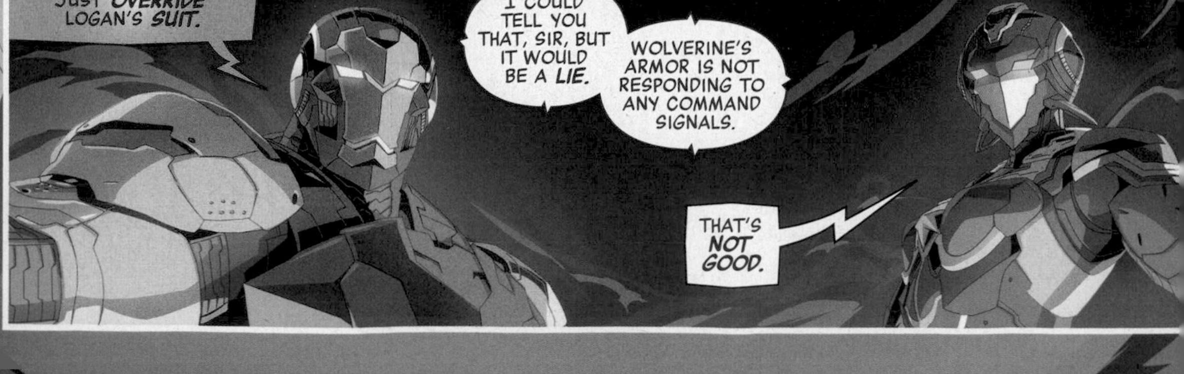

FRIDAY, PLEASE TELL ME THAT SYMBIOTE DIDN'T JUST OVERRIDE LOGAN'S SUIT.
I COULD TELL YOU THAT, SIR, BUT IT WOULD BE A LIE.
WOLVERINE'S ARMOR IS NOT RESPONDING TO ANY COMMAND SIGNALS.
THAT'S NOT GOOD.

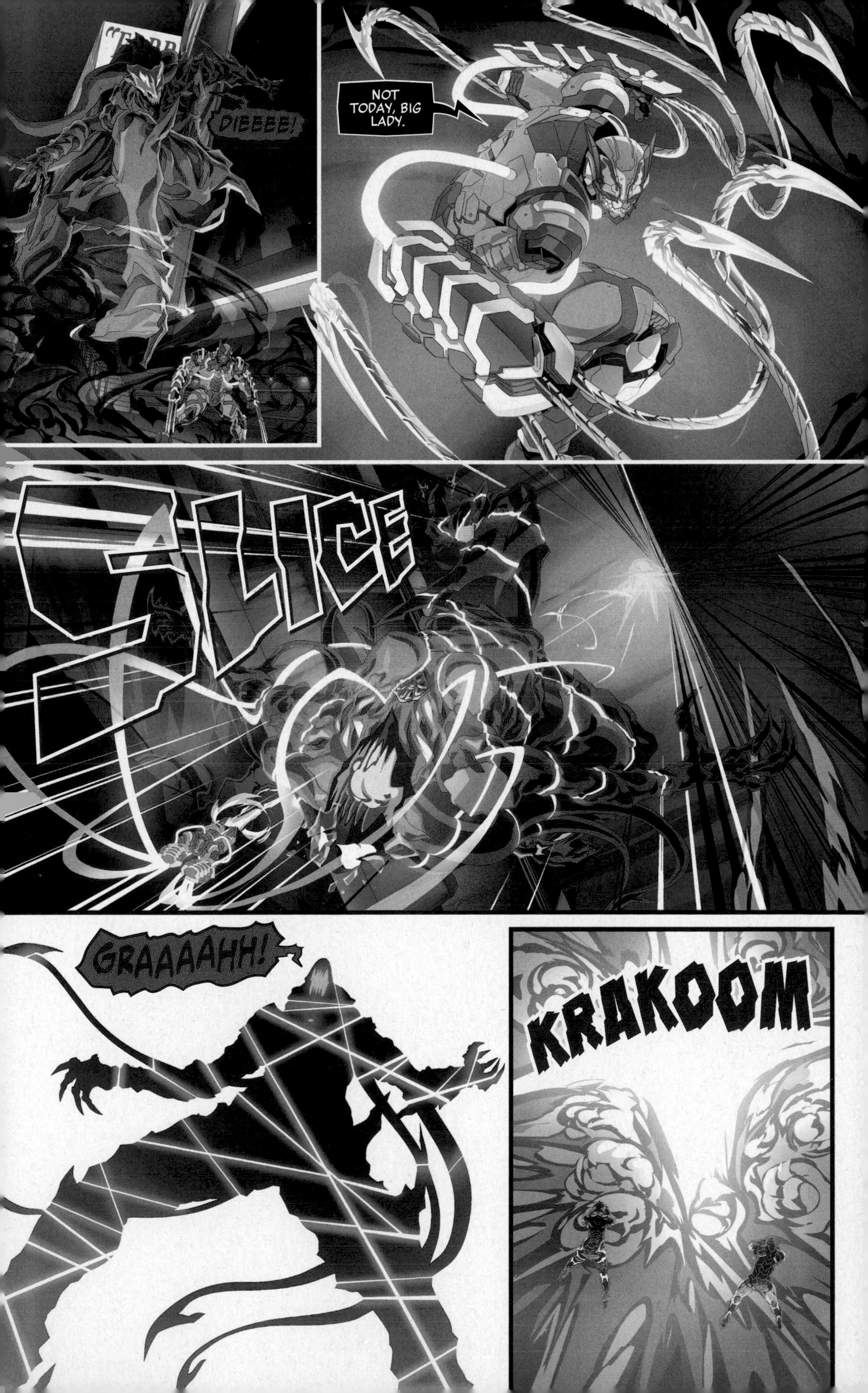
DIEEEE!
NOT TODAY, BIG LADY.
SLICE
GRAAAAHH!
KRAKOOM

ANYONE ELSE WANNA MESS WITH THIS?

WOLVERINE... ...ARE YOU STILL... YOURSELF?

DON'T GET YOUR STARS 'N' STRIPES IN A KNOT, STEVE. I'VE GOT THIS CREEPER UNDER CONTROL.

THAT'S NOT GONNA LAST. YOU NEED TO GET RID OF THAT SYMBIOTE RIGHT NOW!

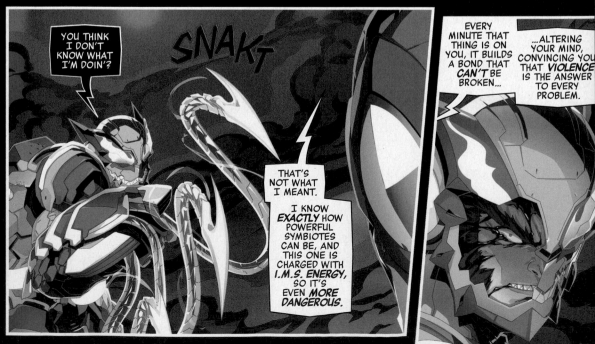

YOU THINK I DON'T KNOW WHAT I'M DOIN'?

SNAKT

THAT'S NOT WHAT I MEANT. I KNOW EXACTLY HOW POWERFUL SYMBIOTES CAN BE, AND THIS ONE IS CHARGED WITH I.M.S. ENERGY, SO IT'S EVEN MORE DANGEROUS.

EVERY MINUTE THAT THING IS ON YOU, IT BUILDS A BOND THAT CAN'T BE BROKEN...

...ALTERING YOUR MIND, CONVINCING YOU THAT VIOLENCE IS THE ANSWER TO EVERY PROBLEM.

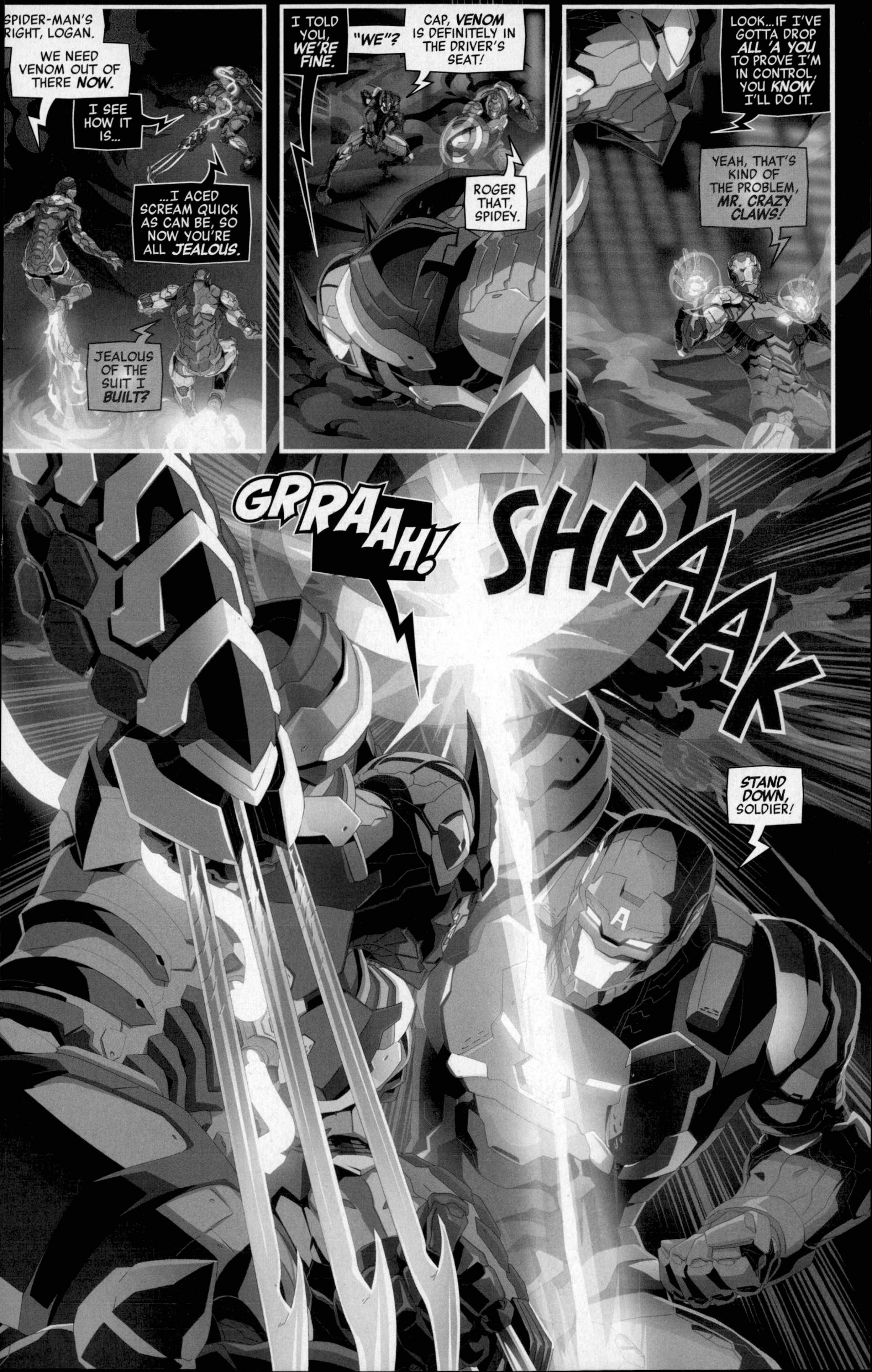
SPIDER-MAN'S RIGHT, LOGAN.
WE NEED VENOM OUT OF THERE NOW.
I SEE HOW IT IS...
...I ACED SCREAM QUICK AS CAN BE, SO NOW YOU'RE ALL JEALOUS.
JEALOUS OF THE SUIT I BUILT?
I TOLD YOU, WE'RE FINE.
"WE"?
CAP, VENOM IS DEFINITELY IN THE DRIVER'S SEAT!
ROGER THAT, SPIDEY.
LOOK...IF I'VE GOTTA DROP ALL 'A YOU TO PROVE I'M IN CONTROL, YOU KNOW I'LL DO IT.
YEAH, THAT'S KIND OF THE PROBLEM, MR. CRAZY CLAWS!
GRRAAAH!
SHRAAAK
STAND DOWN, SOLDIER!

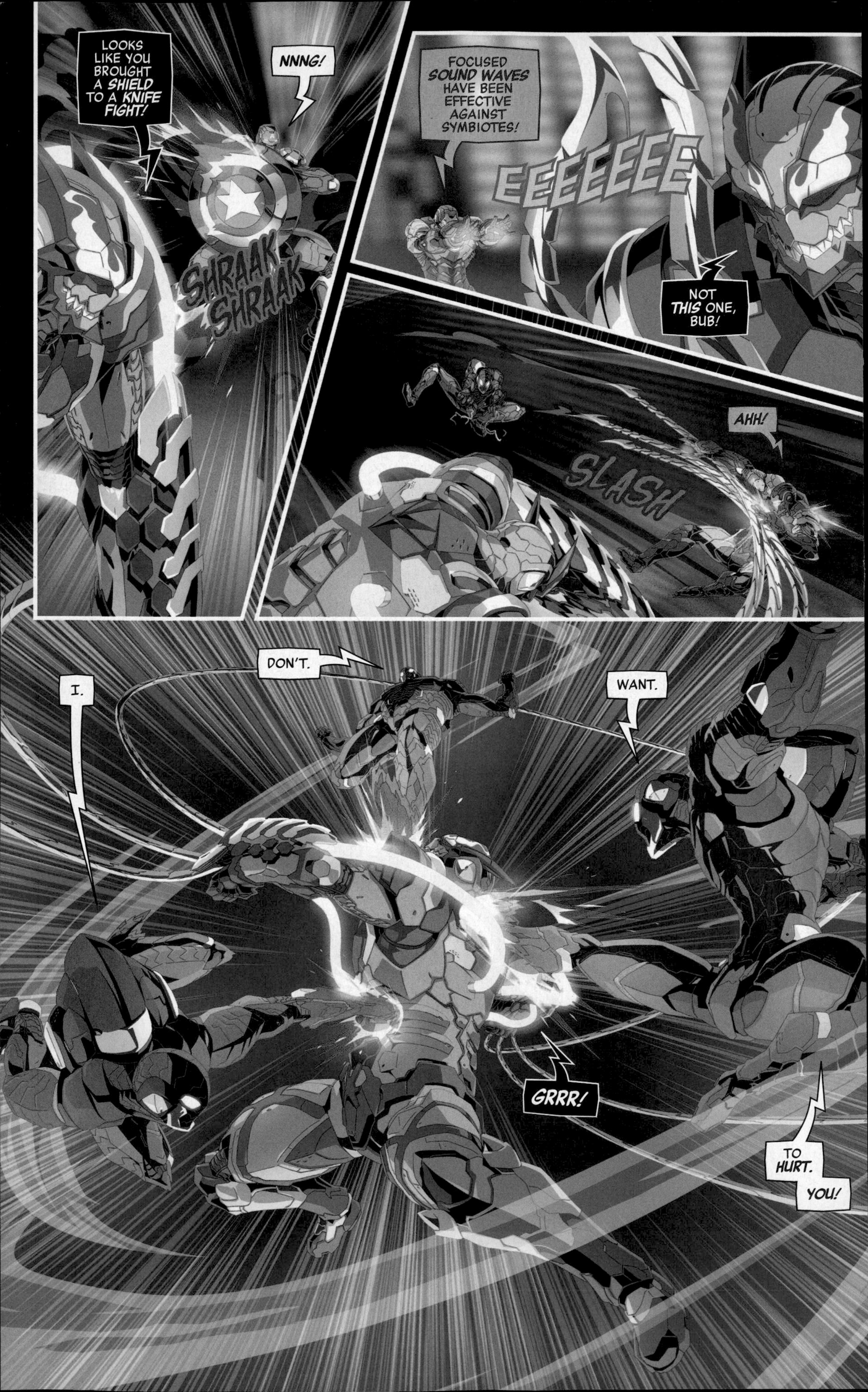
LOOKS LIKE YOU BROUGHT A SHIELD TO A KNIFE FIGHT!
NNNG!
SHRAAK SHRAAK
FOCUSED SOUND WAVES HAVE BEEN EFFECTIVE AGAINST SYMBIOTES!
EEEEEEE
NOT THIS ONE, BUB!
AHH!
SLASH
I.
DON'T.
WANT.
GRRR!
TO HURT.
YOU!

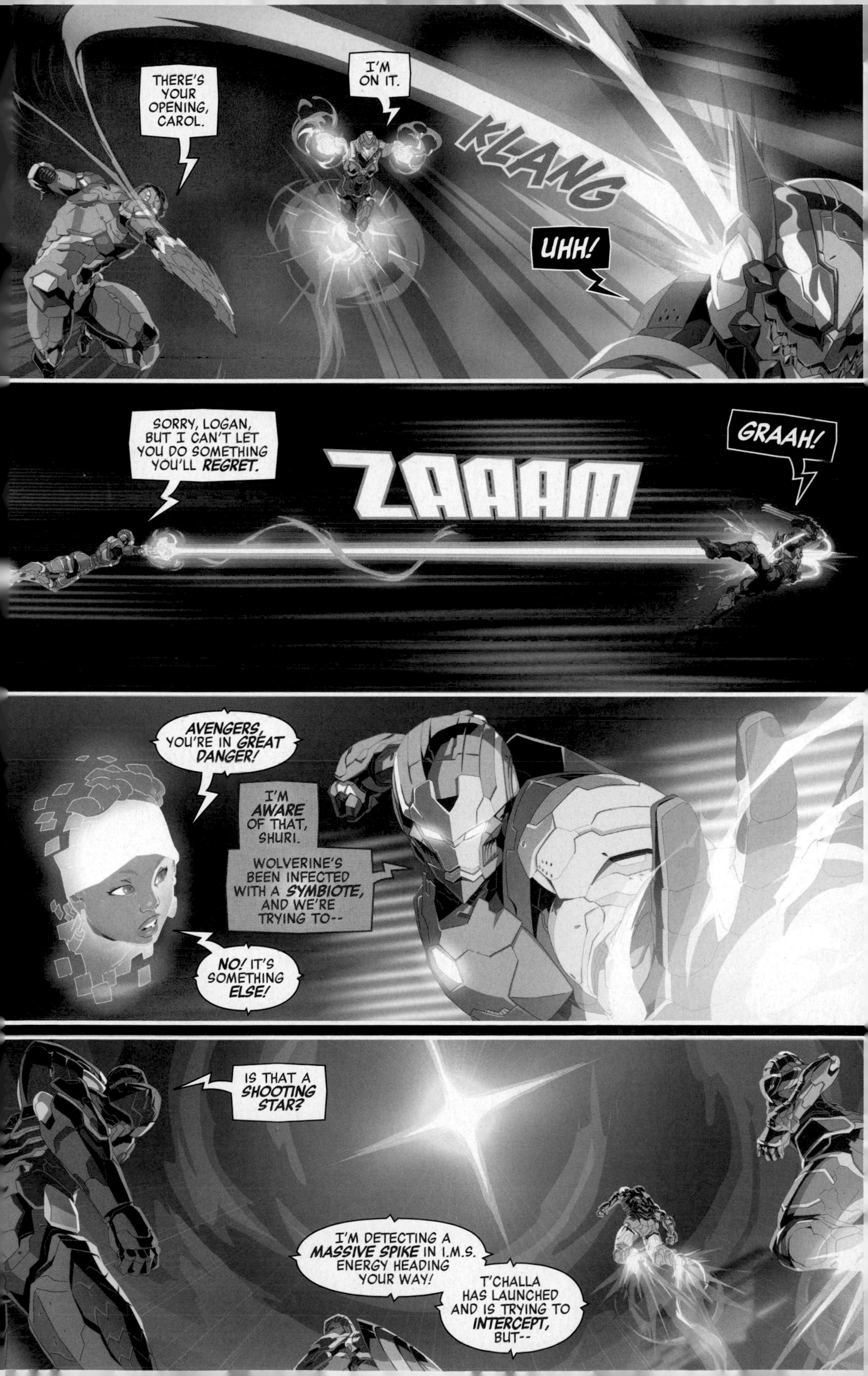

THERE'S YOUR OPENING, CAROL.
I'M ON IT.
KLANG
UHH!
SORRY, LOGAN, BUT I CAN'T LET YOU DO SOMETHING YOU'LL REGRET.
ZAAAM
GRAAH!
AVENGERS, YOU'RE IN GREAT DANGER!
I'M AWARE OF THAT, SHURI.
WOLVERINE'S BEEN INFECTED WITH A SYMBIOTE, AND WE'RE TRYING TO--
NO! IT'S SOMETHING ELSE!
IS THAT A SHOOTING STAR?
I'M DETECTING A MASSIVE SPIKE IN I.M.S. ENERGY HEADING YOUR WAY!
T'CHALLA HAS LAUNCHED AND IS TRYING TO INTERCEPT, BUT--

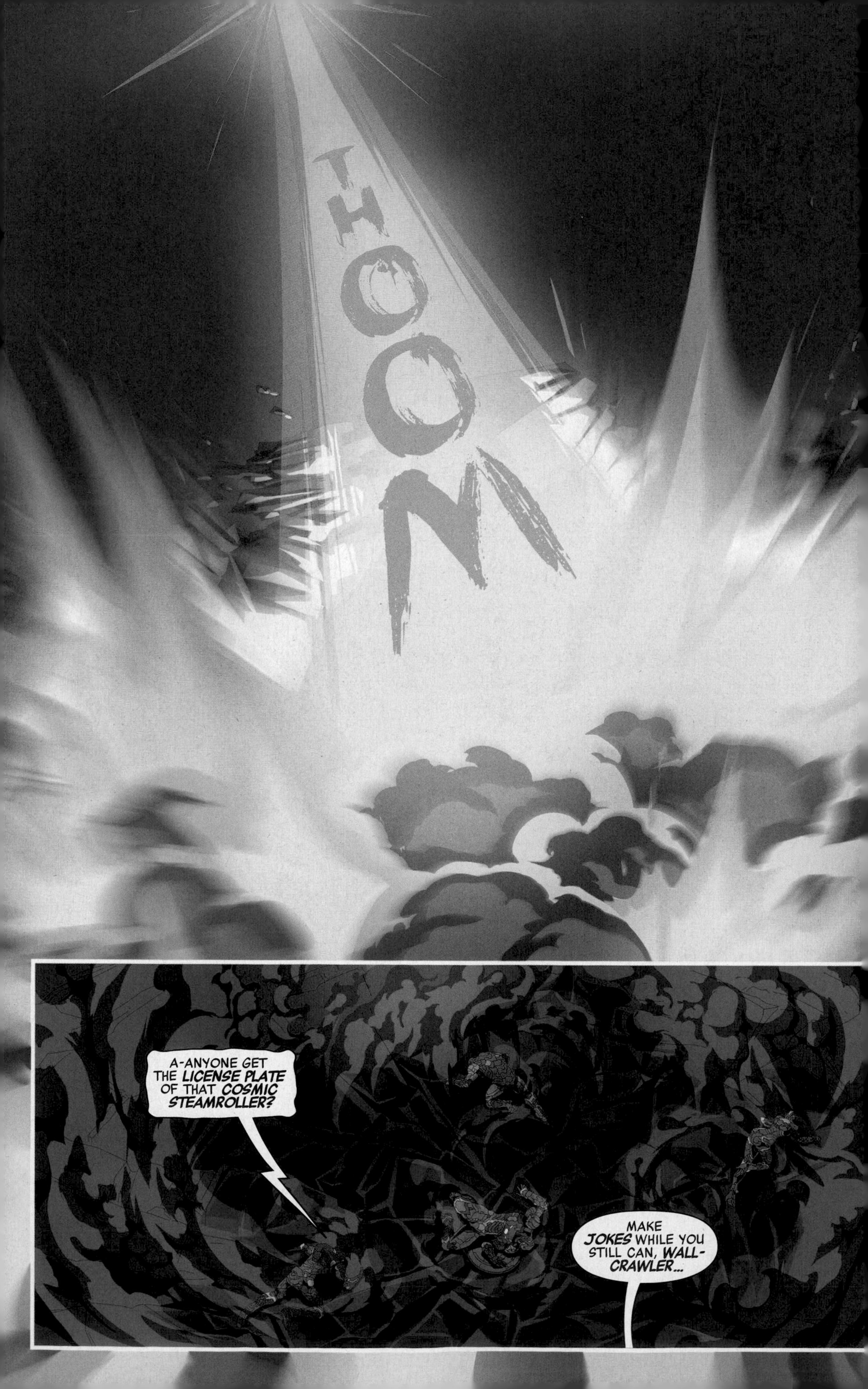
THOOM
A-ANYONE GET THE LICENSE PLATE OF THAT COSMIC STEAMROLLER?
MAKE JOKES WHILE YOU STILL CAN, WALL-CRAWLER...

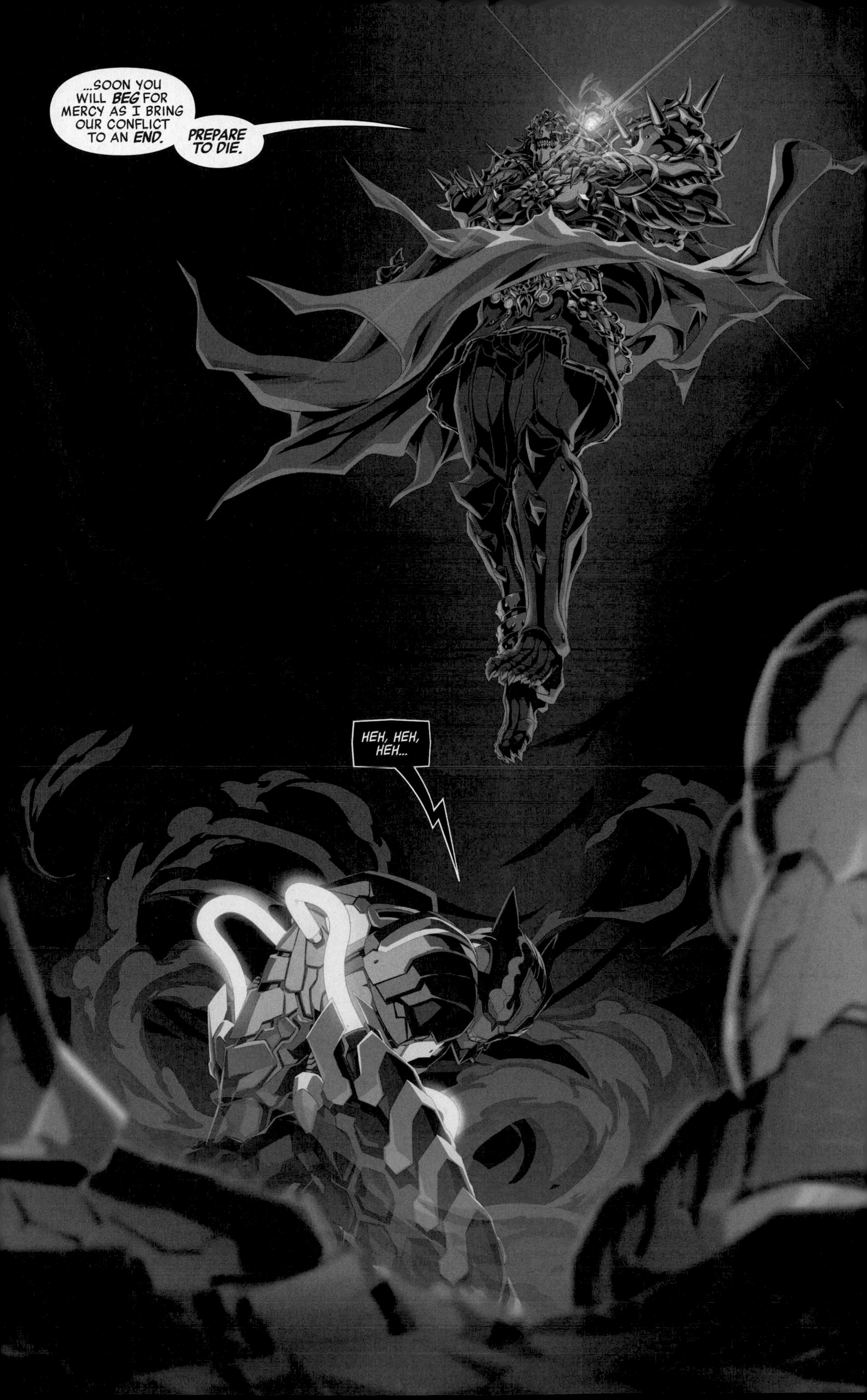
...SOON YOU WILL BEG FOR MERCY AS I BRING OUR CONFLICT TO AN END.
PREPARE TO DIE.
HEH, HEH, HEH...

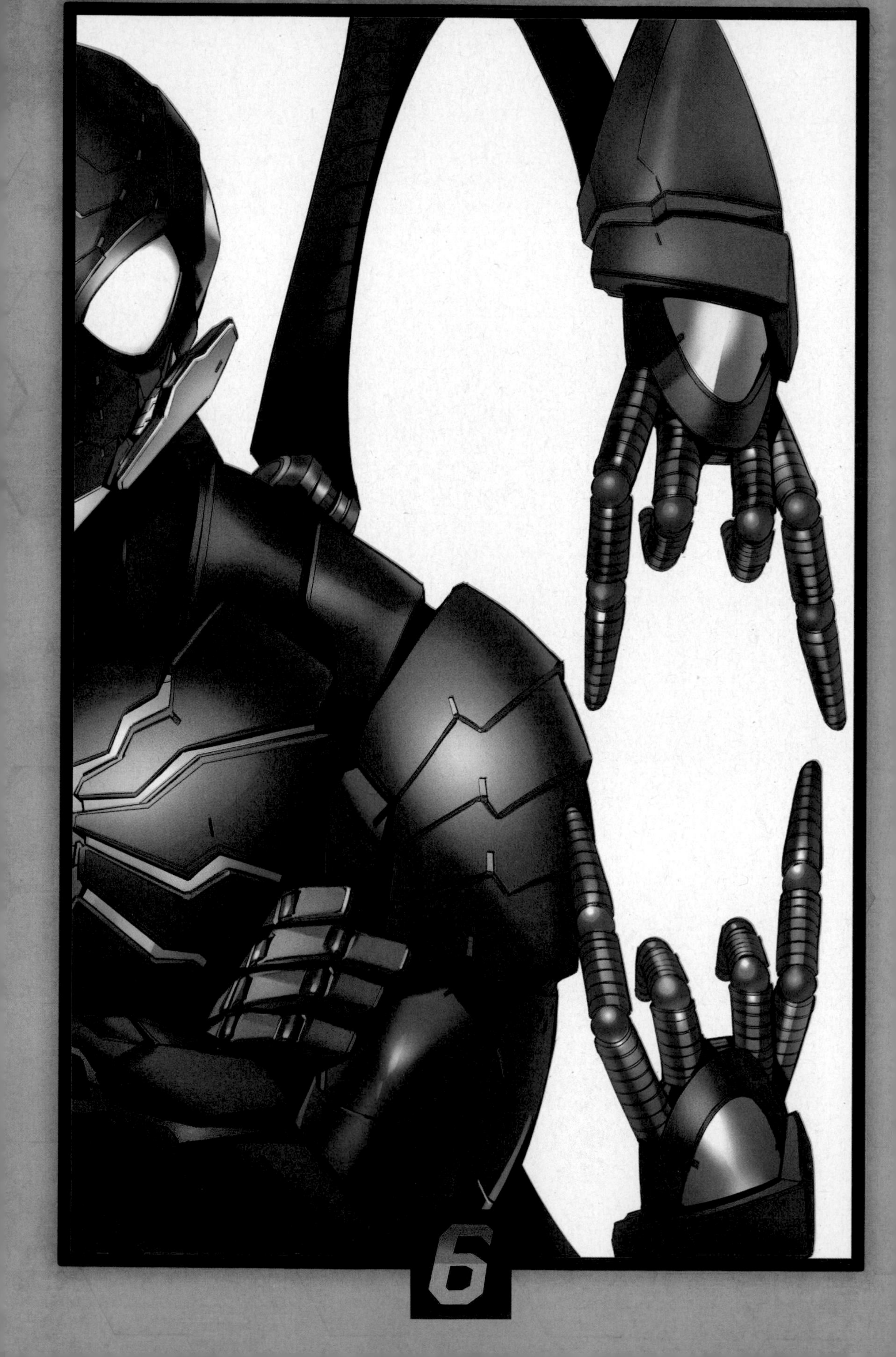

6

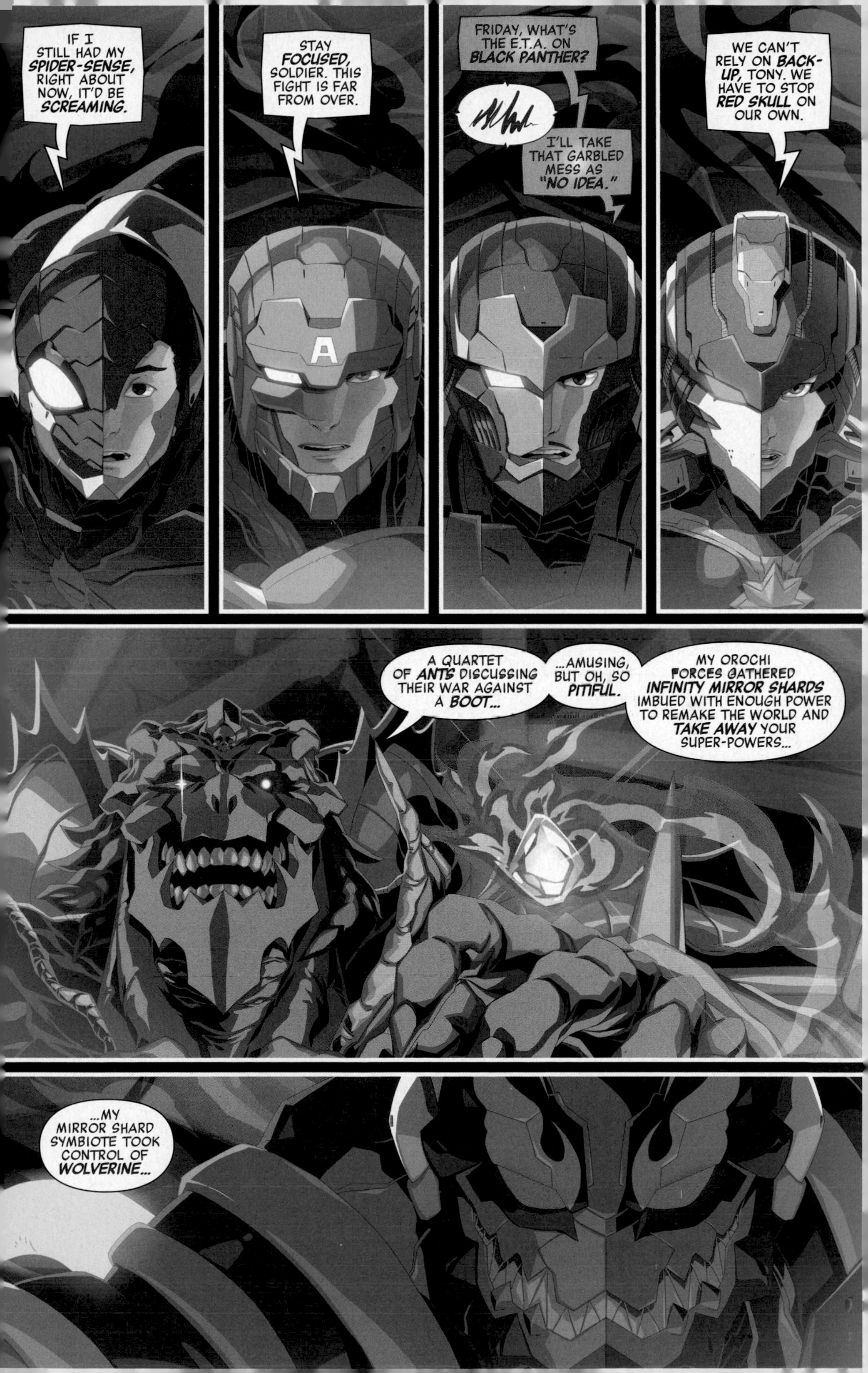
IF I STILL HAD MY SPIDER-SENSE, RIGHT ABOUT NOW, IT'D BE SCREAMING.
STAY FOCUSED, SOLDIER. THIS FIGHT IS FAR FROM OVER.
FRIDAY, WHAT'S THE E.T.A. ON BLACK PANTHER?
I'LL TAKE THAT GARBLED MESS AS "NO IDEA."
WE CAN'T RELY ON BACK-UP, TONY. WE HAVE TO STOP RED SKULL ON OUR OWN.
A QUARTET OF ANTS DISCUSSING THEIR WAR AGAINST A BOOT...
...AMUSING, BUT OH, SO PITIFUL.
MY OROCHI FORCES GATHERED INFINITY MIRROR SHARDS IMBUED WITH ENOUGH POWER TO REMAKE THE WORLD AND TAKE AWAY YOUR SUPER-POWERS...
...MY MIRROR SHARD SYMBIOTE TOOK CONTROL OF WOLVERINE...

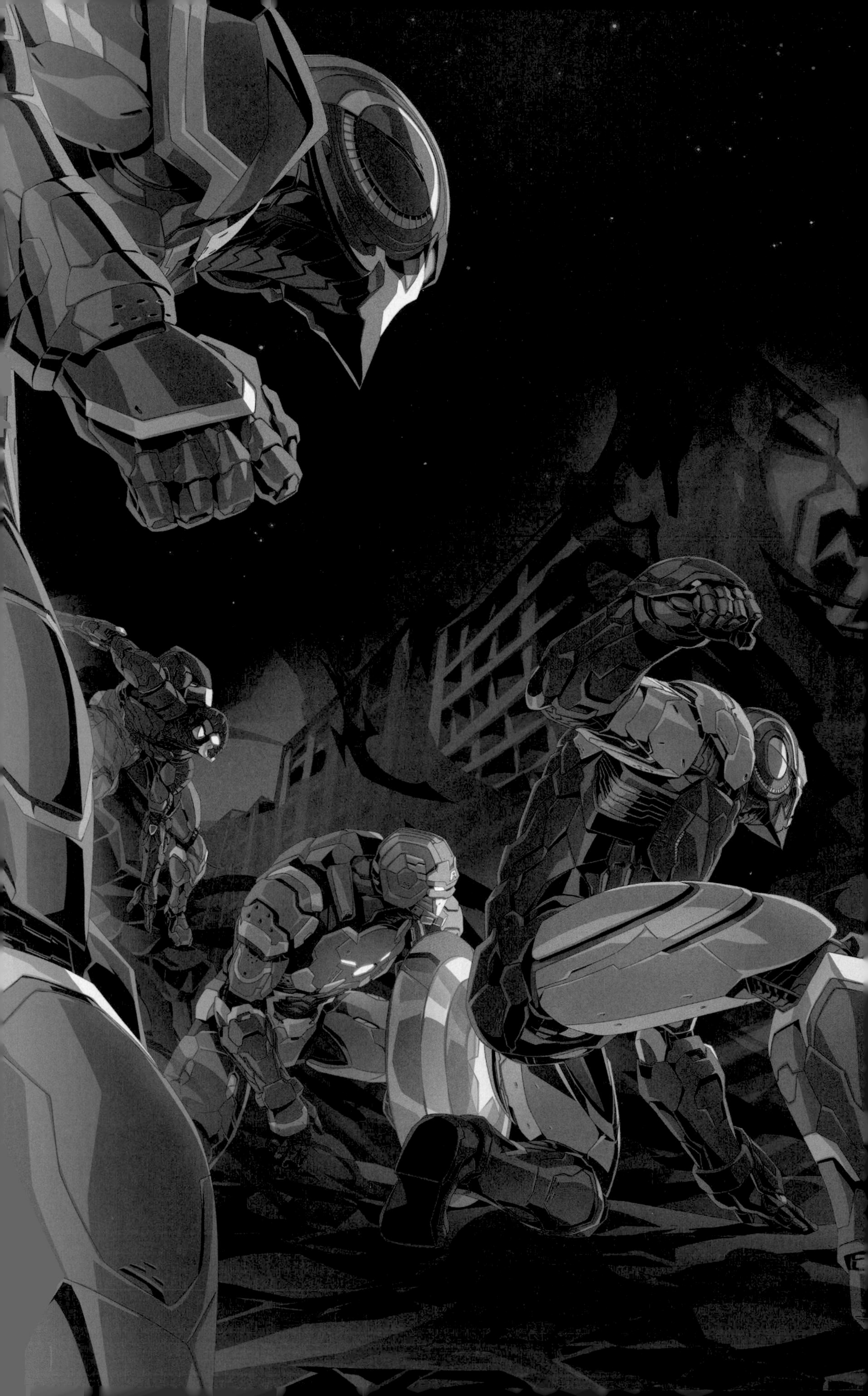

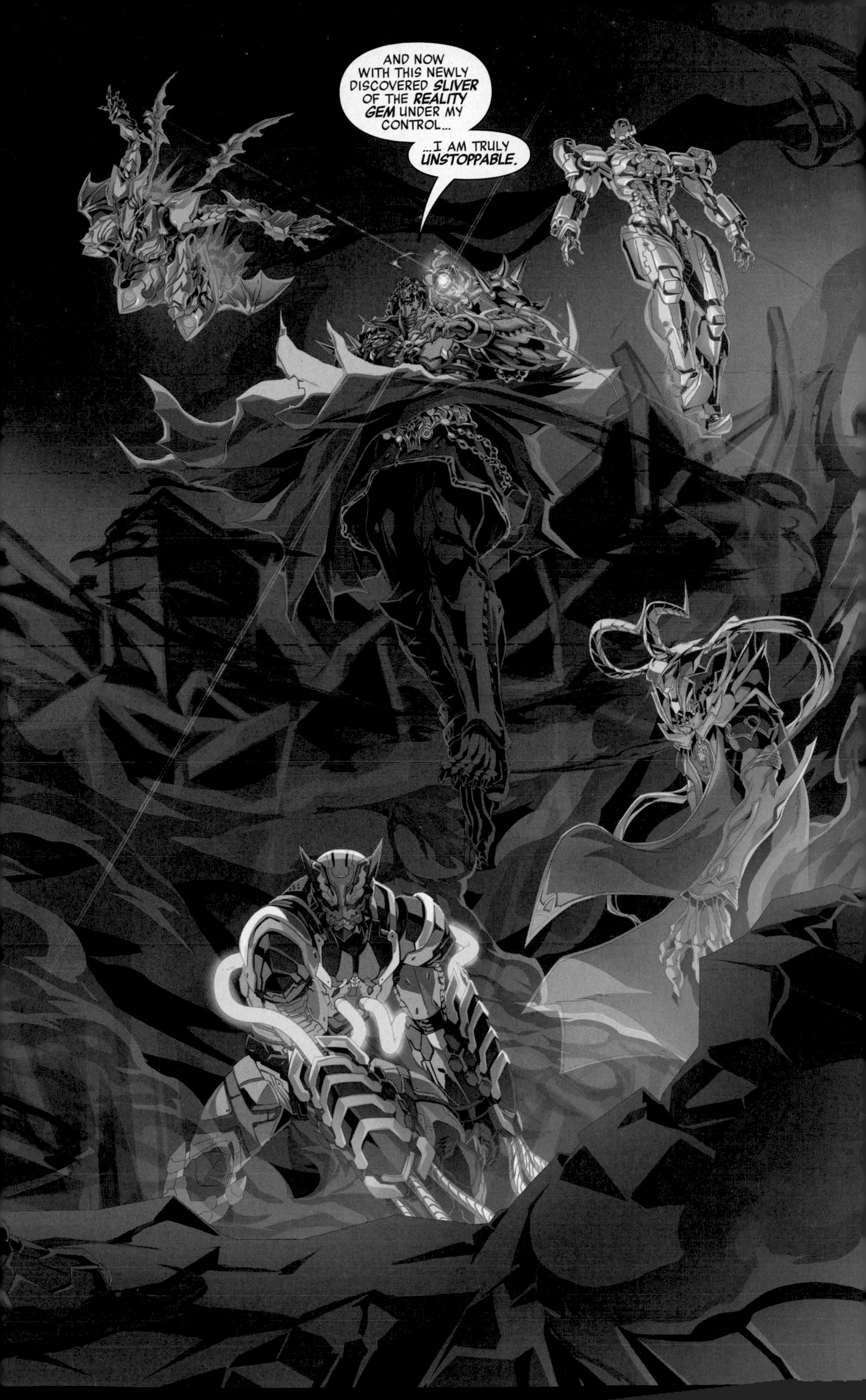
AND NOW WITH THIS NEWLY DISCOVERED SLIVER OF THE REALITY GEM UNDER MY CONTROL...
...I AM TRULY UNSTOPPABLE.

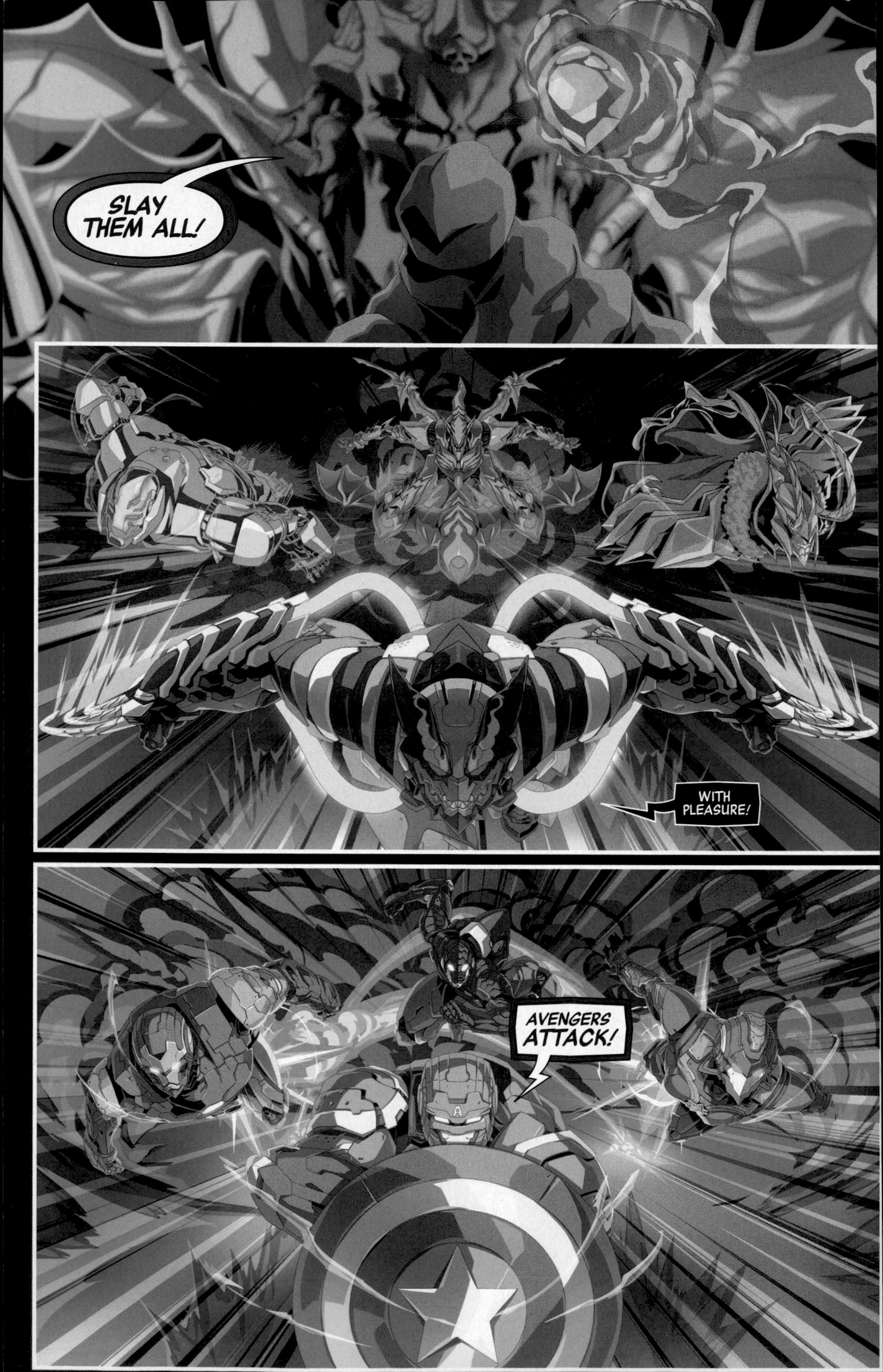
SLAY THEM ALL!
WITH PLEASURE!
AVENGERS ATTACK!

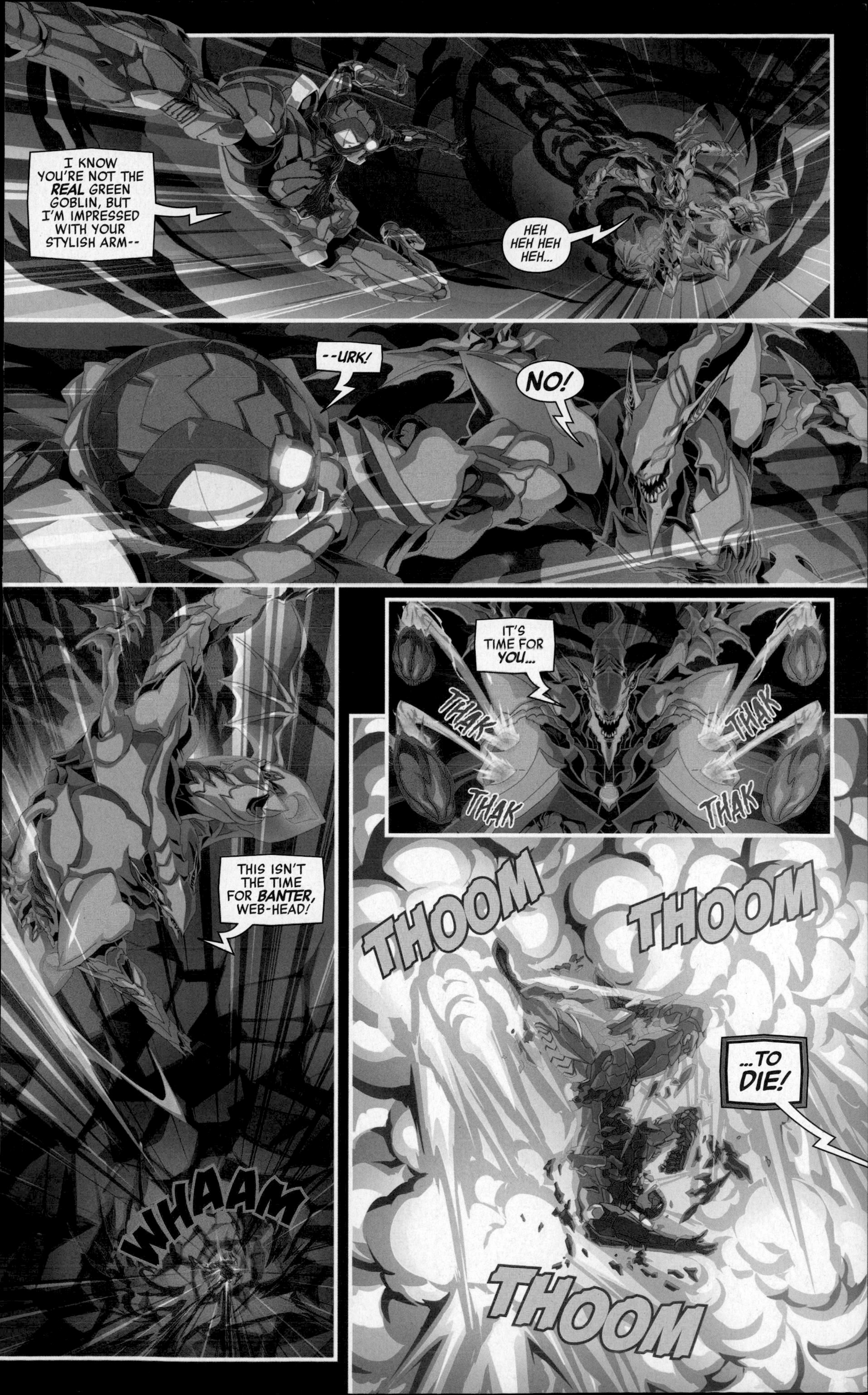
I KNOW YOU'RE NOT THE REAL GREEN GOBLIN, BUT I'M IMPRESSED WITH YOUR STYLISH ARM--
HEH HEH HEH HEH...
--URK!
NO!
THIS ISN'T THE TIME FOR BANTER, WEB-HEAD!
WHAAM
IT'S TIME FOR YOU...
THAK
THAK
THAK
THAK
THOOM
THOOM
...TO DIE!
THOOM

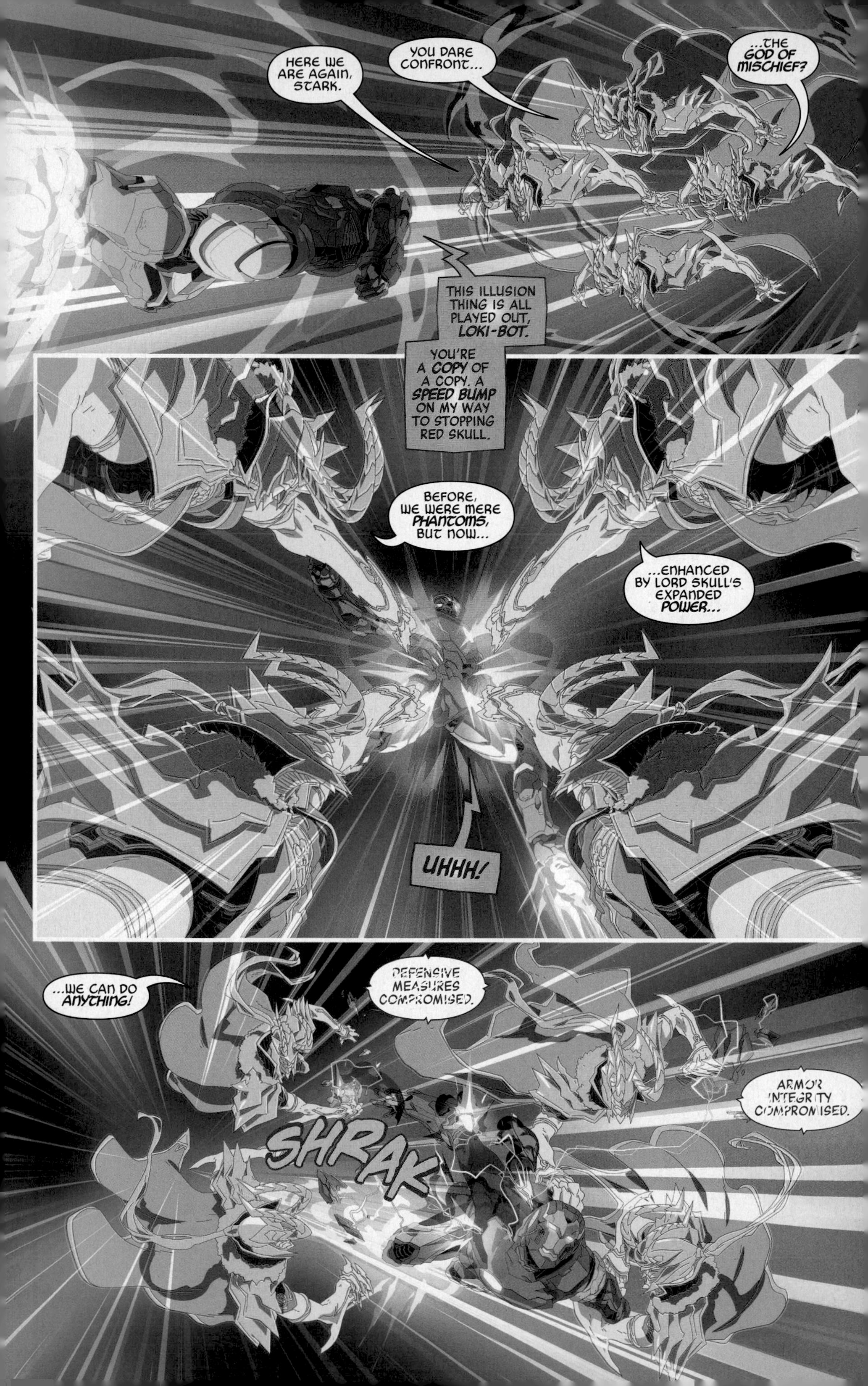
HERE WE ARE AGAIN, STARK.
YOU DARE CONFRONT...
...THE GOD OF MISCHIEF?
THIS ILLUSION THING IS ALL PLAYED OUT, LOKI-BOT.
YOU'RE A COPY OF A COPY. A SPEED BUMP ON MY WAY TO STOPPING RED SKULL.
BEFORE, WE WERE MERE PHANTOMS, BUT NOW...
...ENHANCED BY LORD SKULL'S EXPANDED POWER...
UHHH!
...WE CAN DO ANYTHING!
DEFENSIVE MEASURES COMPROMISED.
ARMOR INTEGRITY COMPROMISED.
SHRAK

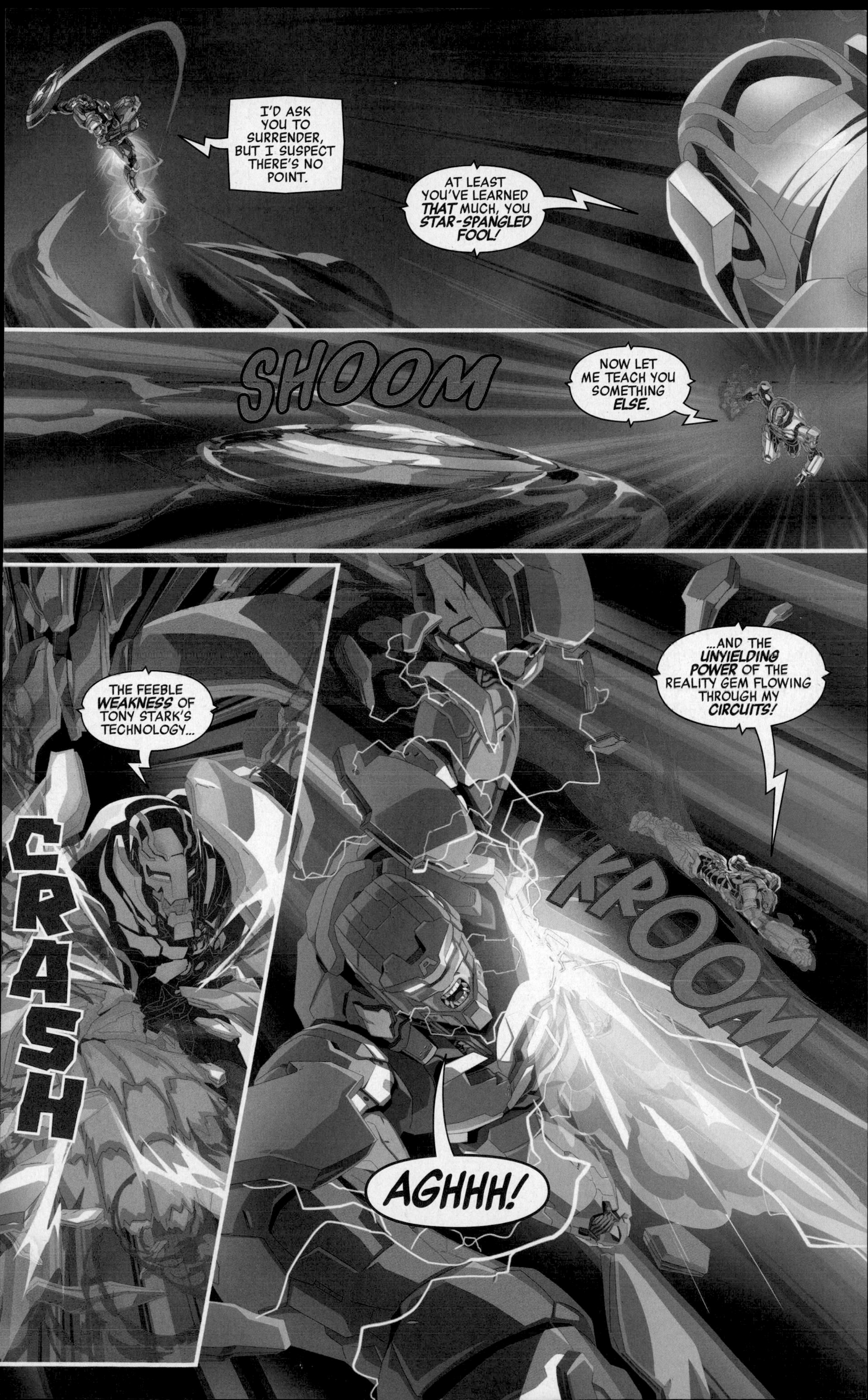
I'D ASK YOU TO SURRENDER, BUT I SUSPECT THERE'S NO POINT.
AT LEAST YOU'VE LEARNED THAT MUCH, YOU STAR-SPANGLED FOOL!
SHOOM
NOW LET ME TEACH YOU SOMETHING ELSE.
THE FEEBLE WEAKNESS OF TONY STARK'S TECHNOLOGY...
...AND THE UNYIELDING POWER OF THE REALITY GEM FLOWING THROUGH MY CIRCUITS!
CRASH
KROOM
AGHHH!

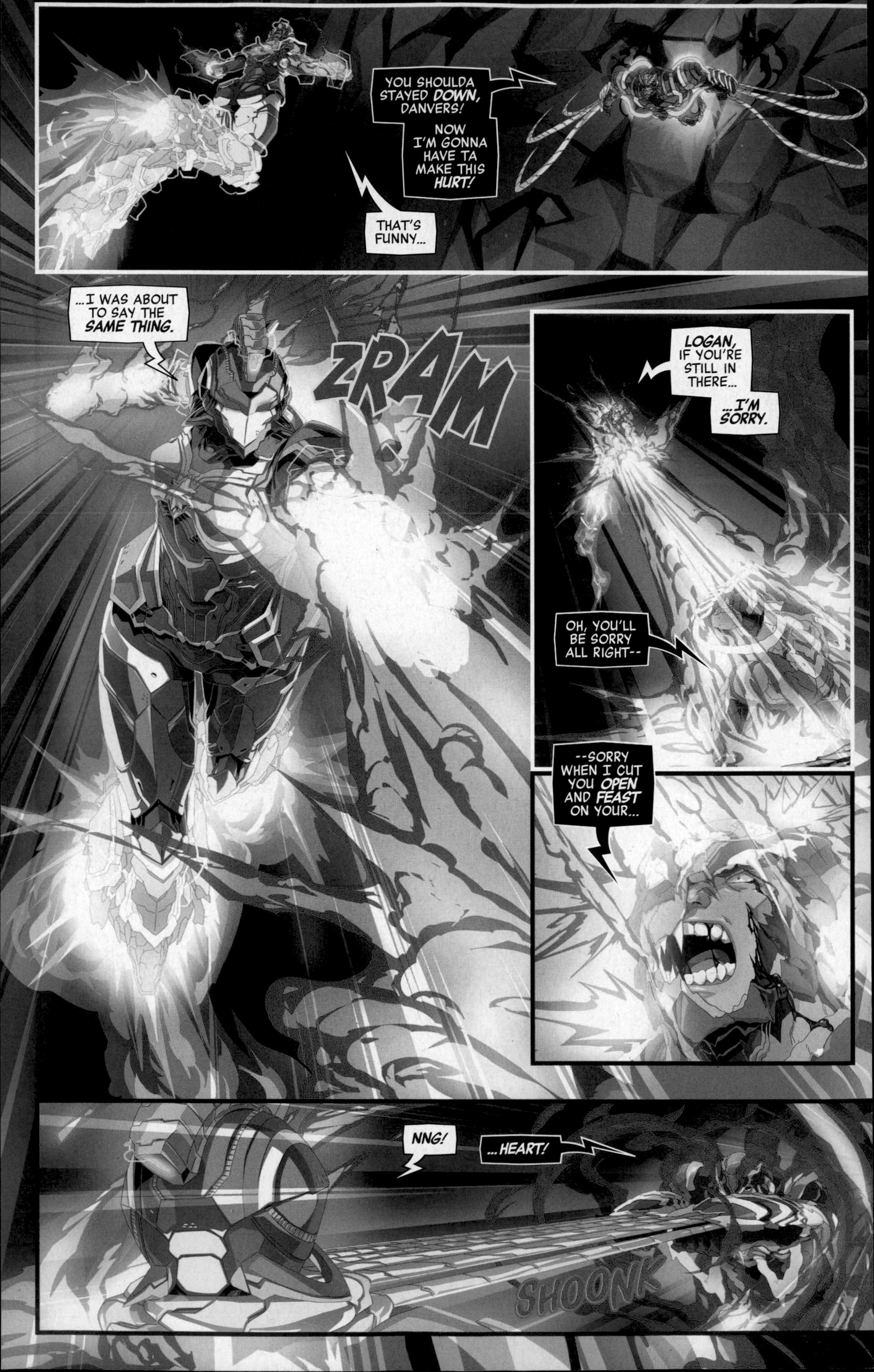
YOU SHOULDA STAYED DOWN, DANVERS!
NOW I'M GONNA HAVE TA MAKE THIS HURT!
THAT'S FUNNY...
...I WAS ABOUT TO SAY THE SAME THING.
ZRAM
LOGAN, IF YOU'RE STILL IN THERE...
...I'M SORRY.
OH, YOU'LL BE SORRY ALL RIGHT--
--SORRY WHEN I CUT YOU OPEN AND FEAST ON YOUR...
NNG!
...HEART!
SHOONK

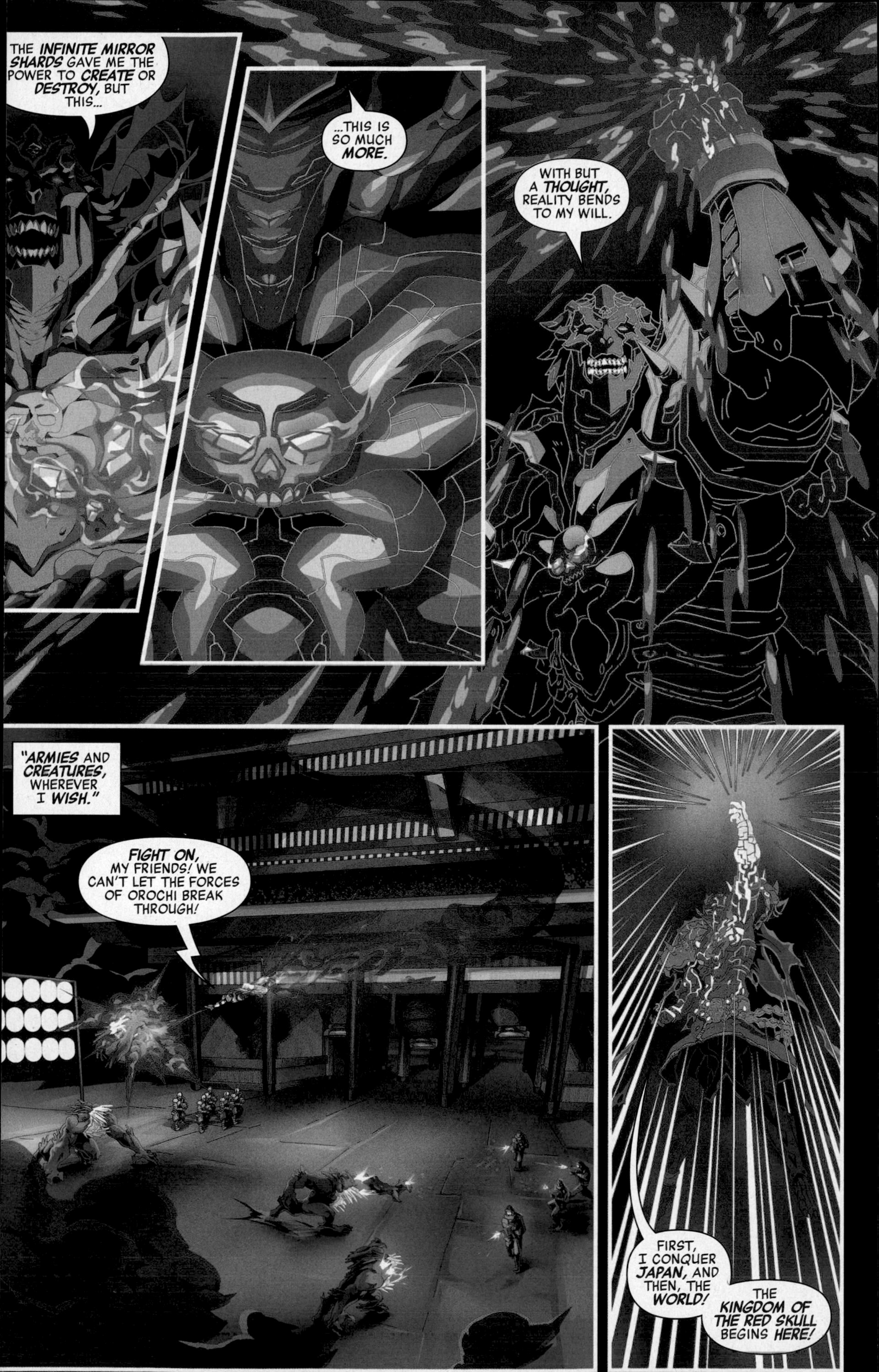
THE INFINITE MIRROR SHARDS GAVE ME THE POWER TO CREATE OR DESTROY, BUT THIS...
...THIS IS SO MUCH MORE.
WITH BUT A THOUGHT, REALITY BENDS TO MY WILL.
"ARMIES AND CREATURES, WHEREVER I WISH."
FIGHT ON, MY FRIENDS! WE CAN'T LET THE FORCES OF OROCHI BREAK THROUGH!
FIRST, I CONQUER JAPAN, AND THEN, THE WORLD!
THE KINGDOM OF THE RED SKULL BEGINS HERE!

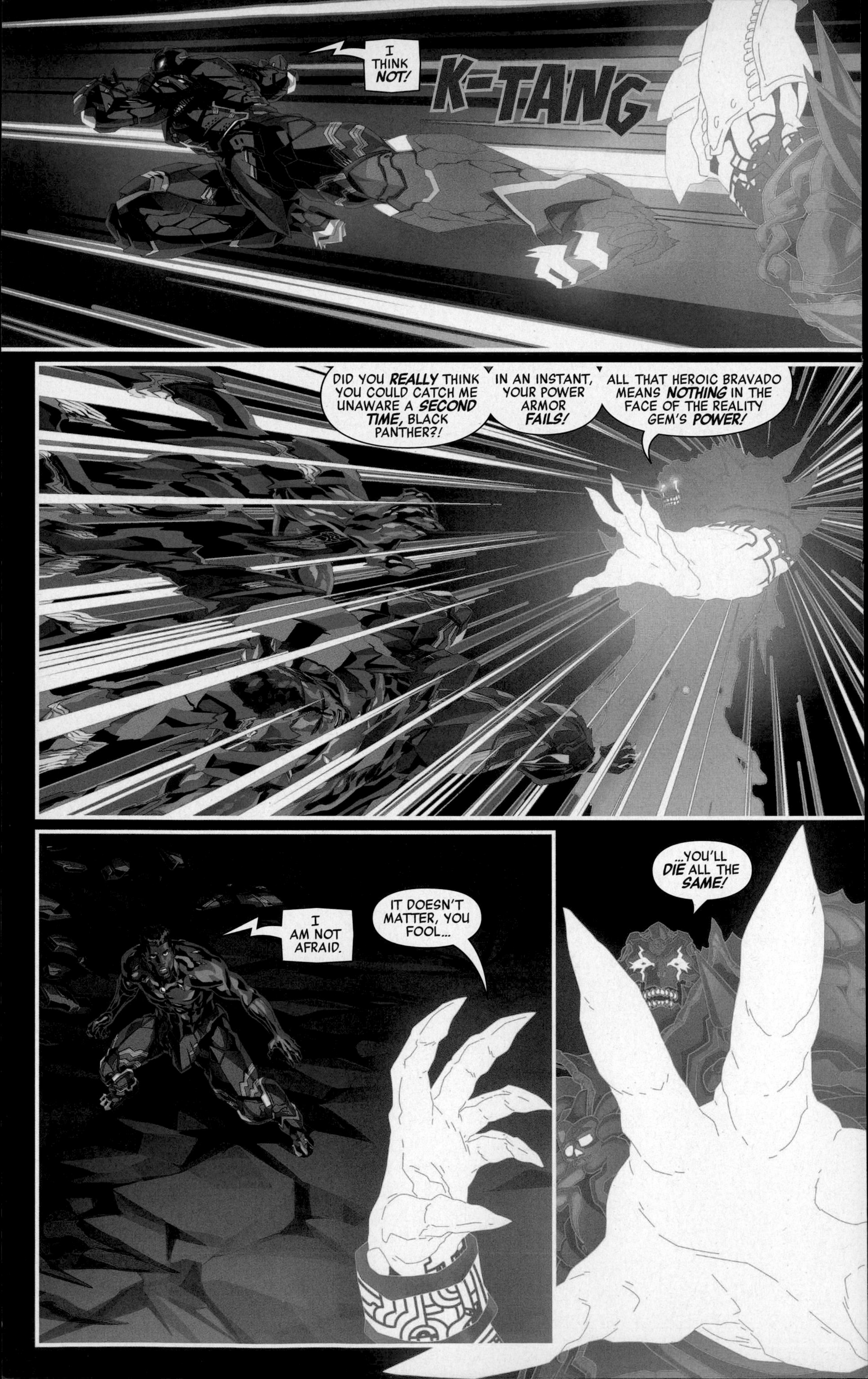
I THINK NOT!
K-TANG
DID YOU REALLY THINK YOU COULD CATCH ME UNAWARE A SECOND TIME, BLACK PANTHER?!
IN AN INSTANT, YOUR POWER ARMOR FAILS!
ALL THAT HEROIC BRAVADO MEANS NOTHING IN THE FACE OF THE REALITY GEM'S POWER!
I AM NOT AFRAID.
IT DOESN'T MATTER, YOU FOOL...
...YOU'LL DIE ALL THE SAME!

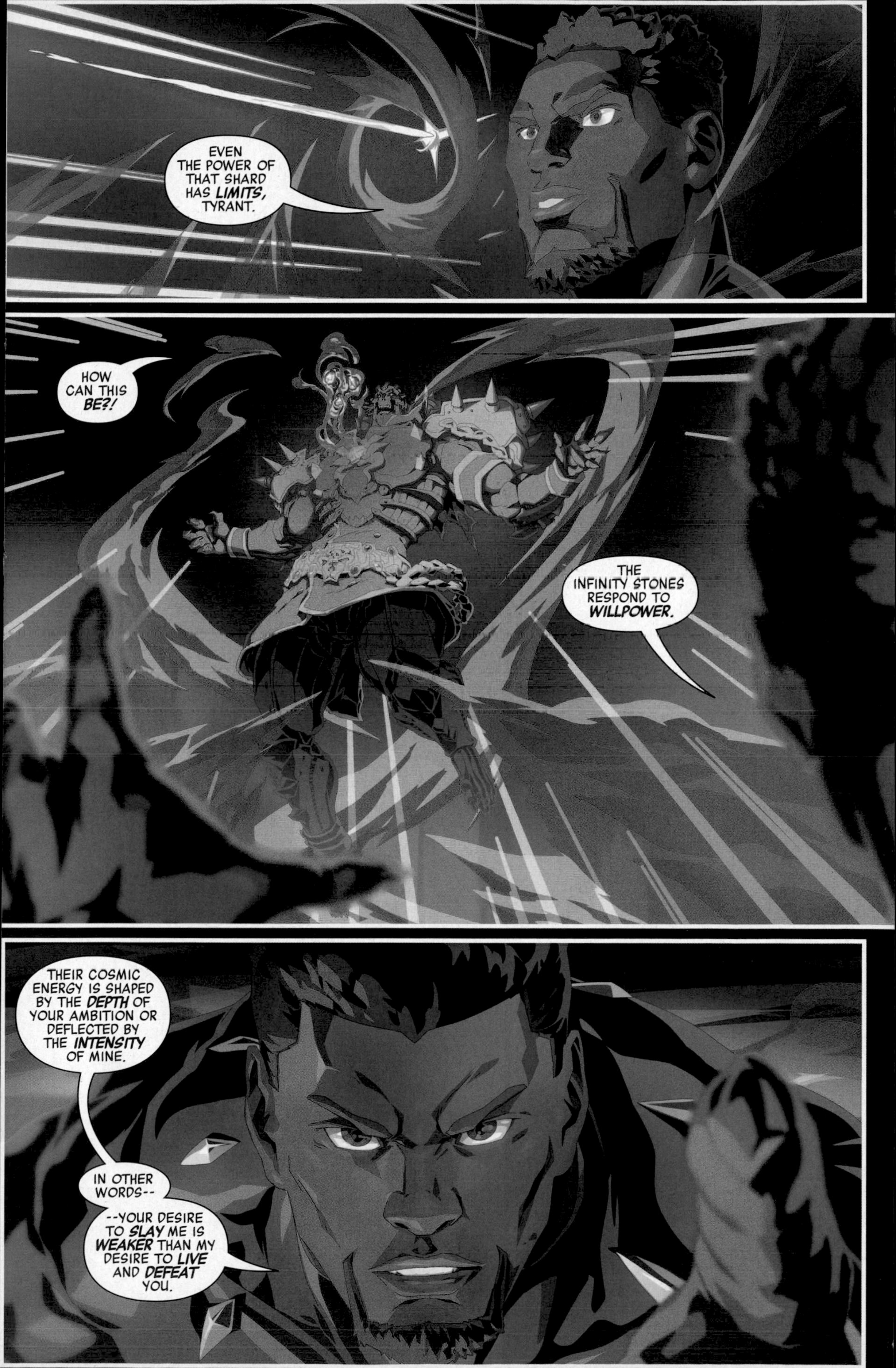
EVEN THE POWER OF THAT SHARD HAS LIMITS, TYRANT.
HOW CAN THIS BE?!
THE INFINITY STONES RESPOND TO WILLPOWER.
THEIR COSMIC ENERGY IS SHAPED BY THE DEPTH OF YOUR AMBITION OR DEFLECTED BY THE INTENSITY OF MINE.
IN OTHER WORDS--
--YOUR DESIRE TO SLAY ME IS WEAKER THAN MY DESIRE TO LIVE AND DEFEAT YOU.

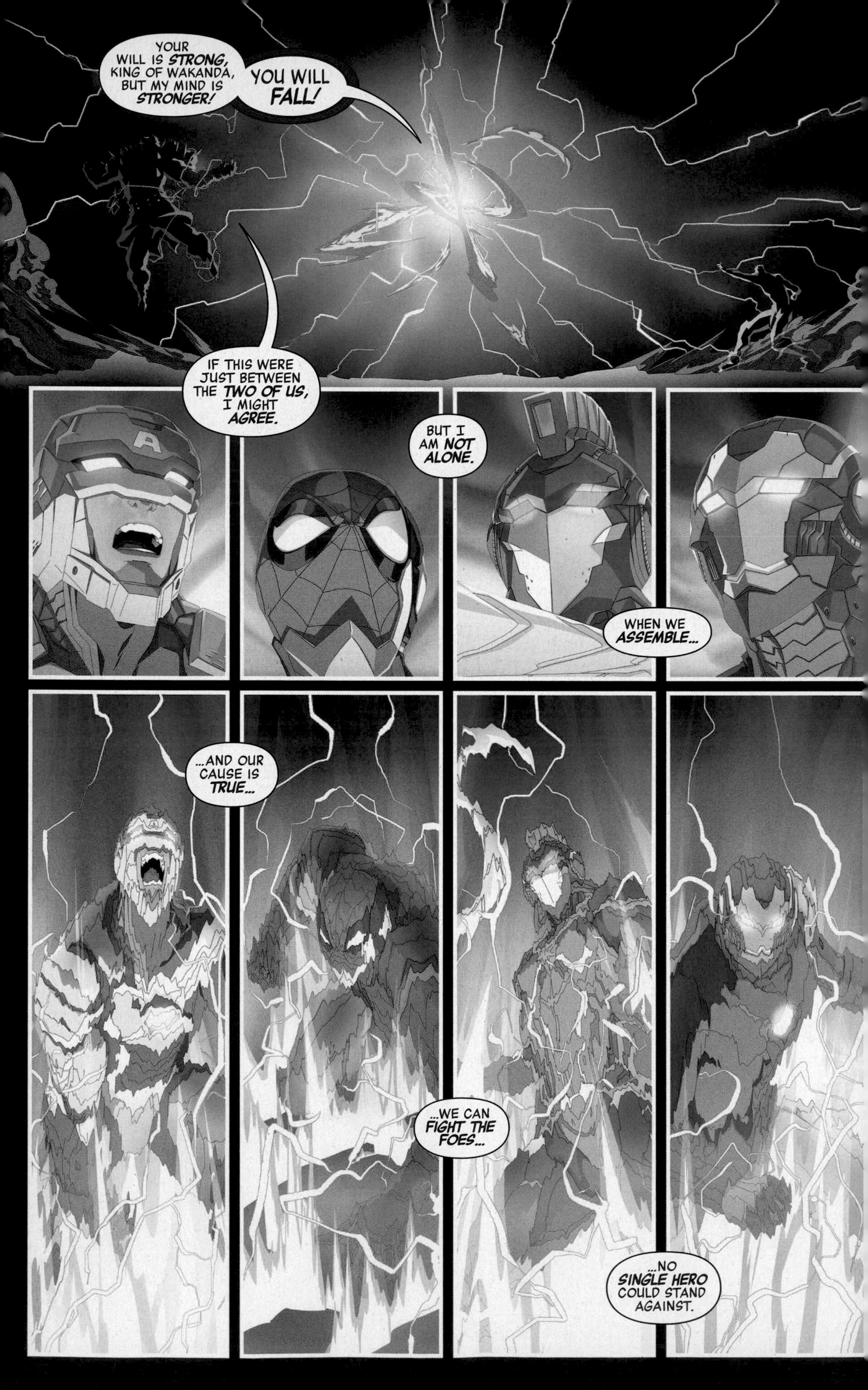
YOUR WILL IS STRONG, KING OF WAKANDA, BUT MY MIND IS STRONGER!
YOU WILL FALL!
IF THIS WERE JUST BETWEEN THE TWO OF US, I MIGHT AGREE.
BUT I AM NOT ALONE.
WHEN WE ASSEMBLE...
...AND OUR CAUSE IS TRUE...
...WE CAN FIGHT THE FOES...
...NO SINGLE HERO COULD STAND AGAINST.

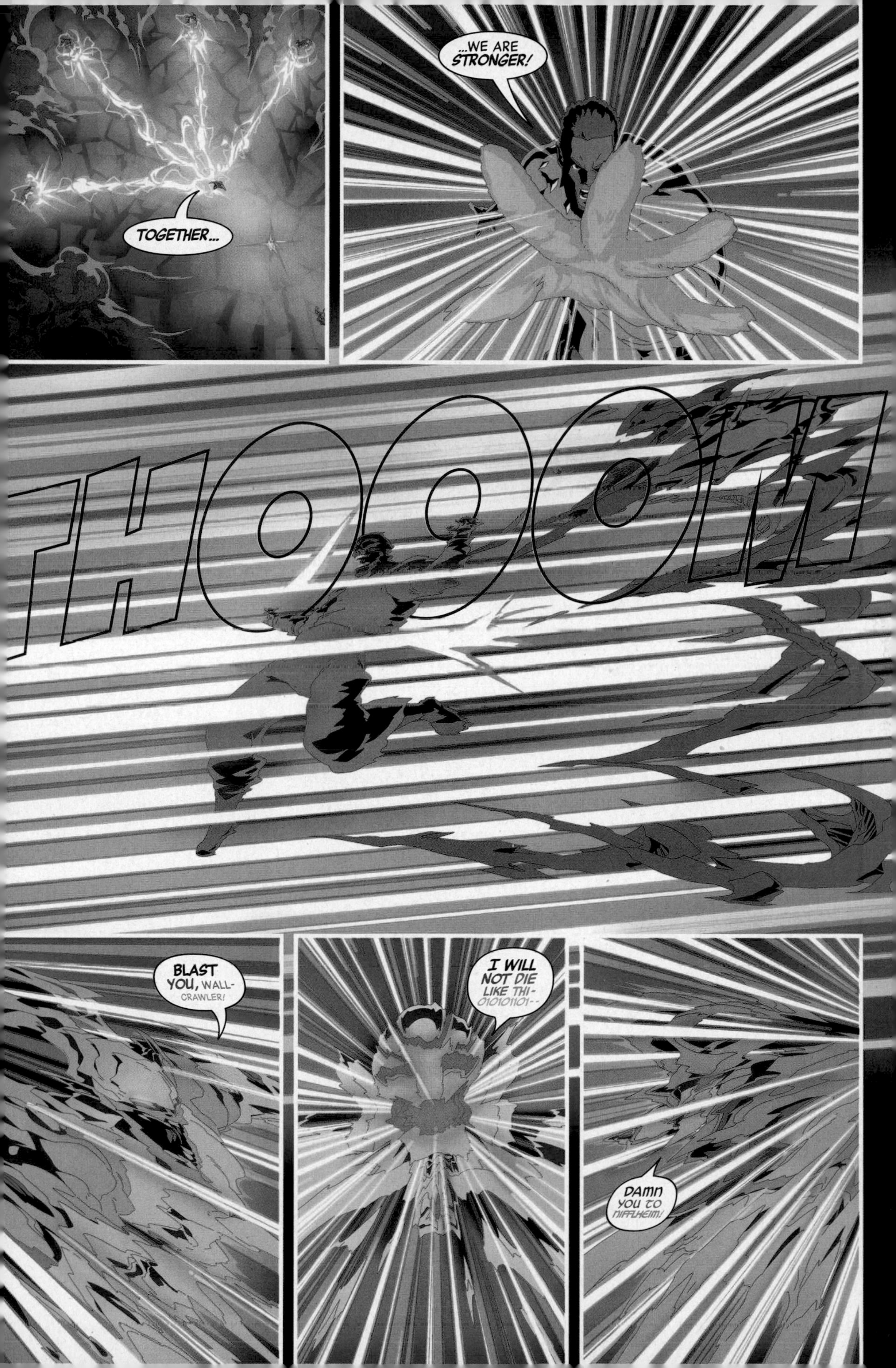
TOGETHER...
...WE ARE STRONGER!
THOOOM
BLAST YOU, WALL-CRAWLER!
I WILL NOT DIE LIKE THI-010101101--
DAMN YOU TO NIFFLHEIM!

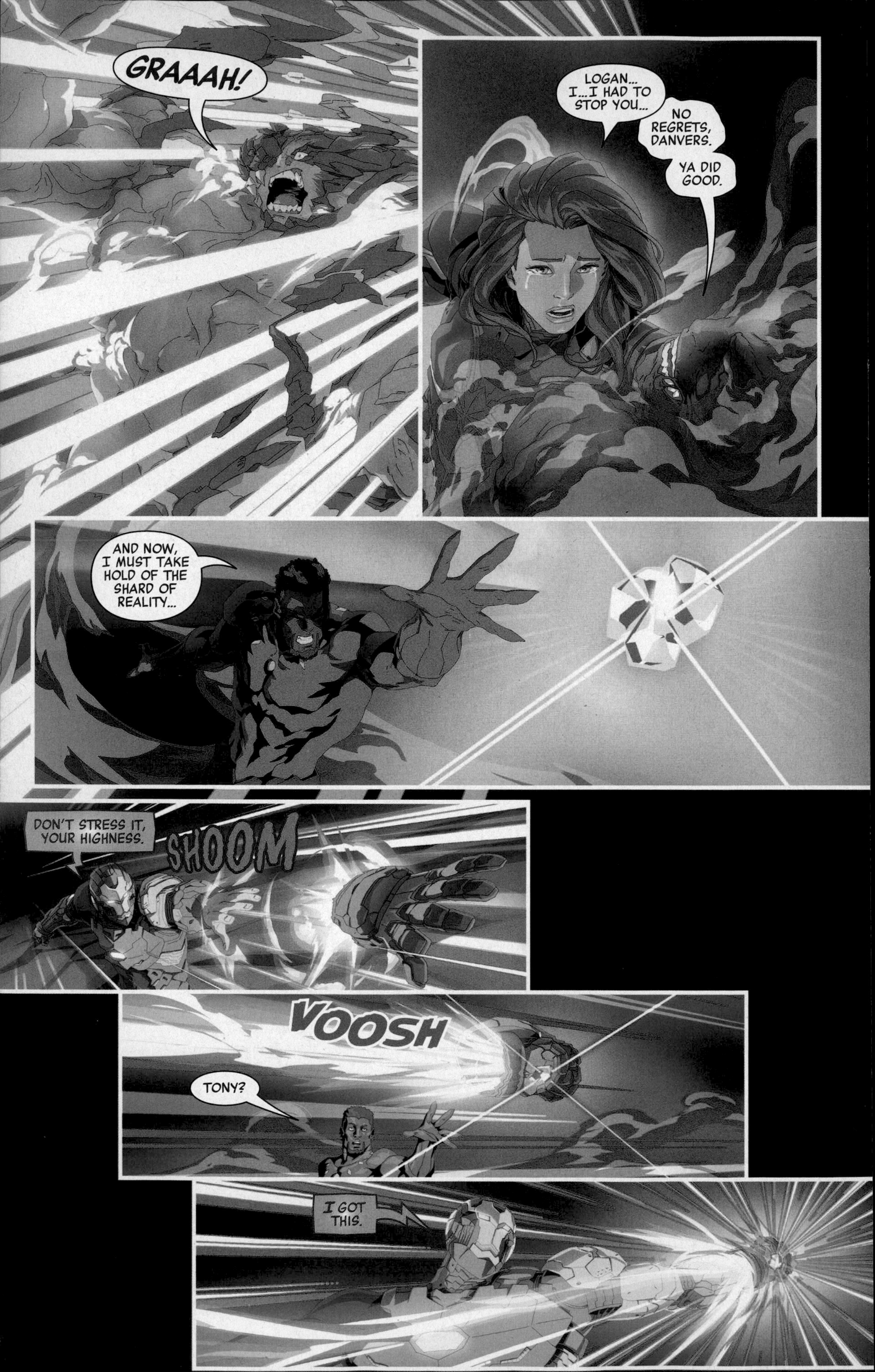
GRAAAH!
LOGAN... I...I HAD TO STOP YOU...
NO REGRETS, DANVERS.
YA DID GOOD.
AND NOW, I MUST TAKE HOLD OF THE SHARD OF REALITY...
DON'T STRESS IT, YOUR HIGHNESS.
SHOOM
VOOSH
TONY?
I GOT THIS.

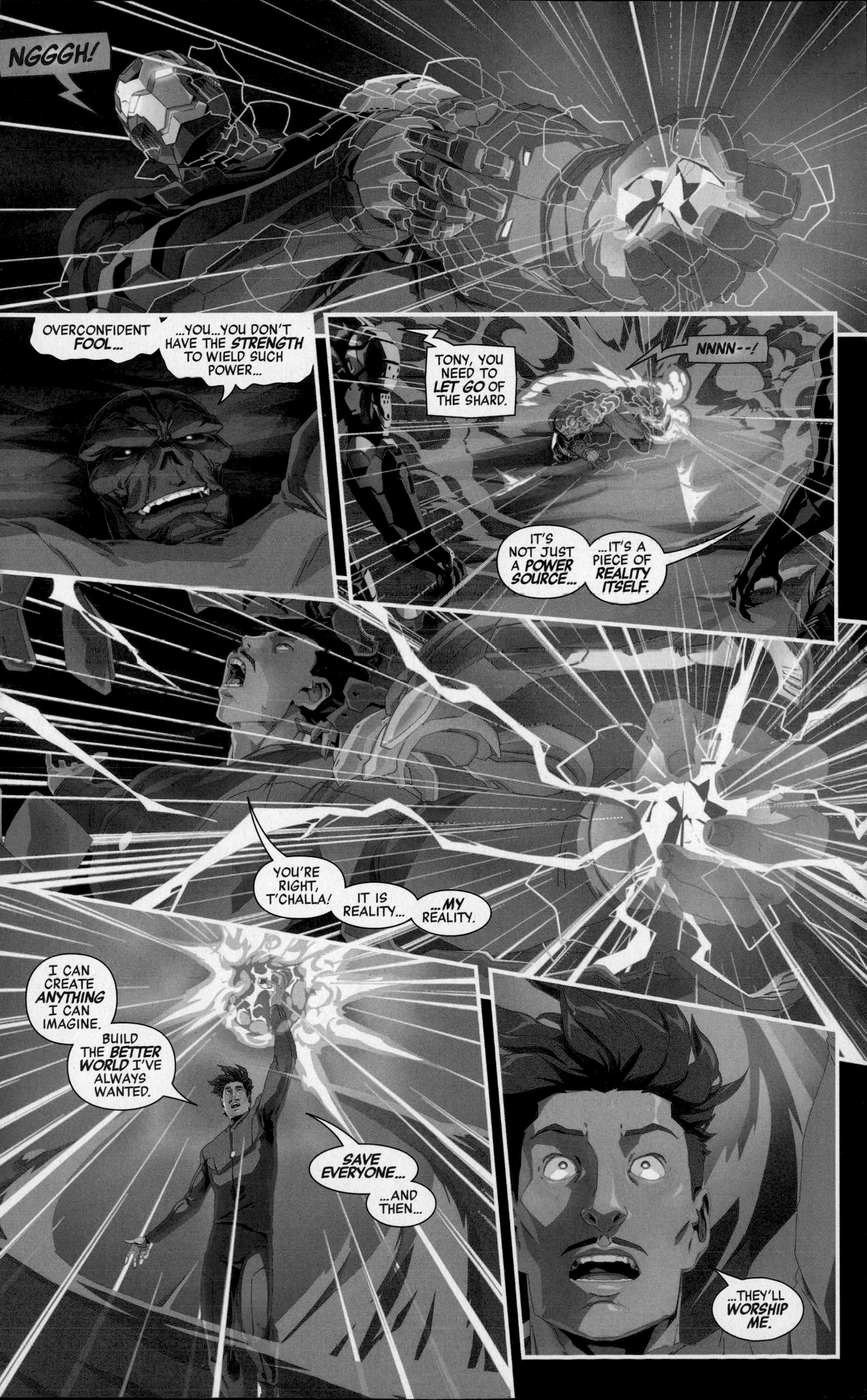
NGGGH!
OVERCONFIDENT FOOL...
...YOU...YOU DON'T HAVE THE STRENGTH TO WIELD SUCH POWER...
TONY, YOU NEED TO LET GO OF THE SHARD.
NNNN--!
IT'S NOT JUST A POWER SOURCE...
...IT'S A PIECE OF REALITY ITSELF.
YOU'RE RIGHT, T'CHALLA!
IT IS REALITY...
...MY REALITY.
I CAN CREATE ANYTHING I CAN IMAGINE.
BUILD THE BETTER WORLD I'VE ALWAYS WANTED.
SAVE EVERYONE...
...AND THEN...
...THEY'LL WORSHIP ME.

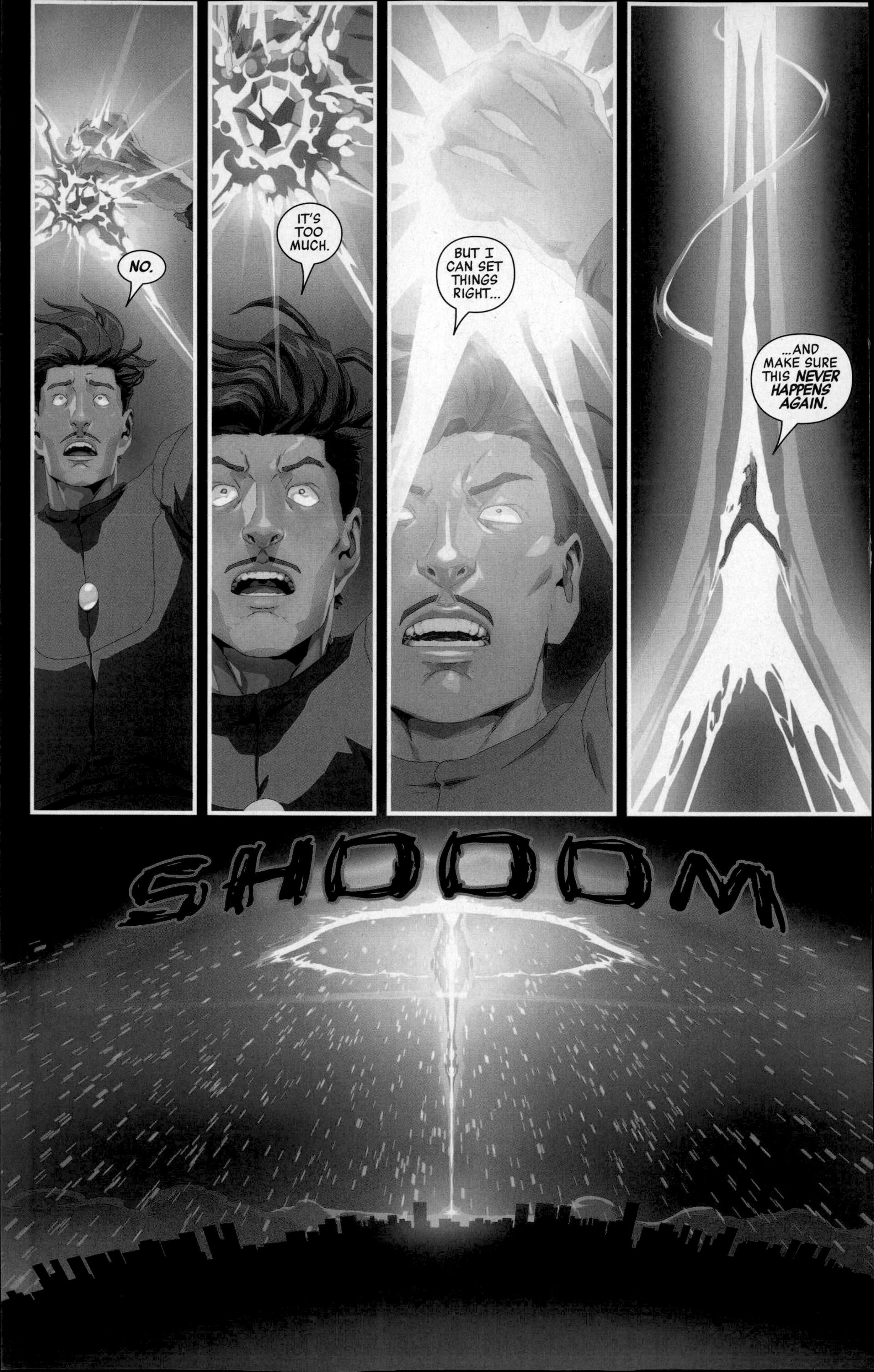
NO.
IT'S TOO MUCH.
BUT I CAN SET THINGS RIGHT...
...AND MAKE SURE THIS **NEVER HAPPENS AGAIN.**
SHOOOM

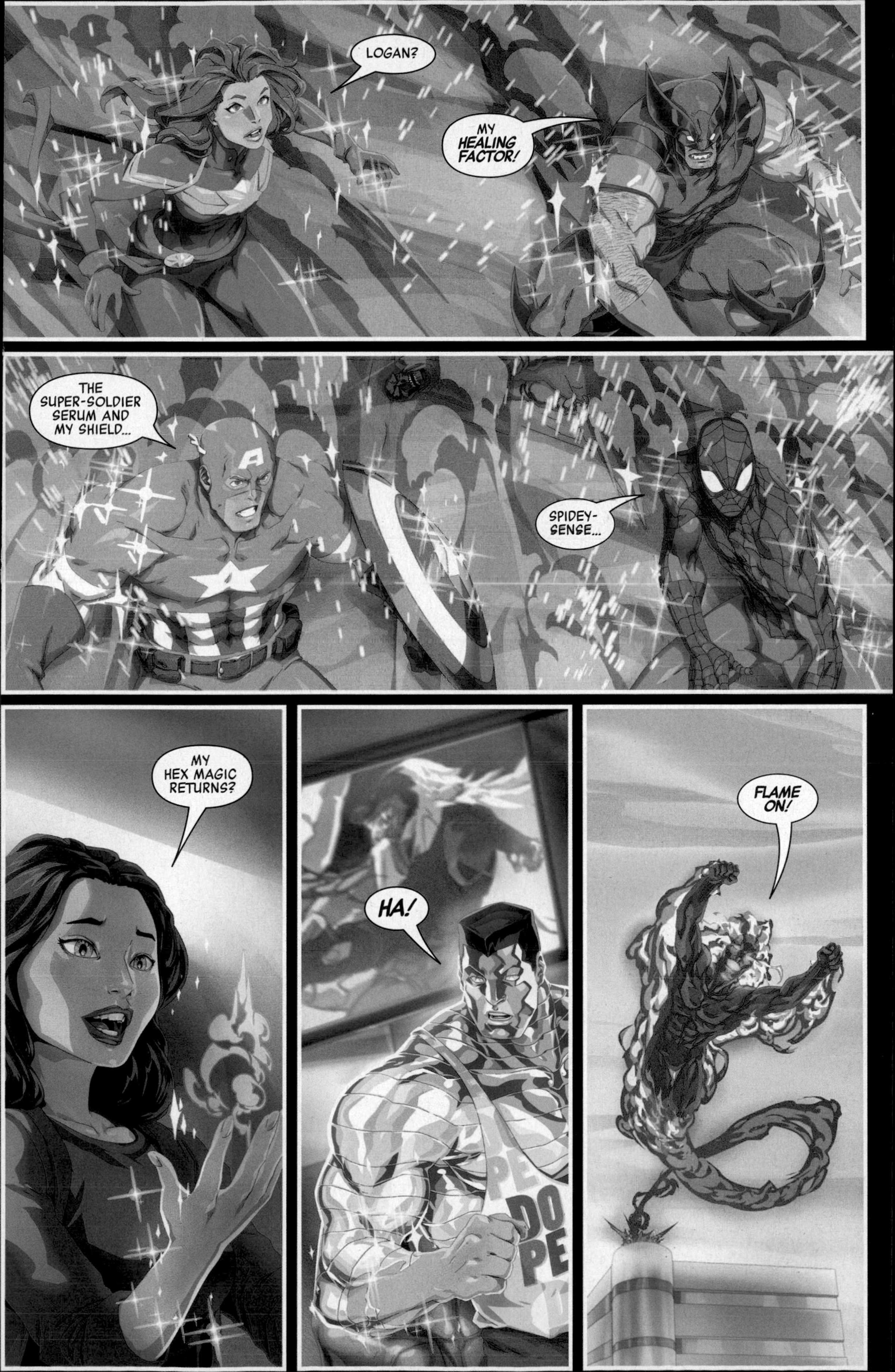
LOGAN?
MY HEALING FACTOR!
THE SUPER-SOLDIER SERUM AND MY SHIELD...
SPIDEY-SENSE...
MY HEX MAGIC RETURNS?
HA!
FLAME ON!

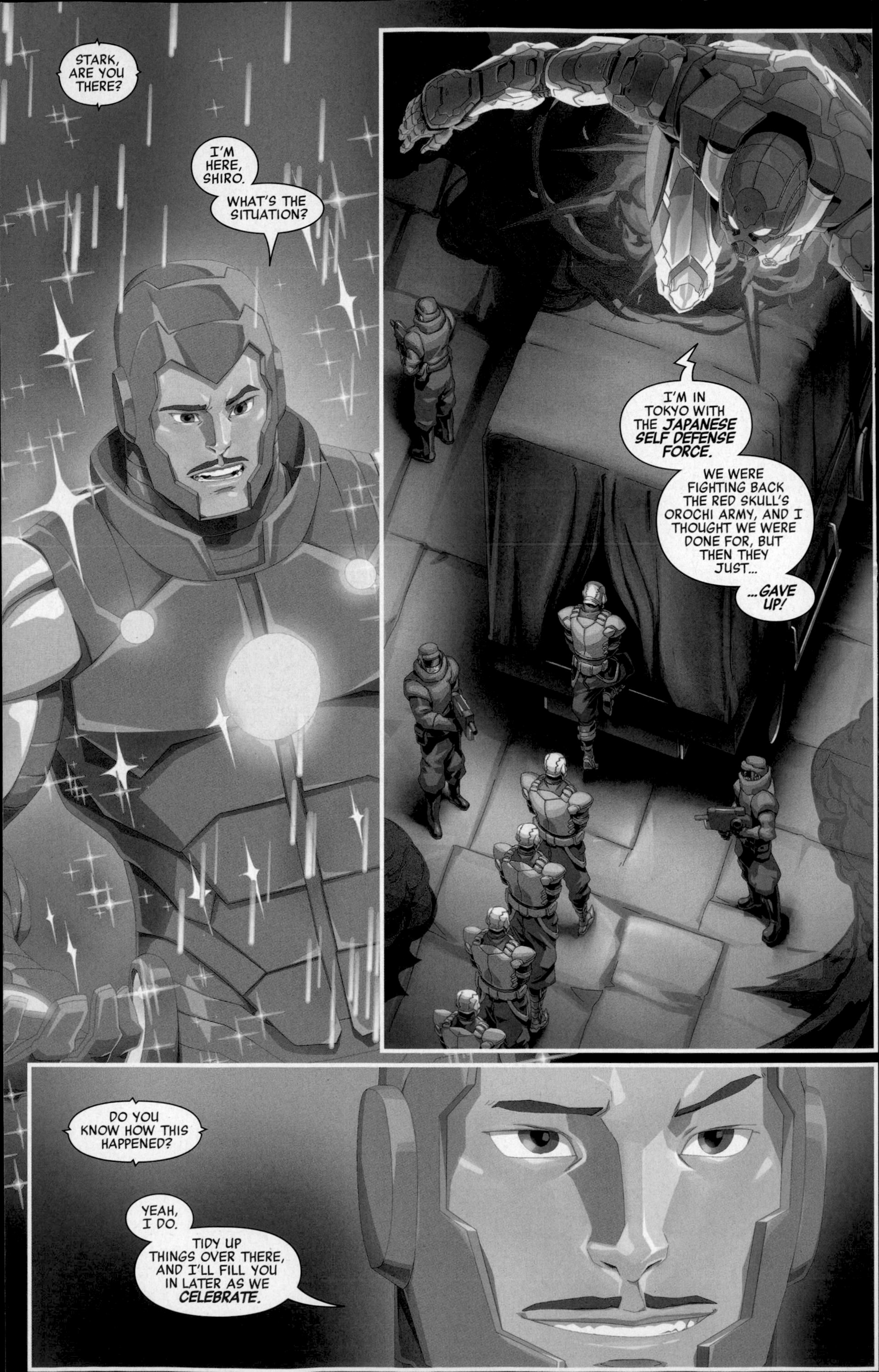

STARK, ARE YOU THERE?
I'M HERE, SHIRO.
WHAT'S THE SITUATION?
I'M IN TOKYO WITH THE JAPANESE SELF DEFENSE FORCE.
WE WERE FIGHTING BACK THE RED SKULL'S OROCHI ARMY, AND I THOUGHT WE WERE DONE FOR, BUT THEN THEY JUST...
...GAVE UP!
DO YOU KNOW HOW THIS HAPPENED?
YEAH, I DO.
TIDY UP THINGS OVER THERE, AND I'LL FILL YOU IN LATER AS WE CELEBRATE.

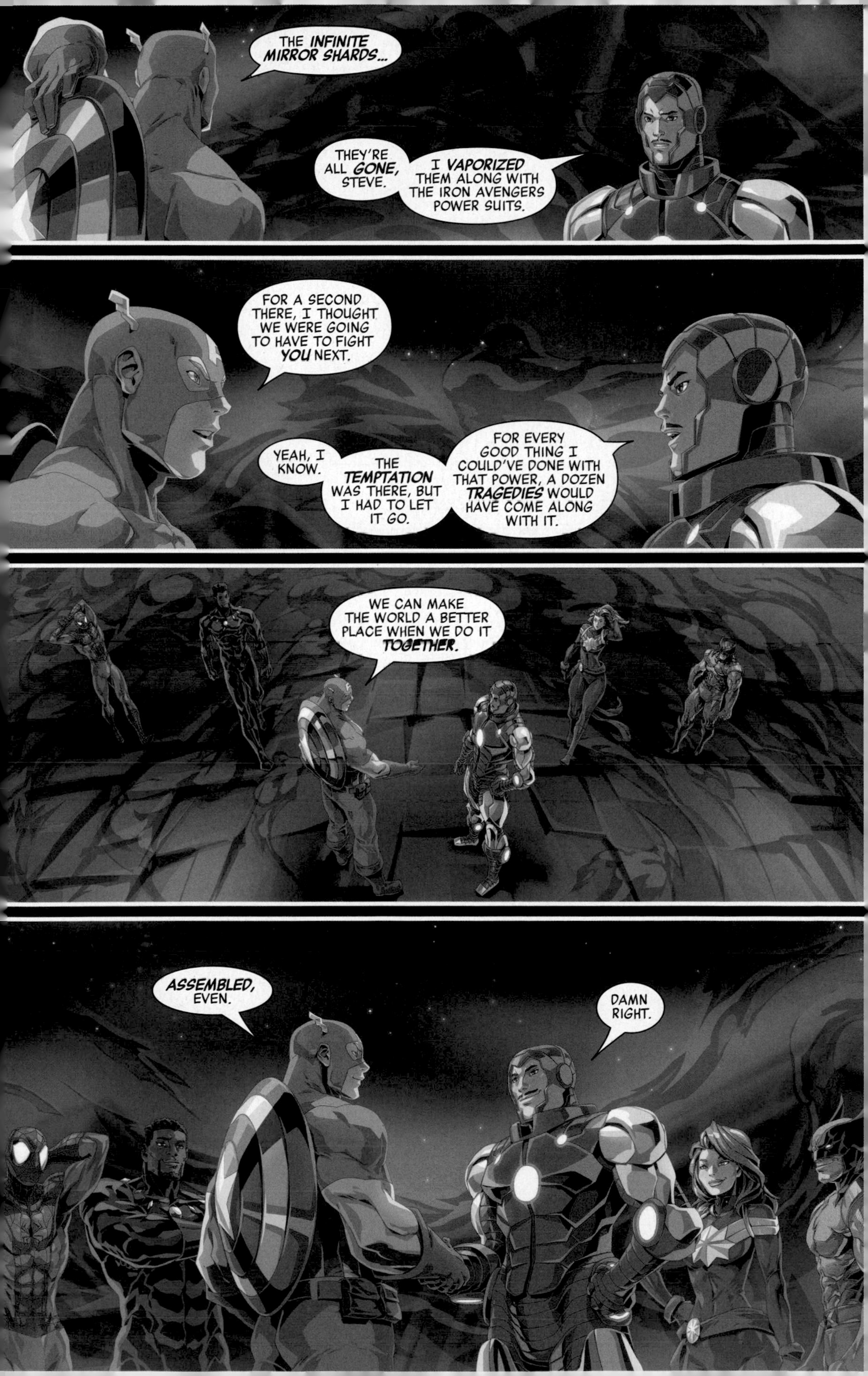
THE INFINITE MIRROR SHARDS...
THEY'RE ALL GONE, STEVE.
I VAPORIZED THEM ALONG WITH THE IRON AVENGERS POWER SUITS.
FOR A SECOND THERE, I THOUGHT WE WERE GOING TO HAVE TO FIGHT YOU NEXT.
YEAH, I KNOW.
THE TEMPTATION WAS THERE, BUT I HAD TO LET IT GO.
FOR EVERY GOOD THING I COULD'VE DONE WITH THAT POWER, A DOZEN TRAGEDIES WOULD HAVE COME ALONG WITH IT.
WE CAN MAKE THE WORLD A BETTER PLACE WHEN WE DO IT TOGETHER.
ASSEMBLED, EVEN.
DAMN RIGHT.

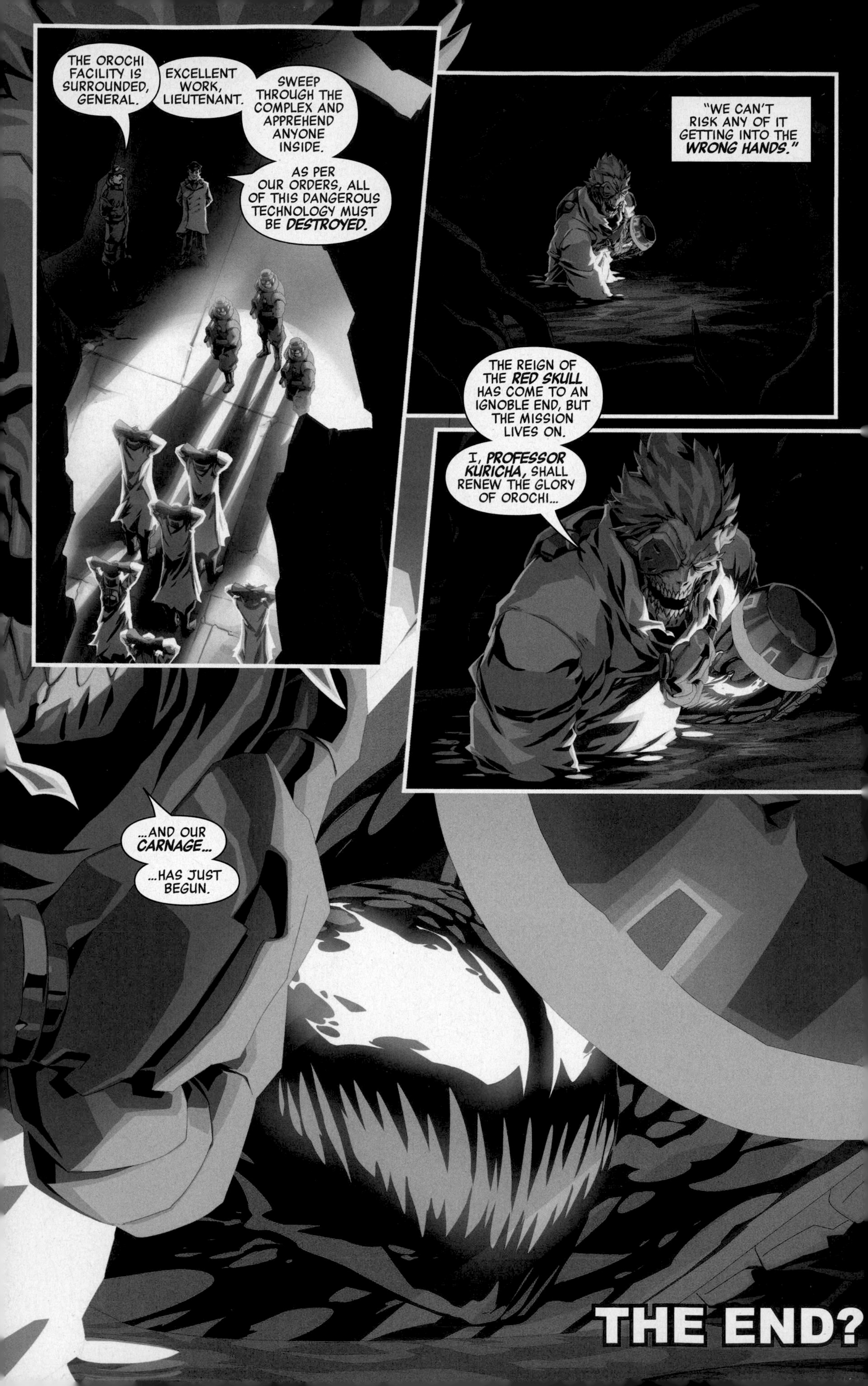
THE OROCHI FACILITY IS SURROUNDED, GENERAL.
EXCELLENT WORK, LIEUTENANT.
SWEEP THROUGH THE COMPLEX AND APPREHEND ANYONE INSIDE.
AS PER OUR ORDERS, ALL OF THIS DANGEROUS TECHNOLOGY MUST BE DESTROYED.
"WE CAN'T RISK ANY OF IT GETTING INTO THE WRONG HANDS."
THE REIGN OF THE RED SKULL HAS COME TO AN IGNOBLE END, BUT THE MISSION LIVES ON.
I, PROFESSOR KURICHA, SHALL RENEW THE GLORY OF OROCHI...
...AND OUR CARNAGE...
...HAS JUST BEGUN.
THE END?

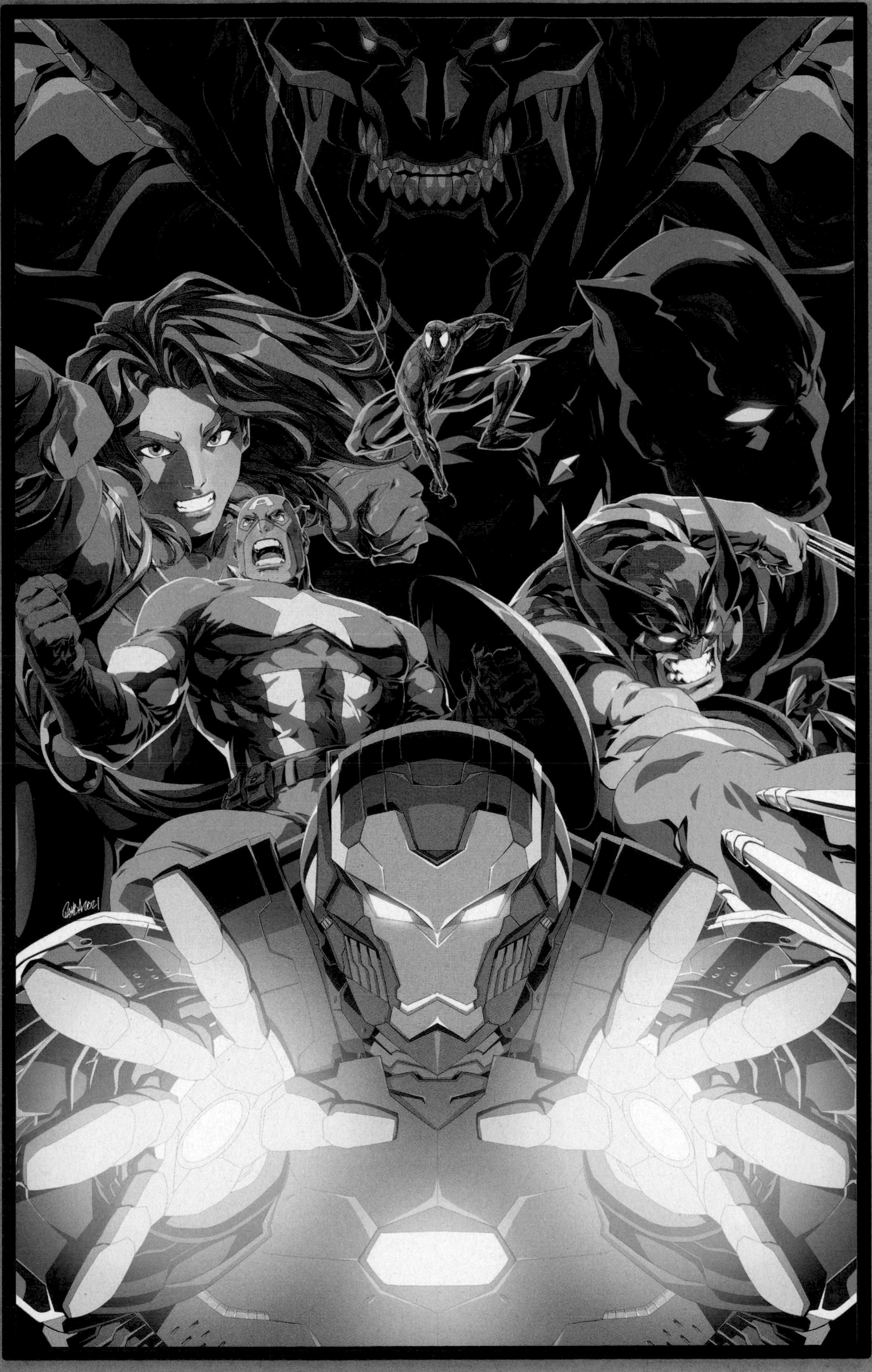

JEFFREY "CHAMBA" CRUZ
#1 VARIANT

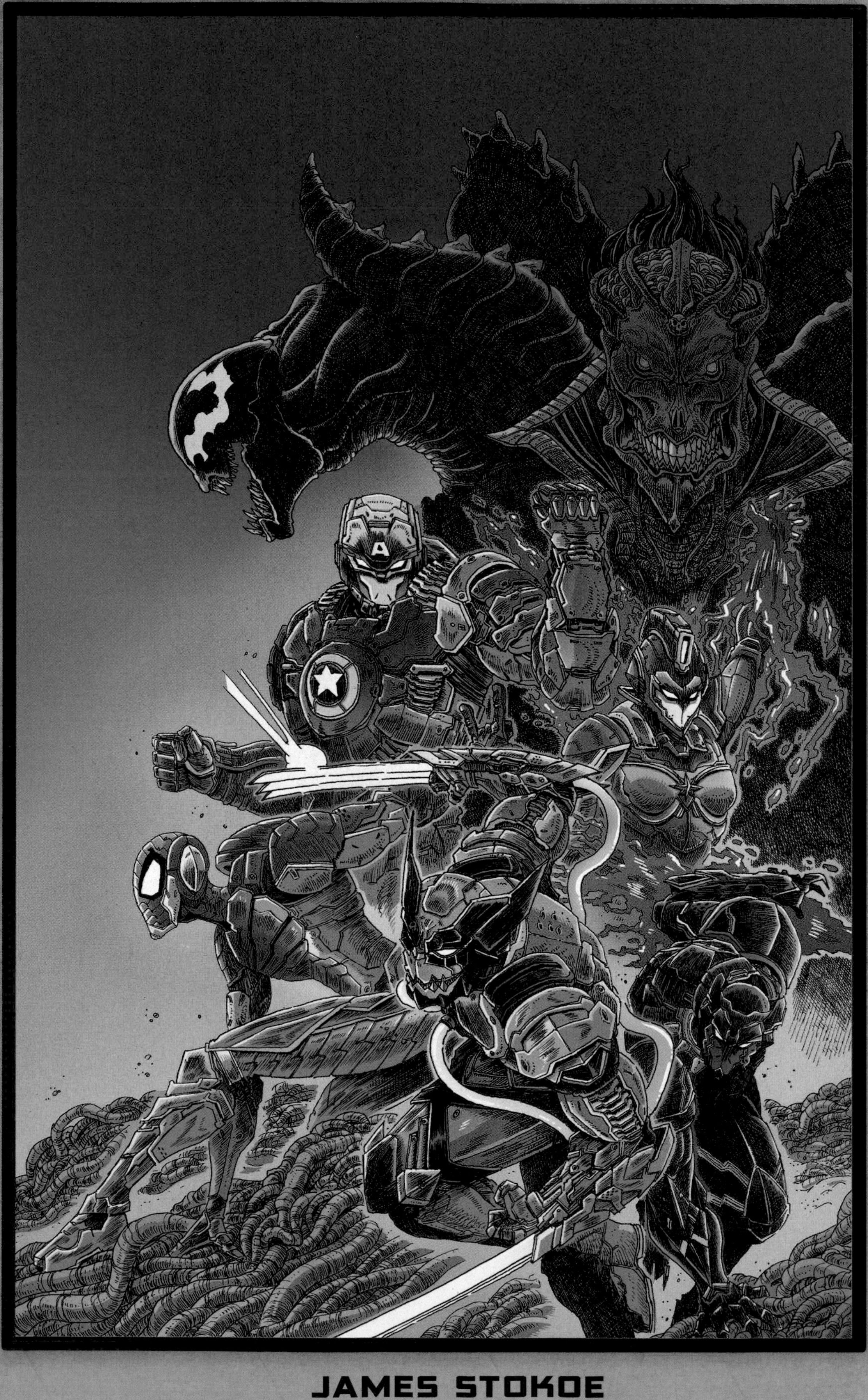

JAMES STOKOE
#1 VARIANT

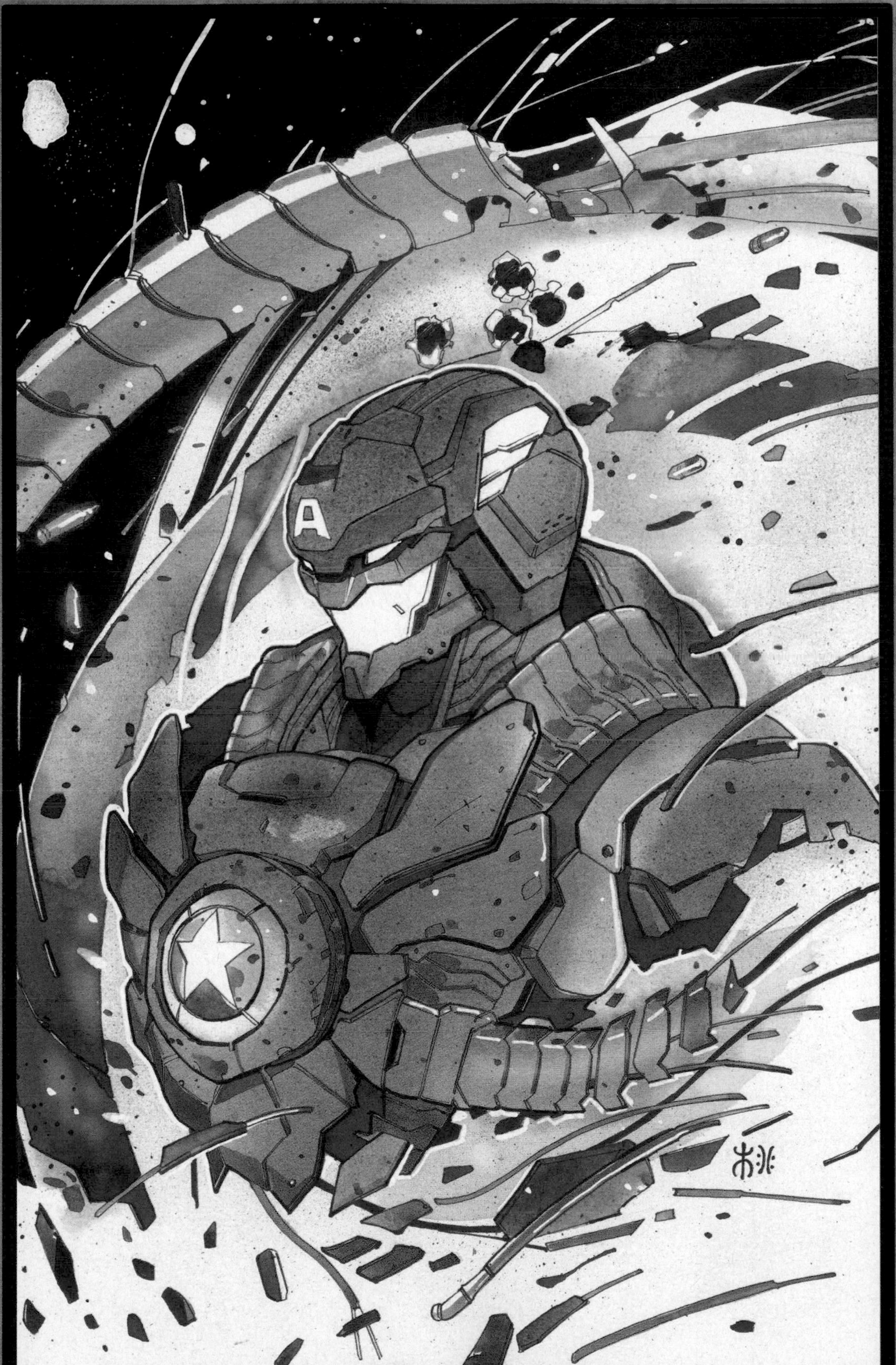

PEACH MOMOKO
#1 VARIANT

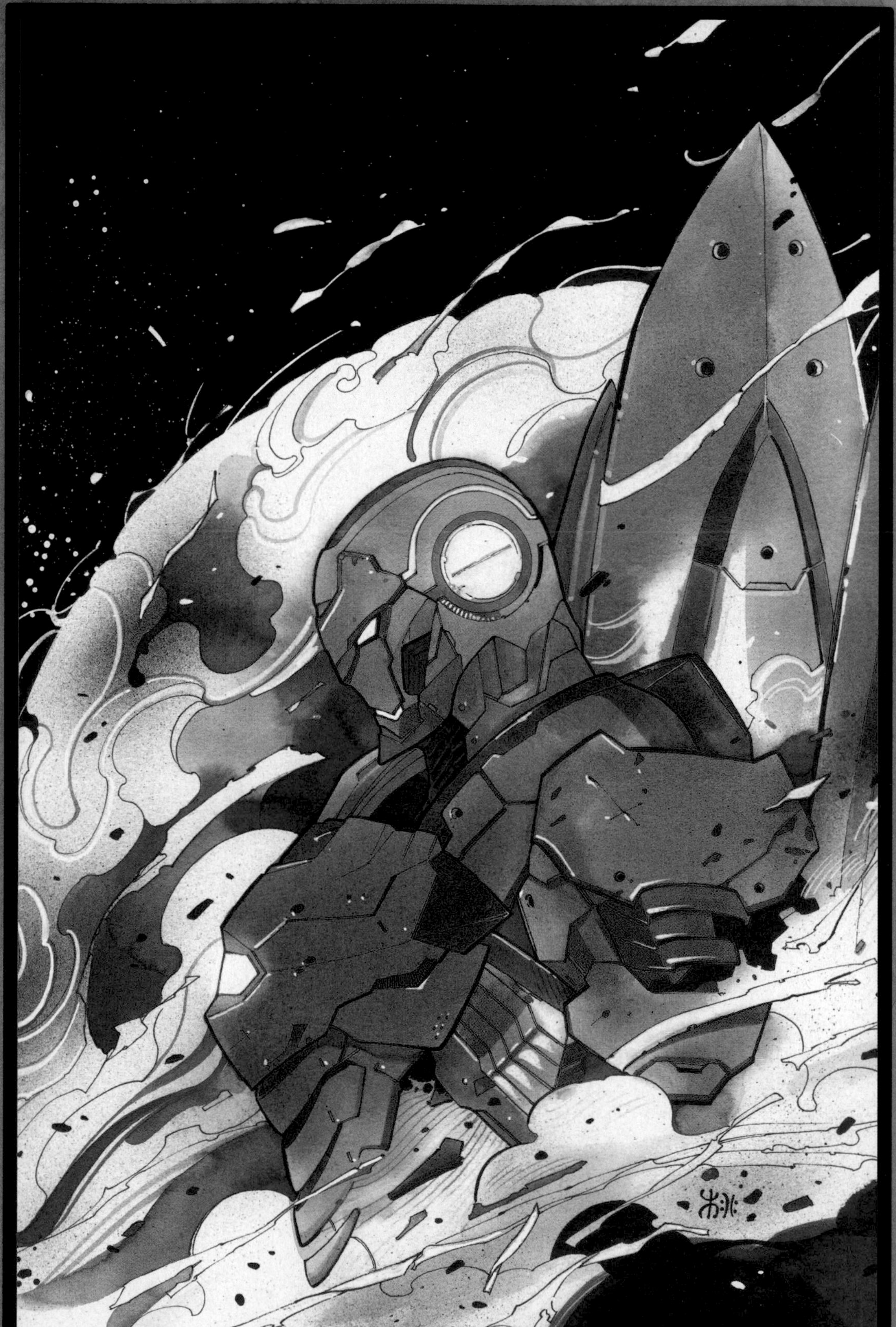

PEACH MOMOKO
#2 VARIANT

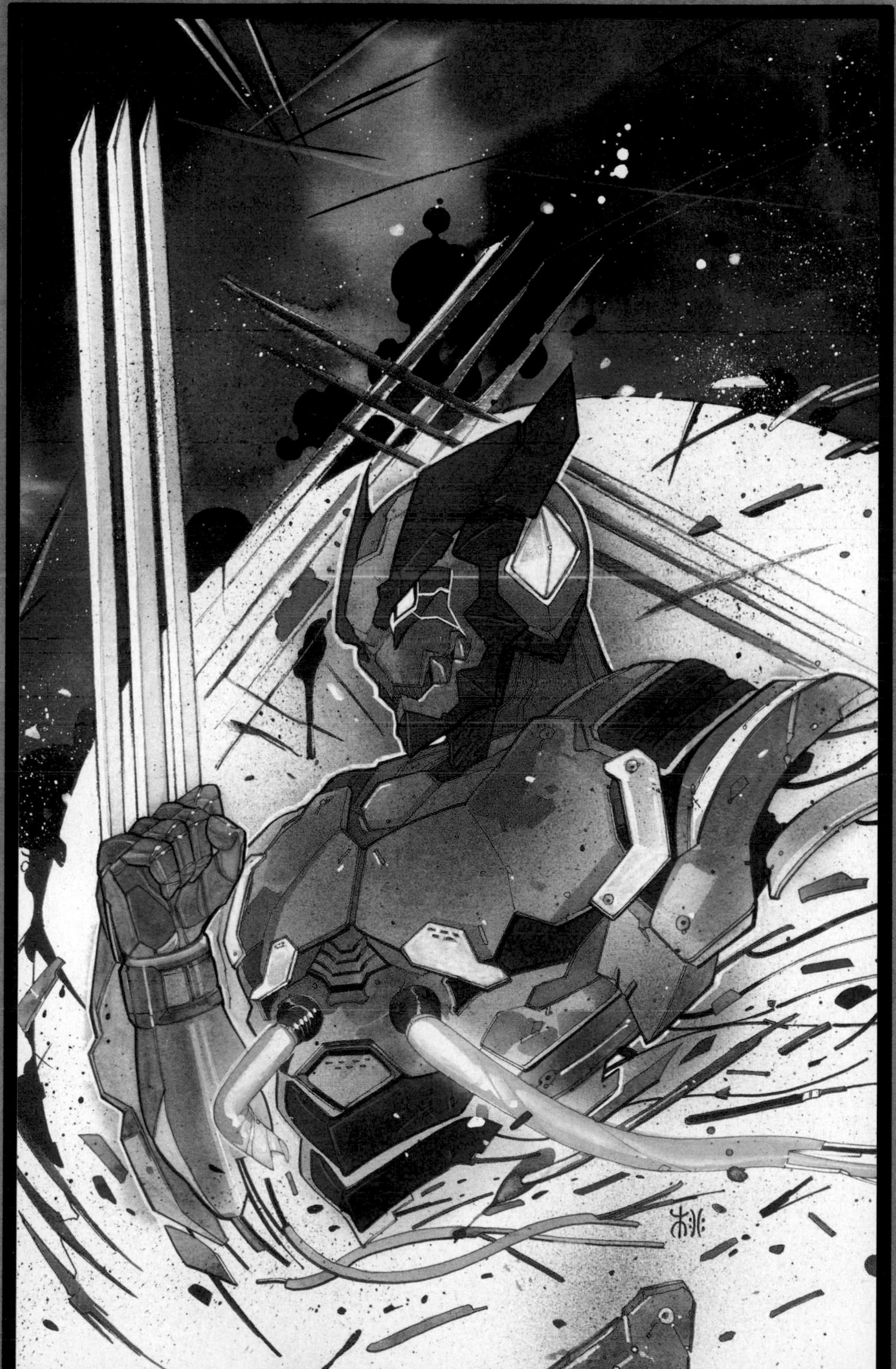

PEACH MOMOKO
#3 VARIANT

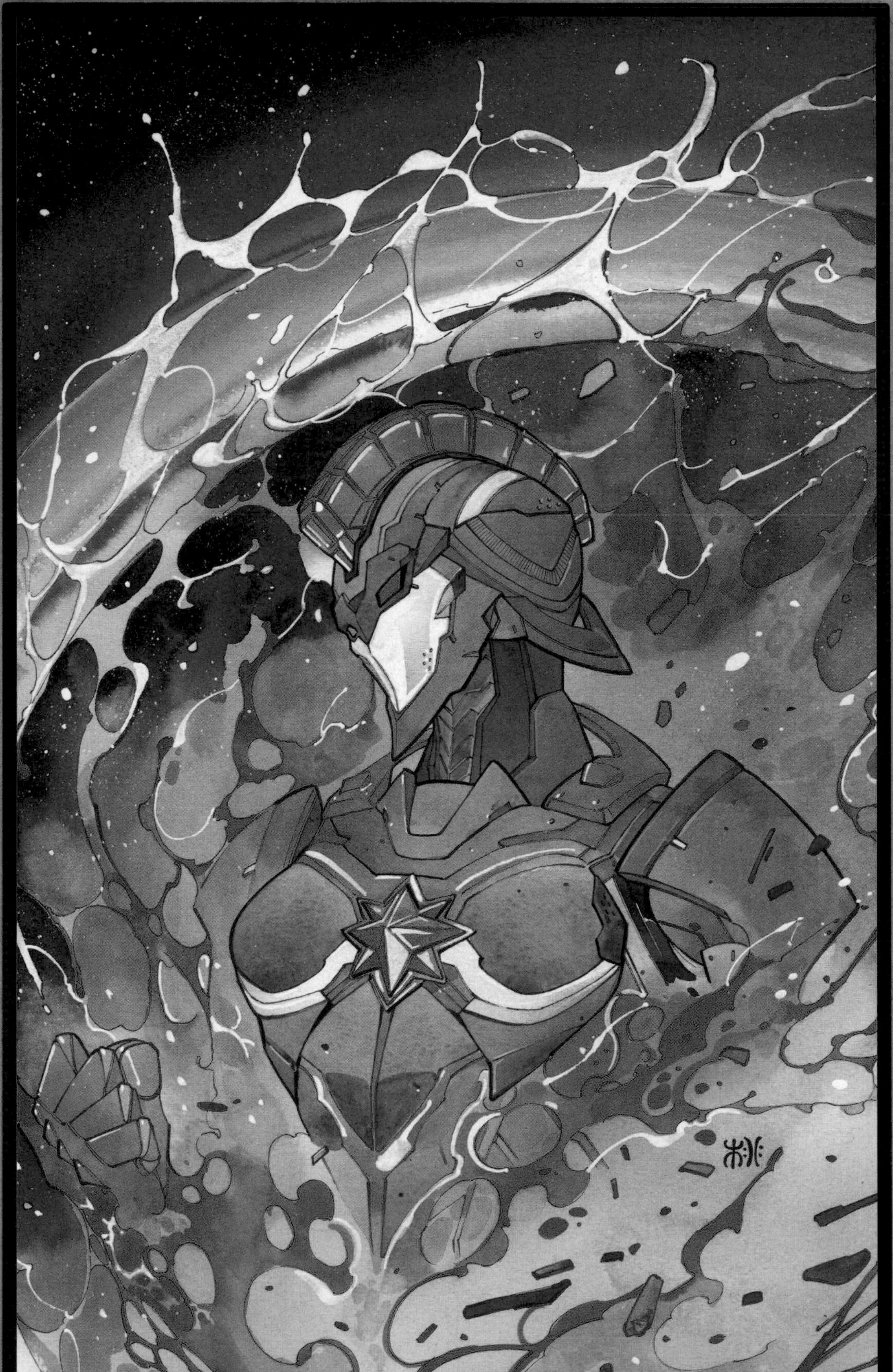

PEACH MOMOKO

#4 VARIANT

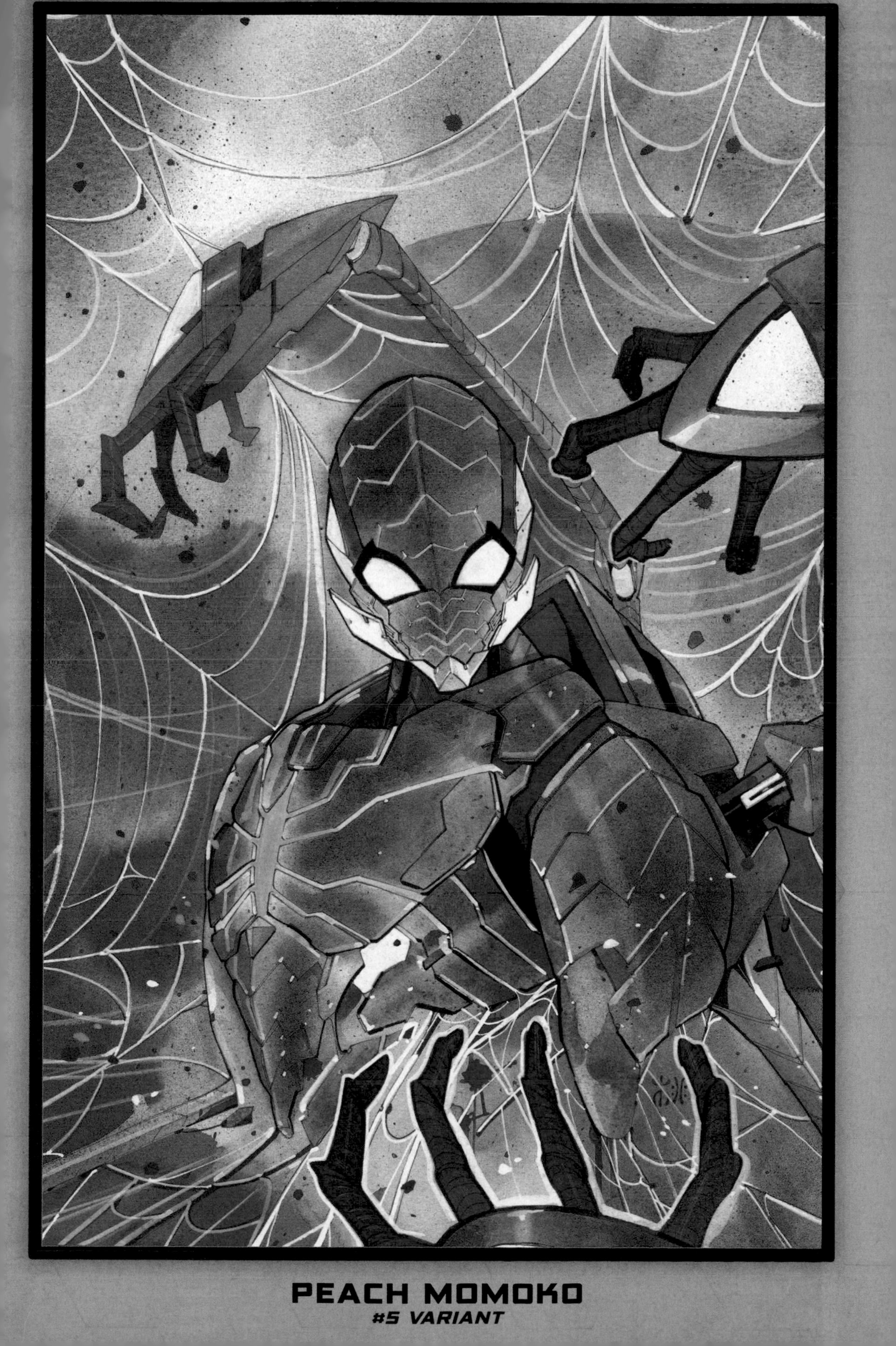

PEACH MOMOKO
#5 VARIANT

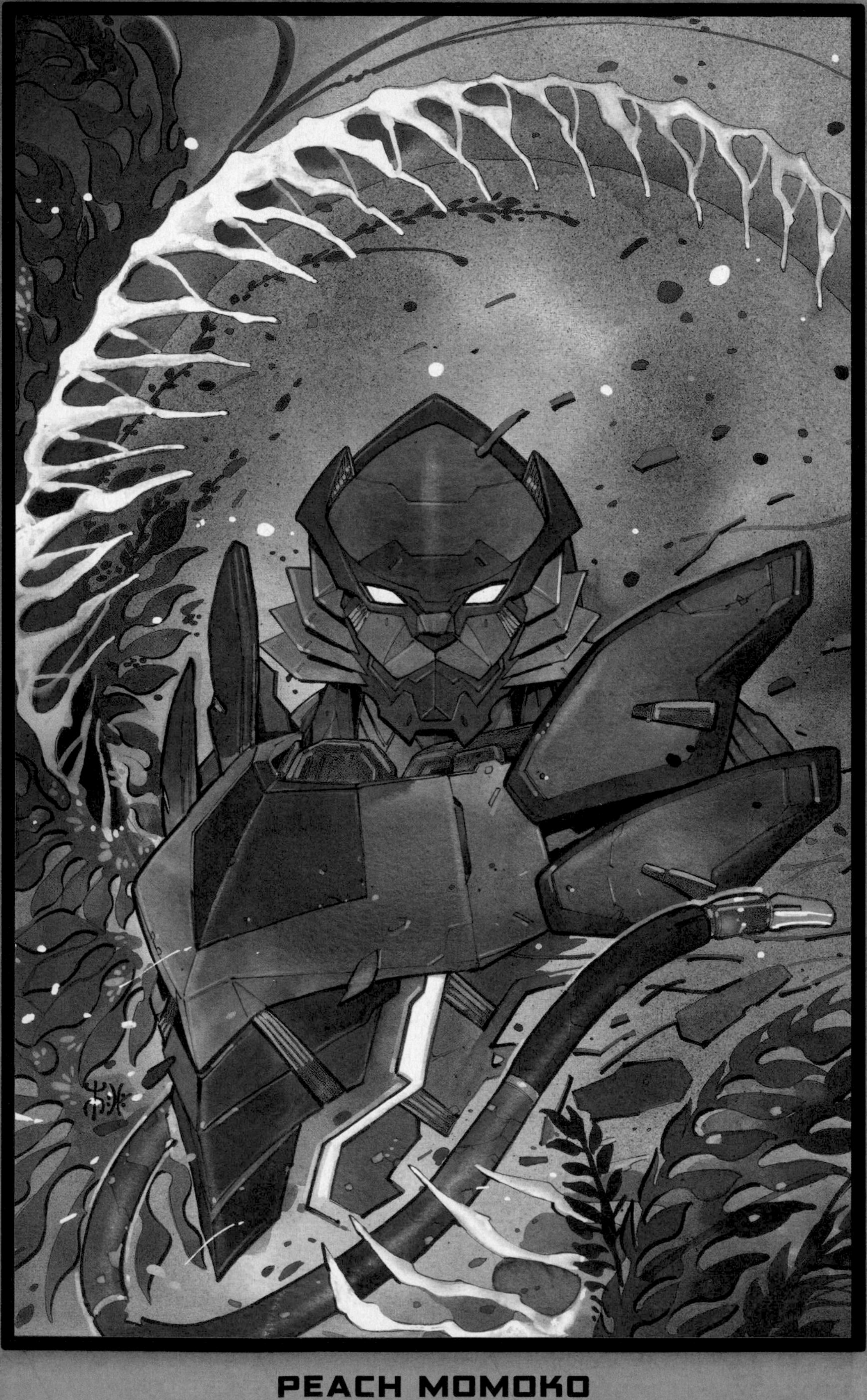

PEACH MOMOKO
#6 VARIANT